The Jack Morton
(Who's He?) Story

THE
JACK MORTON
(Who's He?)
STORY

Jack Morton

as told to
William Fuchs

VANTAGE PRESS
New York / Washington / Atlanta
Los Angeles / Chicago

FIRST EDITION

Published by Vantage Press, Inc.
516 West 34th Street, New York, New York 10001

Manufactured in the United States of America
ISBN: 0-533-06272-1

Library of Congress Catalog Card No.: 84-90224

To all the people who have encouraged
and helped me throughout my life

With Bob Hope at the New York Hilton

April 26, 1984

Dear Jack:

I'm glad that you are finally retiring. It will give you more time to write your book. You certainly must have a lot to write about.

I've met a lot of agents in my time but you were the one that I enjoyed working with the most. Always you displayed a lot of class and possessed such a wonderful personal integrity and you always knew just what an artist needed. I know that every gypsy that ever worked with you appreciated all your talents.

Don't retire. Just take a long, long vacation. Remember, though, if you do retire that when a horse retires they just put him out to stud. How do you feel?

Good luck.

Regards,
Bob

" . . . Jack Morton's shows were always fun to do. . . ."

—Robert Merrill

"The inside of show business is emotion, heartfelt affection and worry for the producer. Jack, a dear friend and real humanitarian, sums it all up. It's an education for those who really want to know about this so-called glamour named the 'lime light.' "

—Red Skelton

" . . . I've never heard anything but praise from the people who have worked for and with . . . [Jack]. [Jack has] . . . class, . . . and that spells it all. . . . time and feelings for the little people. . . . "

—Charlie Dornan

" . . . A *great* man and a *great* talent. What a pleasure it is to work with one of the great pioneers of our business. I have known few men who can even approach [Jack's] . . . show business sense of taste and timing. [Jack is] . . . unique."

—Roger Williams

In my twenty years in show business I have never met a more professional individual than [Jack Morton]. . . . It has been a pleasure working with [Jack]. . . .

—Bobby Vinton

"I first met Jack Morton when he was producing a national meeting for the Royal Crown Cola Company and I was their spokesman for TV and Radio. His presentation of an industrial revue in Florida was actually the first time I had ever seen a sophisticated and original 'book show' for an industrial client. In fact, Jack's production was one of the forerunners of today's highly sophisticated Broadway-like-type presentations, but way back there in the 50s, it was a quantum leap forward from the charts, graphs, and sales manager's reports that occupied most of the routine business conventions. The idea of writing special lyrics and music, as well as adapting popular songs to a company's logo or sales pitch was an innovation, so I kept my eye on Jack for years as he progressed into running one of the nation's top production companies. In the ensuing years, I had informally retired from regular network programming, after doing "House Party" on CBS for twenty-five years, and "People Are Funny" on NBC for nineteen years, to a career of public speaking. Sure enough, Jack Morton contacted me and before long, I was speaking anywhere from eight to ten times a year for all kinds of large business meetings under his banner. Most lecture bureaus are content to write the contract, pick up the speaker at the airport, and deliver him to the hotel. Not so Jack Morton. He is there to check the public address system, the lighting, and other production problems, which his background in show business enabled him to perform. He was also adept at sneaking the speaker out as fast as possible, without offending anybody, and getting him or her on his way to his next date. For this, I thank Jack, and wish he could run a school for many other bookers with whom I have dealt. With the way that communications are expanding into cable, satellite, video-discs, etc., I am sure that Jack has new worlds to conquer, and I hope to be along for the ride."

—Art Linkletter

"The thing I enjoy about working with Jack is his professionalism. I don't like surprises. When I arrive to do the concert, I want the sound and lighting to be the best. . . . Jack always discusses every aspect of the concert with my sound and lighting people, so when we do the show it's always a joy to do. . . . Good luck, Jack, on the book."

—Andy Williams

"The truth is there are 'certain moments' in my life—and they're not necessarily the 'big' ones—that sit on the top of my vivid recollections and are there at all times for me to call upon in my quieter moments. That night at the Orange Bowl with that wonderful rickety surrey and Earl Wrightson and all those special people is one of those events for me, and I know I will never forget it."

—Shirley Jones

"A bumpy ride over back roads in the Washington area in a rainstorm with Jack Morton driving was the beginning for both of us. Jack, an aspiring producer, and an ambitious young comedian were setting out on their first club date. . . . For forty years, Jack Morton and I have been friends. From a young standup comic to a headliner, we have stayed friends. He has *always* treated me the same, trying to get me to cut my price! . . . I'm honored to be included in his memoirs and look back over the years with joy and pleasant memories. . . . I am still available."

—Alan King

"Jack Morton, a man for all seasons and for all engagements. I have played them all, but none better produced than those by Jack Morton. I only wish all engagements were as pleasant as the ones presented by my good friend, Jack Morton."

—Sammy Kaye

"I first met Jack Morton about thirty-five years ago and have since worked for Jack, or one of his associates, in practically every major city in the USA, and foreign places. I have watched his business expand from the simple vaudeville and concert-type shows into a multifaceted company. . . . In the 'good old days,' club dates, casuals, or one-nighters, as they were called, were little more than 'smokers,' where the 'orchestra' generally consisted of a piano player. In those days, a spotlight was a rarity, and good lighting was nonexistent. Jack changed all that! From the beginning, his shows had what we refer to as 'class.' He would arrange for special lighting and professional sound; he blazed a trail that others were to follow. Jack also pioneered the use of large orchestras to accompany performers. . . . I have seen Jack hire directors, writers, production people, conductors, composers, and other specialists who might contribute to a superior show. Today, a typical Jack Morton production is a beautifully constructed presentation. More important, however, is his imagination and creativity. The effect of all this has been to force others in the field to try to emulate what Jack has accomplished. . . . Jack has always been a gentleman, which in this business is truly an accolade. He has undoubtedly been a trend-setter and has set a pace that few will be able to equal."

—Alan "Blackie" Shackner

"For years Jack Morton and his associates have arranged many concert appearances for me, always handled with integrity and good taste. In gratitude, and with all good wishes for Jack and his colleagues. . .

—Victor Borge

"Jack Morton really knows how to take care of business. The dates are always fun."

—Joel Grey

October 18, 1976

Dear Mr. Morton:

Although this reply is somewhat belated, I did
want to thank you personally for your sugges-
tions concerning my appearance on television.
You may be sure your comments have been
carefully considered and that your interest is
very much appreciated.

I am deeply grateful for your support and good
efforts on my behalf. I send my warmest regards to you and your wife.

Sincerely,

Gerald R. Ford

Mr. Jack Morton
President
Jack Morton Productions, Inc.
1225 Connecticut Avenue, N.W.
Washington, D.C. 20036

Preface

THERE WE WERE, three of us, sitting around a table in a hotel coffee shop in downtown Cleveland, feeling relaxed and happy because the show we had just put on was a tremendous success.

"It all worked out very well, Jack."

I nodded gratefully.

The speaker was Jack Benny, and as I lifted my fork, bearing a couple of french fries, I had the sudden compulsion to pinch myself. Here I was, I.L. (Jack) Morton, a nobody out of Wilson, North Carolina, sitting and talking with the great Jack Benny and his longtime manager, Irv Fein.

I am not famous in my own right—which is fine with me—but it has been my pleasure to be associated rather closely with some of the biggest names in show business—Jack Benny, Bob Hope, George Burns, Red Skelton, Eddie Arnold, Jane Morgan—the list is almost endless. These great stars—whom I have found to be human beings, just as you and I—have confided in me, have asked for and heeded my advice, and, most importantly, have come to show me respect and trust.

Jack Benny once told a mutual friend: "Jack Morton is the only person in this business I work for without asking for my money in advance."

You cannot put a monetary value on a tribute like that.

That night in Cleveland comes to mind because it marked the close of what had become an all-too-typical day in the life of Jack Morton, producer of shows for national conventions—one of the services rendered by Jack Morton Productions, a nationwide entertainment and communications corporation.

On this balmy June night in 1967, Jack Benny had been the

headliner of a show at the closing banquet of the annual convention of the Super Market Institute, the national association of the big grocery chain industry.

The show was held in the Cleveland Convention Center, an old, cavernous building that was better suited for an exhibit hall than a ballroom. Entertaining 2,000 people in that barn of a place and making sure they all were able to see and hear what was happening on-stage presented some challenges.

From the very beginning of our planning for the show—about a year before—SMI's convention director, Dick Daspit, made it clear they wanted something special. For one thing, he said, a lot of those planning to attend the convention were not too happy about the location. Now, Cleveland is a grand city in many respects, but other cities offer much more in the way of convention-type accommodations and outside attractions.

But SMI provided a big enough entertainment budget to allow me to bring in from Hollywood Jack Benny, still at the height of a fabulous career. I also assured Dick I would come up with a large orchestra and good supporting acts. Still, he wasn't totally satisfied.

"We're going to have to put a lot of people in there," he said. "That's a big place. If we put the stage on one end, in the conventional manner, some of those people are going to feel like they're not even there. How about putting the show on with the stage in the center?"

I thought about it for a minute. "We have Jack Benny," I said. "Jack literally stands still during his act, so he will be facing a small part of the audience the whole time, and his back will be to the rest."

Dick said, "Can't you get him to move around?"

"You want me to tell Jack Benny to change the routine he's had for fifty years?"

Then I thought of using a turntable. "Where can we get one?" I asked.

Dick put me in touch with Hal Bartlett of Andrews-Bartlett, the firm that was arranging the exhibits. I reached Hal in his office and made arrangements to get a turntable, along with a circular canopy, without which the stage would end up looking like a boxing ring.

On the day of the show, I arrived at the hall to find sound and light people working furiously to get things ready for the rehearsal at 2:30. By 1:30, the grand piano had not yet arrived. I finally traced it to a room two floors above. Getting it moved required heated negotiations with three unions and the exhibit-hall management. But the piano arrived just as the musicians were taking their places.

At about the same time, Jack Benny showed up with his manager, Irving Fein, and I got a sinking feeling in my stomach. Jack did not know he was going to be asked to perform on a revolving stage, and I wasn't at all sure he was going to like it.

Jack walked up to me and looked around the vast hall as workers were setting up the dining tables and others were hustling back and forth with table cloths, napkins, dishes, flower arrangements, and silver. "I've played smaller towns than this," Jack said.

"It is big," I said. "We'll have a good house, a little more than two thousand."

"I see the stage is in the center," Jack said.

"Yes," I said. "It moves."

"It what?" Jack said.

"It moves. It is a revolving stage."

"I know what it is," Jack said. "Look, I'm not too steady when nothing is moving. When I learned in the first grade that the earth was turning, I took the rest of the day off sick."

Irv Fein, who was standing next to Jack taking it all in, broke in to say, "No way! Jack is not going to get on a moving stage!"

There I was with a million dollars worth of staging, crews, and equipment, and two million dollars worth of talent, and the star was balking at using the turntable. We could turn off the turntable, of course, for Jack's act, but the client would be very unhappy, not to mention the thousand or more people who would be at the rear of a fixed stage.

It was then that I noticed the little girl sitting off to the side with her mother, and I was struck with an idea. The girl, about ten years old, was part of Jack's act. Jack would come on stage carrying his violin, all set to play Rimsky-Korsakov's "The Flight of the Bumblebee," when the girl, "planted" in the audience, would walk up the aisle and onto the stage carrying an autograph book and say, "Mr. Benny, will you please give me your autograph?" And Jack would say, "Oh, all right. Here, hold my violin." And, as Jack wrote his name in the book, the little girl (actually an accomplished violinist) would begin to give an exquisite rendition of "The Flight of the Bumblebee." Jack would get that famous Benny look of exasperation and the audience would be in convulsions.

So I asked the little girl to help me convince Jack Benny that a revolving stage was nothing to be concerned about.

She danced up onto the stage—it was now moving—and called to Jack:

"Hey, Mr. Benny, come on up. This is really neat. Come try it."

Jack hesitated for a moment, but the girl kept smiling and beckoning, and he finally walked onto the stage. In a minute he was smiling, too. And so was I—all over.

Following the rehearsal, Jack invited me to his suite for a drink and a talk about the show routine. When I arrived, Jack had the television on, and the news was dominated by the start of the Arab–Israeli war. (The date was June 6, 1967—the start of that war, the anniversary of D-Day, in 1944, and the birthdays of Jack Morton, his fifty-seventh, and his daughter, Mary Lou, her twenty-sixth. Those are the reasons I remember the exact date.)

Jack was so furious at the Arabs that I thought he was going to have a stroke.

After he calmed down, I asked him if I could use the phone to call my daughter and wish her a happy birthday. He said, by all means. "In fact," he said, "let me wish her a happy birthday, too."

Mary Lou was in our Washington home. I wished her a happy birthday, and she wished me the same. Then I said, "Someone here wants to speak to you."

"I'm here with your dad," Jack said, "and I wanted to wish you a happy birthday."

"Who is this?" Mary Lou asked.

"I'm just a friend of your dad's."

"Are you one of the musicians?" Mary Lou asked.

"That," Jack said, "apparently is a matter of much debate."

Mary Lou never guessed who it was, and when I later told her, she was very surprised and pleased.

I went to my room to change and then back to the hall to make sure everything was set.

The show was fantastic.

I have produced a lot of shows over the last forty years, but that one in Cleveland stands out as one of the more rewarding ones. The fears I had over Jack and the turntable never came to pass. The apprehension I had over whether or not the darn thing would work and whether the effect would be what we hoped for proved unfounded. The supporting acts were great, and Jack Benny was never better. The audience response was heartwarming. I know all 2,000 members and guests of the Super Market Institute went to their respective homes with warm feelings about Cleveland.

And so, there I sat late at night, relaxing with Jack Benny and Irv Fein, and Jack turned to me and asked: "Jack, how did you get into this business?"

"It's a long story," I said, "but an interesting one, I believe."

"Then maybe you ought to write it," he said.

And, so I am. Other show business celebrities, along with other friends, family members, and business associates, have been urging me for years to put my life down on paper.

Some of them were thinking mostly of the true stories I have witnessed—funny, sad, and dramatic—concerning some rather well-known people.

Others (business associates included) believe the real story lies in the evolution of Jack Morton Productions, which now has offices in six cities, but which I began in 1936 by booking dance bands out of an apartment in Washington, D.C.

Still others (family members included) believe the real story lies in the life and times of Jack Morton, a life that began in a poor farmhouse in North Carolina and has never been dull for one minute.

Still others, including my coauthor, Bill Fuchs, say the Jack Morton story is all of these. Bill says medical students may be able to dissect a man's body in the pathology lab, but no one can dissect a man's life. Each part has a bearing on the others; each segment affects and is affected by every other segment. Every man and every woman's life, Bill says, is a story worth telling.

It is my fervent wish that everyone who reads this story will agree.

xvii

The Jack Morton
(Who's He?) Story

1

IT AMAZES ME that after all these years, I can remember so much about those early days when we were a real family living on a farm in Wilson, North Carolina.

It seems that from ages three to six, I did an awful lot of living. I know people who cannot remember that far back in their lives. I can. It is like I have a movie projector in my brain, and whenever I want, I can sit back and look at our farm way out on Nash Road, a whole mile, or maybe even a mile and a quarter, from downtown Wilson. I can see in living technicolor the large, green oak trees that guarded our front yard, and across the road, Saul's Country Store, where Papa drank his cider and liquor when he wasn't drinking them someplace else, and I can see the Joyner place and Palmer's place, also across the road. I can see the broad tobacco leaves and the fluffy white cotton growing on the back acres, and I can still see Papa standing there telling the mule to get moving to the tobacco barn.

It's quite a good movie, "uplifting" or "wholesome," I guess the critics would call it. Of course, there are a lot of pages missing from the script. It was produced too long ago. But there is enough there to give me a warm feeling and make me glad that I starred in it.

It wasn't until I was a grown man and had left the rich farm-land and hills and streams of eastern North Carolina behind me that I realized that I was a Southern sharecropper's son.

Words have a way of playing tricks on people. Take those words, "Southern sharecropper's son." To the average person, they conjure up the picture of a raggedy, miserable kid with a pinched, hungry face, a kid whose life was one gray, hard day after another.

1

Well, it wasn't like that at all.

And I am gratified that no Yankee female social worker ever got hold of me, especially in those days when I was being shunted from one home to another. There is no telling what she'd have done to me for my own good.

Yes, my father was a sharecropper. But when I think of that word, I think of a good, hardworking man with a strong sense of right and wrong, a simple man who lived close to the land and loved the land, though he never owned a square foot of it himself, a man who—to use today's idiom—knew his priorities.

My father raised tobacco and cotton for absentee landlords. He did other things, including one time running a boat down the Newport River from Newport to Pamlico Sound, over to Ocracoke, Hatteras, and Beaufort. He was also an expert landscaper and gardener. In later years, he stopped growing tobacco and cotton for other people and instead planted trees and landscaped yards for other people. He was also expert enough in treating animals to qualify as a veterinarian, except for the technicality of never having finished the sixth grade.

I was born in Newport, North Carolina, on June 6, 1910. At the time my father was running a truck farm for George Ives, a New York businessman, doing some commercial fishing and running people and things in his boat, the "things" no doubt bearing some relationship to the distillery business.

I was the fifth child born to Irvin L. and Gertrude Riggs Morton. The fourth child had died, and there was a seven-year gap between my closest brother, Ted, and me. Charlie was ten years older than I, and Otis was eleven years older. For whatever reason—perhaps my father feared he was running out of chances—I was given the dubious distinction of bearing his name. When they christened me Irvin Leonidas, Jr., I had nothing to say about it. Irvin is a grand old Southern surname, I was told when I was old enough to protest, while Leonidas was a legendary Greek hero. Leonidas means "lion-like." There are no Greeks in my heritage and no lion tamers, so far as I know. But my father and I were stuck with that name.

Fortunately, few people ever called me Irvin or Leonidas. For the first fourteen years of my life, I was known mostly as "I.L.," though for a good part of my growing-up years in Wilson, my peers referred to me by the more formal appellation of "Toenail."

I acquired the nickname "Jack" at the age of fourteen while working in a movie theater in Raleigh. It was one of those unexpected, rather important things that happen in life that seem so insignificant at the time. On first hearing "I.L.," most people thought it was a name and a most unusual one at that, and they were always asking me to spell it. The cashier in the Raleigh theater had trouble pronouncing it, so she started to call me Jack. And it stuck. I am grateful she picked a name I liked. She was so attractive she could have called me Leonidas and it would have been all right with me.

But that didn't mean I was through with name problems forever. Before I became Jack, I had started calling myself Irving because I had been reading some books by Washington Irving, and I liked the name better than Irvin.

Well, for some reason, that name continued to crop up now and then like a drinking brother-in-law. There was the time when the word got around that my real name was not Jack, but Irving. I was already in show business, and the natural conclusion was that my last name was a phony, too, and that I was Jewish. Being Jewish can sometimes be a problem. Ask any Jew. Even if they *think* you are a Jew it can be a problem. Ask me. I was rejected for membership at two clubs because of that.

Soon after I was born, the family moved from Newport to Wilson, about 100 miles inland, where my father took over a 200-acre farm. We grew corn, tobacco, cotton, and such truck-farm items as beans, peas, watermelon, cantaloupe, cucumbers, asparagus, potatoes—anything and everything that we could sell in summer and can or preserve for the winter.

We had mules, cows, hogs, a few sheep, ducks, a goat—which I designated my special pet—and some geese—which I designated my special enemies. Papa let the geese roam around so they could help control the grass among the things he had planted. The trouble is, they didn't only go after the grass, they also went after me, nipping me as I ran. I soon learned to keep my distance. To this day, I hate geese, and if you ever invite me to Christmas dinner, serve me anything, but never, never goose.

While Papa knew everything there was to know about growing things and animals, it was Mama who kept the place hum-

3

ming. Mama was poor Southern stock, also. She was not more than fifteen years old when she married my father. Like my father, she was on intimate terms with hard work. She was also scrupulously honest and scrupulously clean.

I can sense her still, a slim, plain woman, who, after all these years, seems more like a presence than a flesh-and-bones figure, a kindly, caring presence who believed love was a verb and was best expressed in deeds, not words.

While Papa was strong in body, the way men are strong, Mama was strong inside. She was the disciplinarian who never had a doubt as to what was right and what was wrong and firmly believed her chief responsibility in life was to impart that same moral certitude to her offspring.

If cleanliness is really next to Godliness, then the Mortons back in those days must have been in heaven and didn't know it. There was a washbasin, soap, and towel on our backporch near the well, and I learned real early what they were for. Some of my earliest memories show Mama turning from the kitchen sink as I walked into the door and demanding: "Did you wash up real good?"

Mama was also a stickler for manners. At the dinner table, if you didn't say "please," you didn't get it. So, at meal times, we always had very "pleasing" conversations.

I don't remember ever seeing my mother when she wasn't busy—churning butter, scrubbing floors, cooking, baking, canning, making clothes. She was also not one to push around.

I remember when I was about five, I went skinny-dipping in a little stream on our farm with Joey Palmer. Joey's father caught us there and decided to teach us both a lesson. He took off his belt and gave us each a thrashing. I didn't really enjoy that, so I went home and told my mother. Mama got a look in her eyes you usually associate with a grizzly bear, stopped canning blackberry preserves, and stormed across the road.

"Palmer," she said, "you keep your hands off my boy. The next time you just as much as put a finger on him, I'm comin' back over here and I'm going to do more than just talk."

Mr. Palmer stared at the ground for a few seconds. Then, without looking up, he allowed as how my mother had a good point there. He said he was only doing what he thought was right at the time, but now could see he was wrong. He told her it never would happen again. And it didn't.

It seems that in the first few years of my life, I was always getting into one kind of mess or another, and the Palmers were always involved.

There was the time Joey and I set fire to the field of dry broomstraw and it almost caught the Palmer house afire before Papa, my brothers, and Mr. Palmer got it out. That was right before I fell down the well and almost drowned.

It was an old abandoned well in the Palmer's front yard that Mr. Palmer had never bothered to fill in. I was sort of half-running across the yard, with Joey chasing me in some kind of game, when I suddenly felt my right leg give way and I was pitched into a gaping hole. As I went crashing down into the darkness, I managed to grab at some roots growing out of the sides of the well just as my head was going to follow the rest of me into black, icy water. The frigid wetness gripped my legs and back and arms like a vise, and I could feel the water sloshing around my neck. I was certain that any second whatever I was holding onto would give way and I would sink and that would be the end of me. I cannot tell you that my entire life passed before me, because I hadn't lived much of it yet—only about five years. Up on top I could hear Joey screaming his head off. Soon—not more than two or three months, I figured at the time—grownups were up there, and somebody reached down and pulled me up and out.

When my mother heard about what happened, I almost felt sorry for Mr. Palmer. But Mama was exceptionally calm about it. She told him very quietly: "You fill in that well—and I mean fill it in right now, today, or else!"

Mr. Palmer allowed that Mama had a fine suggestion, and he acted on it immediately.

Can you imagine what Mr. Palmer would be facing in today's world—criminal charges and lawsuits and who knows what else. Certainly all kinds of government agencies would be involved. In those more simple days, at about the time of the First World War, people managed to solve most of their personal difficulties between and among themselves.

Papa stayed in the background in those personal situations. My relationship with Papa almost always centered around work of some kind or another. And certainly he taught me a lot about farming and animals, landscaping, wells, septic tanks, and machinery.

One thing he never could teach me—how to kill.

I guess it just wasn't in me. Time and again he would try to teach me how to wring the neck of a chicken. Well, I would try. I would get that chicken's head in my hand just right, but there was something about the warm, live feel of it, something about those frightened black eyes, and the next thing you know the chicken would be running off and Papa would be spitting tobacco juice on the ground and saying, "Goddamn."

I remember one time, the day before Thanksgiving, when Papa told me he wanted me to help kill the turkey. If you invite me to Christmas dinner, you surely can serve turkey. But please, don't ask me to kill it for you. I was five years old, and I remember that day as though it were yesterday. Papa had this big ax in one hand, and he was holding the turkey by the feet in the other. He swung the turkey over onto a wooden chopping block and said, "I.L., all you got to do is hold his head. He sure is plump and he's gonna be real good eatin'. So just hold his head." I held the turkey's head, and Papa pulled that ax up, and I could see the blade coming down (and now, when I think about it, I think about the French Revolution and the guillotine and Madame LaFarge knitting while the heads were rolling off into the basket). I saw the turkey's eyes watching that blade coming down, and I let go of his head, and the turkey pulled his head out of the way just in time.

Papa said "goddamn" two or three times and then put the ax away. I don't remember what we had for Thanksgiving dinner, but it wasn't turkey.

Today, I don't chew tobacco, and I don't smoke, and I really can understand the militant opposition to tobacco on the part of a lot of people today. But when you grow up around it, you look at it a lot differently. I started chewing tobacco before I was in the first grade. Chewing tobacco was just as natural as eating apples or watermelon.

For the tobacco farmer, tobacco is a crop, just like cotton or potatoes.

The tobacco cropping season is very short, just a few weeks

6

or so, but I can remember it vividly. It was an exciting time. Our farm became alive with people and activity. It was like a movie production, with everybody doing a certain thing according to the script. We would have several black people and my brothers and Papa all swarming around there cropping off the tobacco leaves, starting at the bottom, because tobacco ripens from the bottom up. Even the mule knew his lines. He would carry the cart between the rows of tobacco, and when the cart was full, he would carry it to the barn where several black women would tie the leaves together and hang them over a stick about four feet long. Someone else would take the sticks and hang them on the rafters in the barn until there was row after row of tobacco leaves hanging in there.

I used to like staying in the barn at night while the tobacco cured. There was the sweet smell of the wood smoke, and the older folks would sit and tell stories. We might have some fried chicken and watermelon, and I would find myself falling asleep and by some miracle I would awake the next morning in my bed.

You have to have somebody in the curing barn all the time to make sure the temperature stayed constant. It took about eight to ten days to cure the tobacco. We had a stone furnace with flues going in and around all over inside the barn, and there was a thermometer inside the barn. I can still see Papa or brother Otis checking the thermometer and hollering for somebody to put on more wood.

After the tobacco was cured, we would take it out of the barn and off the sticks, untie the leaves and let them unravel. And then they would have to sort them out according to quality or grade. And they'd put them on large trays and set the trays on the wagon, and the mule would take the wagon to market.

The big tobacco warehouses were down on Tarboro Street, off Nash Road, and the wagons would start lining up at six o'clock the evening before. You'd think it was the World Series or something. By ten o'clock, horses and mules and wagons would be lined all the way up Tarboro and around Nash up to the Baptist Church. Those mules, horses, wagons, and men would stay there the whole night, and when the market opened at six in the morning, each seller would have to wait his turn. I don't know about now, but in those days Wilson was the biggest bright-leaf tobacco market in the world. All the big tobacco companies were there—R.J. Reynolds, Liggett & Myers, Imperial, American, all of them.

They were looking mostly for the bright leaves, the kind that goes into cigarettes.

When your turn finally came, and you made it into the warehouse, you would be given a spot on the floor for your tobacco. The warehouse was big enough to hold a football game in. Almost as far as the eye could see, were row after row of mounds of tobacco leaves and people moving about conducting the oldest game on earth, buying and selling. Someone would weigh your tobacco and tag it with your name and the tobacco weight, and finally the auctioneer would come by and pick up your tobacco and feel it, inviting the buyers to do the same. Papa would watch them very intently, and I was always afraid someone would say, "Mr. Morton, your tobacco does not measure up," and all of that work, the plowing, the planting, the cropping and curing, would be for nothing. But nobody ever said that, of course, because Papa knew crops, and he wouldn't try to auction off anything that wasn't top grade. At last, the auctioneer would begin spieling off numbers so fast you couldn't keep up with it and finally, "Sold, American!" or "Sold, Imperial!"

Papa—any seller—had the right to refuse the bid and take his tobacco home and wait for another day. If you sold it, they would give you a slip of paper, and you would go to the cashier's window in the warehouse and get your money. Papa would get his money and then turn most of it over to the fertilizer people. Everybody else did, too. For the Southern farmer, credit was only slightly less important than rain.

I can still remember riding back home in the wagon with Papa, Otis, and Ted. Papa would be saying that we had gotten a pretty good price and that the tobacco people knew the Morton leaves were top-grade. I can still recall the grand feeling of those wonderful, exciting times. I would burst forth in the rapid-fire, sing-song auctioneer's chant, but I could never quite bring it off, and everybody would laugh, with me laughing hardest of all.

Our other "big money" crop was cotton. Once again, we'd have the black people over to help pick it. (It is a mistaken Yankee notion that the whites in the South treated blacks with contempt. In fact, while it was a segregated culture, there was more genuine respect and love between the races in any single county in Dixie than in all the rest of the country combined.) They didn't make much money picking cotton—about a cent a pound, if I remember correctly, or about a dollar a day for bent-over, sack-dragging labor. But the black people didn't feel "exploited," because they knew we weren't doing much better.

I used to go with Papa to the cotton gin. I remember the big vacuum pipe that would suck up the cotton, and I was always afraid I was going to get sucked up there, too.

Today they talk about the work ethic. When I grew up, work wasn't an ethic, it was a way of life, a way of staying alive; everyone took it for granted, everyone pitched in and did it. Even as a "little shaver" on that farm, I was expected to do my share, picking potatoes, beans, berries, and whatever. And I wouldn't have wanted it any other way. By today's standards, I guess it was a tough life. Some kids today cut a quarter-acre lawn, using a gasoline powered mower, and think they've done a week's work and, morever, expect to get paid for it while getting free room, board, clothing, and spending money.

But those early years were good years for me. I can still see my father's strong arms covered with red dirt, standing in a field wiping his face with a red and white bandana. I can still see my mother, her face somewhat drained by the weight of those busy, busy days. And pervading all of it, I can still sense the grand feeling of love and security. Nobody said much about love. There was very little hugging and kissing. Love was just there, a warm, comforting presence. Somehow work was part of it. People in families worked together to express their love and concern for one another.

It was, in short, a happy time.

When I was four years old, I was given a little sister, Mary, and two years later, Mama had twins, Luther and Lee. They were numbers seven and eight for Mama, who—I learned later—had a most difficult time. But two months later, she seemed like her old self, washing and cleaning and making clothes. I can still remember underclothes from Dan Patch Horsefeed and Ralston Purina Hog Chow. It took a long time and a lot of washings to get the red checkers out of Purina underwear.

I remember on this particular day, Mama was sewing in the

dining room while I sat on the floor nearby looking at a Sears Roebuck catalog. Mama got up to go into the kitchen. I don't know why I looked up from my book at the precise moment, but I saw her stop in the doorway, put a hand up to her head, and collapse.

The doctor said she was dead when she hit the floor, from what was probably heart failure.

I was not quite six, and I really did not understand death. But I knew my mother had gone. I knew something very important had been taken from me. And, I also knew my life would never be the same again.

But I was not afraid. For those first six years—what the psychiatrists and psychologists like to refer to as the "formative years"—I had something money could never buy, a secure and loving home. For while my poor, Southern-folk parents were never very demonstrative—I suppose they were just too darned busy—their love for one another and their children was a given. And that is the best kind of love there is.

2

THE PASSING OF MY MOTHER left too much of a burden on my father. There he was, with the day's work to be done every day and with seven children, ranging in age from infancy to seventeen.

My family disintegrated.

Otis, seventeen, and Charlie, fifteen, struck out on their own. Ted, fourteen, was apprenticed to a watchmaker in downtown Wilson, a Dr. Blauvelt, who wanted a boy to live with him and learn the watchmaking and jewelry business, because his own son was interested in medicine. Mary, two, went with Papa's sister, Aunt Annie. The twins were divided between my mother's two sisters, though one of the twins, Lee, followed my mother within the year.

That left me, a sandy-haired, skinny six-year-old, who somehow was blessed with the capacity to adjust quickly and happily. I am sure that is a gift. It is known as acceptance, and some people spend most of their lives in miserable frustration because they have never mastered it. I was born with it, so consequently I have not wasted too much of my life in that futile war with fate. I have known very little despair in my life. Disappointments, of course, but despair, almost never.

The memories of early childhood are often hazy, almost dreamlike, with shadowy figures moving about stealthily, like players in some half-forgotten silent movie.

I was boarded out first to a middle-aged couple named Riley. I remember her as a small, wizened woman who wore her hair in a bun and who was always fussing and fidgeting. He was a large man with a flowing moustache. It was a happy time, but as I said, it didn't take a lot to make me happy.

11

At the age of six, a chaw of tobacco would do it.

By that time I was a veteran chewer. The discovery of that fact almost sent Mrs. Riley into nervous convulsions. I tried to explain to her that a man needed a chaw to spit on his fishbait for good luck and to soften up the leather in his fielder's mitt. But so far as I know, Mrs. Riley never indulged herself, so she was somewhat biased on the subject.

I confined my chewing to the great outdoors, hiding my tobacco outside, but it seems like Mrs. Riley had the instincts of Sherlock Holmes. She was always finding it and looking heavenward for guidance.

I can recall, too, a short but happy friendship with a boy named Bunny Farrell, who lived next door and who had a pony, a brown and white spotted pony that he shared with me. We really took care of that pony. We would curry him and feed and water him and ride him, and we would even feed him sugar, which Bunny would get from his kitchen.

We were encouraged not to do that anymore, when the pony bit off the ends of a couple of Bunny's fingers. It wasn't really the pony's fault. Unlike human beings, animals don't go around inflicting harm on others for no reason. But if you stick your fingers inside a pony's mouth, he has no way of distinguishing fingers from sugar. Bunny, of course, sensed the difference almost immediately.

In the late fall of 1917, I got pneumonia. In those days—in fact, until the advent of the so-called miracle drugs much later—people spoke about pneumonia in whispers, like it was the Black Plague.

The memories of that experience are quite subdued—faded visions of a serious-faced doctor with white hair; a basket of fruit on the dresser that I got out of bed to sample, only to be told I could die doing that (I decided not to do it anymore); and through it all, the genuine concern and tender care of the Rileys.

I remember, too, that my brother Otis, only nineteen himself, and his seventeen-year-old bride, Elsie, came to see me, their eyes filled with compassion, and told me they were going to take me home with them.

And so I went to live with Otis and Elsie in their one-bedroom apartment on the second floor of a private home in Raleigh and left behind forever a middle-aged couple named Riley. I never saw them again, and my time with them was brief—less than a year—but in that short span, with their love and kindness, they helped shape a small boy's feelings and attitudes, and the happiness and success I have known in this life is due in no small measure to their unselfishness. They have long since departed this earth, and I am thoroughly convinced that the first person to greet them on the other side, with much love and gratitude, was the former wife of a sharecropper.

Let me tell you something now about my oldest brother, Otis, with whom I was next to take up lodgings. He was a hard-working, honest man, even as a teenager, and he was always helping other people. Helping other people was just as natural to him as it is for some others to stomp on other people.

When he first left home after Mama died, Otis went to work in a music store in Raleigh. Later he worked for the Pillsbury Flour Company, going around the country selling flour, giving out samples and prizes and putting on demonstrations. Putting on demonstrations on how to cook and bake with Pillsbury must have made an impression on Otis, because later on in life he opened his own bakery. He did quite well with it, too.

Otis was a tall, thin, blondish young man who never had any trouble with women for the simple reason that he only wanted one woman in his entire life, Elsie, whom he married at the age of nineteen and stayed married to until his death parted them sixty-one years later.

Otis met Elsie at a church supper. He saw her standing near the punch bowl across the room, and it was like lightning struck.

He said to someone next to him: "Who is that girl over there?"

"Why, that's Elsie Poole," the other person said.

"She may be Elsie Poole now," Otis supposedly said, "but not for long. Pretty soon she's going to be Elsie Morton."

Well, he managed an introduction and sure enough, after dating her for only a week, he asked her to marry him. And Elsie didn't even hesitate in answering him. She said no.

But Otis persisted. After a little while, he landed a job in Richmond with the streetcar company there. Feeling the way he did about Elsie, I never have understood why he took it. Besides, they weren't hiring him as a vice-president. His job was to sit in a room with several others and count the money in the fare boxes brought in by the conductors.

After three months in Richmond, Otis returned to Raleigh to propose once more. This time Elsie had hit on a plan to keep him from asking her anymore. She said yes. They were married and went back to Richmond, where Otis took up his thrilling duties of counting streetcar tokens.

He finally quit that job. It wasn't so much that he couldn't stand the job any more. It was that Elsie couldn't stand Richmond. She told Otis, "Grant can have this place. Let's go home." And back home they went.

Lest anybody from Richmond take offense, I am sure it's a very nice place. But North Carolinians have a very difficult time feeling at home anywhere outside of North Carolina.

Elsie's father owned a grocery store, and Otis worked there for a while and then took a job with the Railway Express Company. If you are young and are wondering what transported everything between train stations before trucks took over, it was the Railway Express.

That is where Otis was working when I went to live with him and Elsie in December of 1917.

Elsie was a pretty girl, dark-haired and brown-eyed and a little on the plump side, but not too much so. Even today, at the age of eighty-three, with her hair now snow white, Elsie is a striking woman.

Elsie was fairly easy to get along with, but one thing she was totally against, was alcohol. Otis never was much of a drinker anyway, so after marrying Elsie he just never bothered with it again.

Papa drank, of course; sometimes too much, and my next-to-oldest brother, Charlie, drank an awful lot at one time. But he quit suddenly, and some people said he "got religion," because he became a lay preacher and even founded a mission, which is thriving to this day in Raleigh. Dr. Carl Jung, the eminent psychiatrist, once said the only release for the chronic alcoholic lies in a vital spiritual experience, a principle that serves as the basis for the highly successful Alcoholics Anonymous program. I believe that is what happened to Charlie. Saying he "got religion" sort of cheapens what I firmly believe was a genuine spiritual

14

conversion, which resulted in something that was truly miraculous.

At the time I went to live with Otis and Elsie, the big war was in progress, the one they always called the "World War" until they decided to have a series of them and give them numbers. I don't remember much about it. I do remember going with Papa to visit Charlie in an army camp over in Goldsboro, but the war ended before Charlie had the chance to become a hero.

I also have some vague memories of a cousin on Papa's side who really was a hero, a much-decorated army captain who was wounded and gassed in France. He died shortly after the war. I heard my Papa and others talking about him in hushed tones, and I dimly recall some references to the way he died—suddenly, I think, by his own hand.

There are parts of my brain that maybe weren't working too well back in those days, or perhaps they aren't working too well now. At any rate, trying to focus in on events of three score and more years ago is a chancy business.

But all the memory cells aren't in the brain. A lot of them are in the nose. At least, it seems I can remember almost as much with my nose as with my brain.

I stayed with Otis and Elsie that first time only about seven or eight months, and every time I think about that, a heavy, pungent smell of burning coal envelops me, and even my eyes smart a little. It was not an unpleasant smell; it was the same kind of coal-smoke smell you'd get at the train station, the heavy smell of a big industry.

The source of this continuous presence was the gasworks located across the street from Otis and Elsie and right next door to the Poole's house.

The gasworks was a sprawling mass of wood, stone, and dark gray metal, with large pipes sticking out through the roof; outside, all around, were mountains of coal. So far as I can remember, we kids never ventured inside—I don't think they would have allowed us anyway—but the place had such a forbidding look we no doubt decided that if it would leave us alone, we would leave it alone. And except for the smell, it left us pretty much alone.

We knew, of course, that they made gas there and the gas

15

was sent through pipes to people's houses for cooking mostly, though at one time the gas was also used for lighting. Still later, of course, they discovered large deposits of natural gas, and the smell of burning coal began to lessen, if not disappear altogether, from America's towns and cities.

But in those days every town smelled like Pittsburgh. I learned later that they heated the coal until it turned into coke and gas.

One Sunday afternoon, while everybody was having dinner at the Pooles, I found out why coal burning in the gasworks smelled with so much authority. I heard Mr. Poole saying that coal was actually the remains of plants and animals that had been dead for millions of years, all crushed together in those black lumps. I remember later asking Charles Poole about it, and he said, "Well, if Papa said it, it must be true. But how do they know about that? They weren't around then when it was happening. So how would they know it?"

I had planned to ask Mr. Poole that, but I don't remember whether I ever did.

The only other thing about the gas that I remember is that Mrs. Poole was always running out. She was always sending me next door to the grocery store to get quarters to put in the coin meter in the kitchen. You'd put a quarter in and it would turn the gas back on. Later someone from the gas company would come by and collect all the quarters.

The Pooles were really something. Elsie was one of about ten or eleven children. Her mother was one of those short, plump women who are constantly busy and are always laughing and singing. Though I lived with Otis and Elsie across the street, I spent most of my time at the Pooles, and in no time at all I was one of the family.

Mr. Poole was a big, gray-haired man, with a big gray mustache. He was the head of the clan and presided over everything, like a kindly Prussian general. In personality he was quite the opposite of his wife, stern and quiet and all business.

Of all the offspring, Charles was the one I gravitated to. He was about five or six years older than I was, but I was naturally attracted to him because it was obvious that he was a cut above the rest of the Pooles. He chewed tobacco, smoked and cussed.

16

Charles and I both worked in the store. Our main job was delivering the groceries. We would pack them in cartons or crates, hitch up Nellie and drive all over Raleigh delivering "Poole's Groceries." People didn't go shopping for groceries the way they do now.

Nellie, the mare, had only one eye, and she was as mean as a pirate, but she was a good worker and she was smart. When we got all our deliveries done, we would wrap the reins around the buckboard, cluck to old Nellie, and she would find her own way home. Then Charles and I would settle back, pull out our tobacco, and do some serious chewing.

But what I remember most about those days was the Sunday dinners. The married members of the family and their spouses and children, including Otis and Elsie, would attend every single Sunday. That dining room, with the big oak table, looked like a banquet room. The rule was that the adults would eat first, about a dozen or so of them, gathered around that table, while we kids would hang around outside on the porch looking in at them through the windows.

When it came to cooking, nobody, absolutely nobody, at any time or anyplace, could excel Mrs. Poole. Not that there was much variety. You didn't need, or even want, variety when something was that good.

The main course was always fried chicken. The Pooles had their own chickens; in fact, they slaughtered them and sold them in the store.

There was always potato salad, big yellow gobs of potato salad with mustard and eggs to give it that special tang. And hot biscuits. Mrs. Poole would bring in a plate of hot biscuits from the kitchen, and that plate never touched the table until it was empty, which took all of about four seconds flat. There were vegetables of all kinds, butter and preserves, and for dessert, homemade cakes and pies and ice cream. Homemade? Naturally. Everything was homemade.

The adults-first, children-last rule had a terrible disadvantage if you were a child. Looking through the windows from the porch at all that eating was downright frustrating.

I remember one time hanging on that window and looking inside and saying, "That chicken sure looks good." Well, it was

17

summertime, the windows were open, and I carefully picked a time to open my big mouth when there was a sudden lull in the dining room conversation.

Mrs. Poole was out on the porch in a second. "All right, you young'ns," she said, "there's plenty of food and you'll all get your turn. Meanwhile, get off the porch and leave the grownups be. I'll call you when it's your turn." Our turn always came, and that is where I learned that waiting is a seasoning itself and will enhance the taste of anything in life worth waiting for.

Soon it was time for me to move on again. Otis and Elsie had very cramped living quarters on the second floor of Mrs. Hinnant's two-story house, and now their first child was due. And I was sleeping in that child's crib. They named the baby Minerva after the kind and bubbly Mrs. Poole.

It was Mrs. Poole, as I remember, who helped me get scrubbed and dressed and put me on the train for Walstonburg, a sleepy little town about seventy miles from Raleigh and only eighteen miles from my original hometown of Wilson.

3

WE DIDN'T HAVE MUCH MONEY when I was a boy, but one thing we did have in our family, and that was people. I had more relatives—aunts and uncles and half-aunts and half-uncles, and half-this and half-that—it was just impossible to keep track of them all.

There I was, eight years old, and a veteran tobacco chewer, and I was off to live with an aunt and uncle I had never laid eyes on before, to my knowledge. Aunt Matt was my father's half-sister. But she and Uncle Kib proved themselves to be worthy guardians right off the bat, when they offered no objection to my chewing.

They had a grown daughter, Lizzie, who worked at the local telephone exchange. She was a very sweet person, but one side of her face was disfigured by a fire when she was a child. And she always carried a gun, a loaded revolver, which she let me handle on occasion.

Their house was very small, and the only place for me to sleep was with Lizzie. She always slept with the gun under her pillow and me beside her. I vaguely recall the sweet smell of her powder or perfume, and I think I got some of my earliest vibrations about the "benefits" of sleeping with a woman. They were, of course, the purest thoughts—my being so young—but I wasn't exactly stupid even at that early age.

There isn't an awful lot one can say about Walstonburg. It was so small it was almost not there. During that summer, I used to walk down the dirt road to the railroad station and watch the train come in and depart. I also remember that somebody had a monkey down there. He was tied out there on the depot platform,

19

and people would feed him peanuts and play with him. The monkey and I became good friends. I made a deal with him from the very start: I wouldn't put my fingers in his mouth and he wouldn't bite them off.

As I recall, Uncle Kib and Aunt Matt were getting up in years. They grew a few things in the fields, but Uncle Kib was not very active.

The big thing I remember, and I wish I didn't, was hog-killing time.

One thing about hogs: Once you get to know them, they turn out to be pretty good people. They have a lot of personality, and they are quite smart. One of my chores was to feed the hogs every day. I guess I never realized what I was feeding them for, but I found out one cold December day when Uncle Kib mentioned that it was hog-killing day and a couple of Negroes were coming over to help out.

Killing a hog isn't easy. For one thing, it is pretty obvious that they want to keep their porkchops inside them, not put 'em inside somebody else. You can tell 'em it hurts you a lot more than it does them, but they won't believe you.

There were a couple of ways to kill a hog back then. Some people would shoot 'em in the brain, but I understand that takes a measure of skill to do it right. Some people knocked 'em in the head with an ax and then cut their throat. That's how we did it.

Then they tied him by a rope to a block and tackle, hoisted him up, and dunked him in a big tub of boiling water; then they took scrapers and worked all the hair off the hog. And finally, they hung him up and disemboweled him and took all the fat off to boil down to make lye soap. The fat that was left over was used for crackling. It was real crunchy, and people ate it and made crackling bread out of it.

In those days, there was no refrigeration, like today, so they had to kill the hogs on a cold day. As soon as possible they would cut the meat out and pack it in salt.

And while I admit I didn't like the hog-killing part, I had no objection to the hog-eating part. Pork was our main meat—porkchops, pork roasts, ham, bacon, all kinds of good things.

And I still like pork. But I can tell you: If I had to kill an animal in order to eat, I would go hungry a long time.

I remember my first and last Christmas in Walstonburg. There was about two feet of snow on the ground. I got a stocking that was filled with apples, oranges, dried raisins, peppermint sticks, and rock candy. It seems like I also got a horn, but I'm not sure. What I do remember is standing out there knee-deep in snow, eating an orange and sweating like it was the Fourth of July. It wasn't until years later that I found out I had a peculiar allergy to citrus fruits and had to give them up altogether. It was a shame, in a way, because I never did mind slaughtering an orange.

It was at Christmastime that Aunt Matt took me aside and told me I would soon be leaving. They told me my father had another wife and I was going back to Wilson to live. I didn't like that idea at all. Maybe it was that I liked where I was and was tired of moving around. Maybe it was that I resented my father for remarrying. I don't know. Besides, I figured it would be only temporary, so what was the use?

Two days later, we walked to the train station, where the monkey played on the freight platform. That monkey was quite impersonal—he liked everybody, and naturally, everybody liked him. He was about the most interesting thing in Walstonburg, which had no moving picture show. The train ride to Wilson was real short, and when we pulled into the station, I saw Papa. My mixed feelings and emotions were still in me, and when I stepped off the train, I took off through the train yard—away from Papa. I just decided I didn't want to go home with him—I wanted to go to Aunt Annie's. He caught up with me and "convinced" me about where to go. My anger didn't last long—I guess it was more confusion than anything else—and very soon I was settled in another "new home." My stepmother did more than her share to make me happy. In the following years she became my "protector"—it was always easier to go to her with my problems than to Papa. Love—something I never was able to define—comes in many ways.

21

4

My NEW HOME WAS A SMALL, white frame house on Rountree Street just off Nash, across the street from the Atlantic Christian College. We used to pass Rountree, going down Nash Road with our mule, tobacco, and cotton when we lived out on the farm. Now, we were right in town, almost, although "town" in those days still smacked pretty much of country.

I spent the next six years there, so it proved to be the most permanent home of my life until I married and found a real sense of permanency.

And yet I never felt orphaned or at loose ends. My roots seemed securely planted, and there was all about me a sense of family, even though the family was made up of "halves" and "steps" and people who hardly knew each other.

Perhaps the lack of the orthodox solid family structure gave me the sense of independence that propelled me into the world of business at an early age, leading me to work in theaters and eventually into the fascinating glitter of show business.

My first recollection of life with Papa and my new stepmother and her daughter Gladys, was seeing great leaping tongues of fire across the street at the college and hearing screaming and chanting and turning to my stepmother and asking her if the college was burning down. She told me they were hanging the Kaiser in something over there. I remember thinking we must have captured the Kaiser and brought him to Wilson. It wasn't until much later that I realized what the college students were hanging the Kaiser in was effigy.

My Aunt Annie lived across the street, next to the college toward Nash, with Uncle Ben and Aunt Annie's daughter, Charlie

22

Gray; Grannie, Aunt Annie' and Papa's mother, and my sister, Mary. Charlie Gray, who was by Aunt Annie's first husband, long deceased, was an accomplished pianist. She tried to teach me to play the piano, but either she was a terrible teacher, or I was a terrible pupil. I'm sure it was the latter. I do believe, however, that she, ever so briefly, kindled a fire of music appreciation in me. I loved the melodic sounds, the variety of tempos, and I was enchanted with the skill and dexterity used to bring it all forth.

My stepmother was a frail woman of medium height, a very pleasant woman, and like so many Southern women of that era, a hard worker who put great store in keeping a good house, setting a good table, and having mannerly, respectful children.

A word about my brother Ted, who was fifteen when I moved back with Papa and was already an accomplished watchmaker and jeweler. Ted also moved into Papa's new house (which actually belonged to Aunt Annie and Uncle Ben). He had been living with Dr. Blauvelt, the jeweler, but I guess he longed for family and preferred sharing a room with me than having a room of his own at the Blauvelts. I sure took advantage of Ted. I would hang around out in front of the jewelry store, knowing full well he could see me through the window from his repair bench. Sure enough, it wouldn't be long before he would come and give me a nickel or a dime, and off I would go to the ice-cream parlor, the popcorn stand, or the soda fountain. Sometimes he would tell me to go up to Taylor's Cafe and charge a meal on him. I always had my favorite—a fried ham sandwich that cost fifteen cents.

I remember one time losing Ted's diamond stickpin, and on another occasion I appropriated his .22 rifle and traded it for a make-believe saxophone. I don't even know where I got the urge to own a musical instrument, even a fake one. I certainly didn't have the talent to play either kind. Nevertheless, the urge to play a musical instrument was slow to go away. Although this desire got me into trouble during my childhood, later in life it proved to be a valuable asset—not in playing—but being better able to understand and appreciate those who possessed such talent.

To me, Ted was a big success. And he was, when you stop to think of it—a boy of thirteen when he went out to earn his own keep, and today, at the age of eighty, he can still hold his head up high and say he earned his way, all the way. Ted was a nice-looking youngster, with Mama's sandy hair and brown eyes with a fleck of green in them. He had the kind of open, happy face and outgoing personality that made people like and trust him on first meeting. More importantly, they never had reason to change that initial impression.

Besides letting me sponge off him, Ted also took me along hunting and fishing. Ted was the kind of guy who believed life was something to be enjoyed, no matter what kind of cards you were dealt. I think a little of that rubbed off on me. I never saw a man or woman complain who improved the situation by doing so.

But the lead role in my early life was played by my father, and I guess Ted and I both got a lot of our basic philosophy from him. He never complained. Curse? Oh, my, yes, he could give lessons in that. What he lacked in variety he made up for with force and frequency. Papa never said "darn." It was always "goddamn" this and "goddamn" that, with a little "son of a bitch" here and a "bastard" there; but never the ace of profanities, the "f" word so much in vogue these days. As blue as Papa could make the air, that word, I am sure, would have shocked him.

A little private profanity never bothered me, but I have always had a distinct distaste for it in public places. In all the years of putting together shows, I have studiously avoided the profane act, the smutty comic. And in this day and age, that certainly narrows the field.

Sometimes, there is a good reason to profane the air. Like the time Papa was cranking the Model T pickup truck he had bought secondhand and the crank recoiled, striking him on the wrist, a frequent hazard in starting cars those days.

"Goddamn it, the son of a bitch!" Papa shouted, and I laughed my head off until Papa looked up at me—he was kneeling on one knee—with an expression that was more pain than anger. I stopped laughing. It turned out that Papa had broken his wrist.

Later—after supper—Papa took me for a walk down Rountree toward the Whitehead School, where I was in the fourth grade. It was one of those blessed June evenings, warm, the sun gleaming yellow-white in a gray-blue sky, all of nature—birds, bees, cicadas, crickets, and dogs—joining in a symphony of summer

24

sounds. As we walked past the school, I could hear, from somewhere, the faint strains of "Moonlight Bay" coming from someone's phonograph. We went on past the school and into the cemetery at the foot of Whitehead, into the hallowed grounds of the Confederate dead, where just a couple of weeks before, the students and teachers of Whitehead had marched to place our flowers in grateful remembrance of their last full measure of devotion. Once in a while I would glance over at my father's wrist, bound in plaster of paris, and I wondered if he was going to say something about it. He finally did, but when he spoke there was a softness in his voice that one seldom heard.

"I.L.," he said, "never, never laugh at someone else's misfortune. No matter how funny it might look, it sure ain't funny to the one that it's happening to."

I think that was the time that I realized that Papa was not all red dirt and shovel, that beneath that hard-working, profane, liquor-drinking, tobacco-chewing dirt farmer was a gentleness that was always trying to get out.

For example, when people would steal his liquor, you would think that would be a time for some real foot-stomping, fist-shaking anger. In those days, almost all the men drank corn liquor—there were stills everywhere. I suspect even some of the preachers drank it. My mother, who was against liquor in all forms, would not allow Papa to keep it in the house, so he kept it in the barn, and he continued that practice after he married my stepmother. Every Saturday at noon, during those times when Papa had helpers, passing around the fruit jar was a ritual, as it was on other occasions of male get-togethers.

"Goddamn! Goddamn!" Papa would say. "I cain't understand it. I cain't understand it at all. Why would a man ruin the liquor for someone else?" You see, drinking the liquor didn't bother Papa much. What bothered him was discovering someone had ruined the liquor by watering it. That was worse than horse stealing.

There is another scene starring Papa that I will happily carry to my grave.

It was the night Louise was born and I lay there in my bed, my eyes wide open. The entire house had settled down to the old, familiar, late-night summer quiet.

And then I heard my father come into the room. He undressed quietly and got into bed with me, trying to shift his big weight easily so as not to disturb my sleep. I was still wide awake, but I did not say anything. And then I felt that big, hard-working arm drape around my shoulder and hold me. And I heard his voice, a soft whisper: "Good night, boy."

And that night I learned something else about my father. He was not one to go around huggin' and kissin' and saying pretty things. But down deep inside, something in him wanted to.

I can tell you something else about Papa. Had he been an educated man and become a surgeon, he would have been an excellent one. Or an attorney. Or a bank executive. Today I hear and read references to "overachieving." I am not sure what that means. I presume it means doing more than the job calls for. I'm not sure whether Papa was an achiever or an overachiever. He certainly wasn't an underachiever. He did his job. He did it well. And he did it all—landscaping, gardening, farming, taking care of animals, digging wells, putting in septic tanks, fixing wagons, repairing houses. If you had something that needed to be done and you wanted it done right the first time, you got hold of Irvin Morton over on Rountree.

In time, Papa became the number one landscaper in Wilson. I have not been to Wilson lately, but it was a pretty town, with a lot of beautiful homes and gardens and yards. I would guess that Papa's green thumb was involved in ninety percent of them.

There wasn't anything he didn't know about trees. If he was doing somebody's yard and wanted to plant a few trees, he did not go to a nursery. He would go out in the swamp and pick out the right trees for the job, and then he would dig 'em up and bring 'em in and plant 'em. He would cut those trees back to the nubs. "If you want something to grow, I.L.," he told me, "prune it."

I remember one story Papa told about the woman who had asked him to plant red roses in her yard. Papa couldn't get any at that time, and she finally told him, "I found someone else who has come across some red roses. He's going to put them in for me."

But when they bloomed, they were white, and Papa could not resist chiding the woman about it. "I thought you wanted red roses," he said.

26

She said, "I thought you knew something about roses. The man told me red roses always bloom white the first year."

That's a funny story and may even be true. It's the kind of thing Papa was always coming up with—wryly humorous, maybe true, maybe not.

I remember one time a man and a woman that I had never seen before came to the house and talked for a long time in low voices with Papa in the kitchen. Later I heard Papa tell my stepmother: "They came here wantin' me to help 'em kill their neighbor."

My stepmother gasped. "Well, you surely aren't getting involved in that!"

"I reckon not," Papa said. "I just told 'em how to go about it."

"Irv!" my stepmother said. "Maybe you should go to the sheriff."

"Over a tree?" my father said.

Having had his fun, Papa finally supplied the details. The intended victim was a tree in a neighbor's yard. Its crime was shedding leaves across the property line. I heard Papa say he never would kill a tree, himself, but he knew how to get the job done, if somebody else was of a mind to do the dirty work.

When Papa mentioned "dirty work," he never meant working in dirt. He was always doing that. And nothing was dirtier than working with septic tanks. A lot of times he gave me the opportunity of helping him install one or clean one, and I can assure you, working with roses was a lot easier on the nose.

Papa was also in demand as an amateur veterinarian. Lots of times, they would bring their ailing animals to our place, or else they would send for Papa. He even had a black bag that he kept various medicines in. He concocted the medicines himself, and apparently he knew what he was doing, because the cows and mules and horses he treated invariably got better, and the people kept coming back and sending others.

I had a couple of regular chores. One was working the vegetable garden, keeping it weeded and watered and the like. And when I say "vegetable garden," I don't mean one of those postage-stamp-sized things you find behind the typical suburban house. Ours was a mammoth garden, covering an acre or more, and I had a hard time keeping up with it, particularly with somebody always getting up a baseball game across the road at the college.

My other big regular chore was delivering the milk from the dairy farm, which was a half-mile from the house on the other side of the Whitehead School. Papa managed the farm, which was owned by Mr. Harrell of the Barnes-Harrell Bottling Company. Mr. Harrell also owned the Cherry Hotel, an exquisite, new hotel down at the foot of Nash Road across the street from the railroad station. Papa and I and his helper would milk all the cows—about thirty of them; then they would load some of the milk on my wagon in ten-gallon cans, and I would deliver it to the hotel.

It was a grand life, and in a lot of ways I was richer than the sons of Rockerfeller. How many pets did they have? I had rabbits and bantam chickens and pigeons, which I kept on top of the chicken coop, and they would fly away and always come back. I had names for all of them. I had dogs, but I never had much luck with dogs. It seems they were always dying, or going out on the road and getting run over. And there was baseball. We would play regularly on Sunday after church, just a bunch of us from the neighborhood; we would pick up sides and hope that we had an even number, but so what if one team had an extra player?

I remember one time, Mr. Ford came out and pitched and got three of his teeth knocked out by a line drive. Fortunately, one of his sons had hit the ball, which at least kept it in the family. The odds were in favor of it being one of the Ford kids, being as there were five of them. (Any time the Fords went by in their car, somebody was bound to quip, "Seven Fords in a Reo.")

Anyway, Mr. Ford never returned to the scene of combat.

In fact, it was unusual for adults to play or even watch, let alone take over and supervise children's play, as they do today. I have watched children corralled like cows into organized teams, uniformed, numbered, supervised, and officiated, the stands filled with involved parents, the whole thing more highly orchestrated than a Cecille B. DeMille biblical epic, and my heart goes out to those "little leaguers." We have put in equipment, coaching, official rules, schedules, and umpires, and have taken out the fun.

I made two special friends in those days, George and Larry

Dew, both about my age, who lived nearby. It was the Dews who introduced me to organized religion. Papa and my stepmother were not churchgoers. I guess Papa thought Uncle Clem would take care of things in the hereafter for them. Uncle Clem, who went by the more classy nomenclature of C. Manley Morton, managed to get himself accepted by Atlantic Christian College the first year it opened, even though he had been only to the seventh grade. He went on to get his degree and was graduated in Atlantic Christian's first class. Uncle Clem became a minister and missionary, spending years in Puerto Rico and Paraguay, where he helped found a university that is ranked among the top universities in that country today.

The Dews were real church people. They never missed a Sunday at the First Baptist Church on Main Street. Once they asked me if I wanted to come along, and I accepted, not because I was suddenly overcome with a yearning to be saved, but because I wanted to be downtown on a Sunday. That was my second reason for going to church. My first reason was the minister's daughter, Miss Mercer. Miss Mercer was one of my teachers at Whitehead School. Seeing me praying piously in church, I reasoned, might induce her to look on me with special favor.

And so I began to go to the Baptist Church every Sunday, and while I figured I might be getting prepared to meet my Maker, I hadn't figured on meeting Him real soon. But for a couple of minutes one Sunday evening, I was sure I was practically there. That is the day I got baptized, which, the way Dr. Mercer did it, was another word for being almost drowned.

I do not know what induced me to get baptized. I guess the Dews were pushing me forward. At any rate, I found myself standing, along with a half-dozen other kids and as many older people, by this pool of water. It was almost as big as a wading pool. It was deep, too, up to Dr. Mercer's waist and up to my shoulders. Dr. Merver took hold of my shoulders and pushed me over backward into the water and held me there. It was then that he decided to give a little speech about Uncle Clem, though I couldn't hear any of it as I was too busy drowning. Just as I was beginning to hear the flapping of wings and the blaring of trumpets, Dr. Mercer brought me back up out of the water, coughing and spitting and wondering where I was.

29

I remember Mrs. Dew saying later, "There, don't you feel a lot better now?"

And I said, "Yes, Ma'am, I sure do."

And she said, "You are spiritually reborn."

And I said, "Yeah, that, too." What I really felt better about was still being alive.

Being regular churchgoers didn't exactly make saints out of the Dew boys or me. We continued to steal Mr. Dew's car. Mr. Dew was a very successful businessman—I think he was in tobacco—and he owned a new Ford touring sedan. After Mr. and Mrs. Dew went to bed, Larry, George, and I would push the car out of the barn and down the hill until we got far enough away to crank it and get the motor running. Then we would ride all around town, with Larry and George and me taking turns driving. After a couple of hours or more, we would bring the car back the same way—pushing it when we got near enough to wake the Dews.

I often wondered if Mr. Dew ever complained to the dealer about his awful gas mileage. We certainly never put any gas in the thing.

I had one memorable year at the Whitehead School, the fourth grade, the only year I ever made the honor roll—which proves the important role a teacher plays in a child's classroom performance. Miss Bass inspired me to excellence. It was just a question of love. One thing about me: Even at that age, I didn't pick any dogs. Miss Bass was a knockout, about twenty-one years of age, with dark hair and eyes the color of the Gulf Stream, dark blue and hundreds of fathoms deep. She was a stunning dresser and had that certain kind of poise I later came to associate with women of class.

At that age I was plagued with intense headaches, particularly if I was in class and unprepared. I had a headache one day, and I guess it showed, because Miss Bass asked me what was wrong.

"I have a headache," I said, almost crying.

She walked over to my desk and began to stroke my brow. Some of the other kids giggled, but I didn't care. Her cool hands on my hot brow, combined with the heady smell of her perfume, made me feel as though Dr. Mercer had succeeded in dispatching me to the Great Beyond.

For some reason, the frequency of my headaches increased

30

after that, and so did my undying devotion to the comely Miss Bass. I couldn't do enough for her. I would empty the wastebaskets, fire the stove, wash the blackboards, dust the erasers.

George Dew once asked me, "What are you doing, becoming the teacher's pet?"

I didn't even hesitate to answer: "You bet I am."

A man will go to great extremes for the woman he loves. Just ask Edward VIII. But all he did was give up a kingdom. I went a lot further. I studied. Boy, did I study! And I never missed a day at school. At the end of the term, my report card showed straight A's. In those days, the students who made the various honor rolls had their names listed in the Wilson Daily Times. And it was then that Papa paid me the highest compliment he could pay to anyone. The two of us ran into a friend of Papa's downtown. I remember the man saying, "I saw your boy's name in the paper. Made the honor roll. That's quite something!"

Papa said, "Well, he did it by himself."

"He did it by himself." In Papa's world, calling someone self-reliant was the supreme compliment.

It was about that same time, when I was about ten, that I received my introduction to the world of business. I learned the fascination of earning money.

It all began when the town officials came to Papa and asked him if he would help construct a baseball park and then continue on as chief groundskeeper. The town was entering a team in the new Atlantic League and they needed a suitable place to play. It seemed like a fairly good job, and Papa accepted.

Papa helped build a wooden fence about six feet high, which surrounded the park, the grandstand, the bleachers, and the dugouts for both teams. He was in charge of constructing the grounds, including the drainage system. Papa put in a system of tile and dry wells that gave that little park a drainage system equal to any in the major leagues.

After the season began, Papa kept everything in working order, and I helped him. We had to keep the grass cut in the outfield. Before each game, we would drag this leveling thing around the dirt infield, adding bricks to it for additional weight, if needed. The baseball may have been Class D, but the facilities were Class A all the way.

Of course, I got into all the games free and I got to know the

31

players, who would give me balls and bats and caps and things and also kept me supplied with chewing tobacco. One of my jobs was cleaning up under the grandstand after each game, and I got to keep whatever money I found there, which sometimes was not inconsiderable. People were always dropping change down there. Sometimes people would drop a lot of money down there—like a quarter—and then they came looking for me to ask if it was all right for them to go look for it. I would go along and pretend I was really helping. But even though I was baptized and saved and all, I really didn't put my heart into it until I was searching alone after the game.

But the big job—the one that made me feel like a true entrepreneur—was working for the concessionaire. I went through the stands carrying a box full of cokes and candy, cigarettes and cigars. And I got a commission. I didn't make a lot of money, but I made enough to realize that working for money beats working for no money every time. I was only eleven years old, but I had been working practically all my life already for no wages, unless you count room and board and clothes. They do count, of course, and I really did not expect to get paid for working at home or for Papa away from home. But there is nothing that beats the jingling of coins in the pocket when accompanied by the grand feeling that you earned them—that people paid you because they thought you were worth it. I liked that feeling and I wanted more of it.

5

A SALESMAN, Arthur Miller said in his famous play about the death of one, is "a man way out there in the blue, riding on a smile and a shoeshine."

That was me.

From my part-time job as an assistant concessionaire at the ballpark, I moved farther out in the blue to the heady outer reaches of door-to-door selling. I answered the ads in magazines, and as soon as I received my merchandise, I was on my way, riding on a smile and a shoeshine, huckstering such exotic wares as Rosebud salve, pictures of Jesus and the saints and circus animals, remedies for colds and itchy scalps, shoe laces, and lye soap. I went from house to house, up and down the streets of Wilson, and I did pretty well. This was selling on the front lines, where you learn real quickly the value of a smile in one-on-one relationships. I also learned that most people are basically of good will. They didn't slam doors on me, even those who didn't want to buy, and I made money.

Later I became the Wilson sales representative for Grit, the conservative weekly newspaper published in Williamsport, Pennsylvania, and extremely popular in small-town and rural America, and, incidentally, now in its second century and still going strong. Every Monday afternoon I would walk down to the railroad station across from the Cherry Hotel at Nash and pick up my bundle of fifty newspapers. I sold them for three cents—and I made one cent and Grit got the other two cents. Still, that was another fifty cents a week for a couple of hours' work.

I also shined shoes. I found an old piano box, and that was my storefront. The trouble was, I was too far from the center of town, and I didn't have many customers. So, I built a small shoeshine kit and walked downtown, and business boomed. At five cents a shine and occasional tip, I felt like Rockefeller. Know something? I had my shoes shined just the other day in the Hilton Hotel in Manhattan, and the price was $1.50. You used to be able to buy a pair of shoes for that. If I had stayed in the shoeshine business, I might be Rockefeller!

The truth is, I wasn't in the shoeshine business all that long. I moved on to a more permanent kind of employment.

But before that occurred, I had a brief encounter with love. I was about twelve at the time, and I looked back on the Miss Bass affair as pure kid's stuff. This was the real thing. She was a niece of my stepmother's, and she came to the house with her parents for a visit. They decided to go from there to see the operetta *Blossom Time*, which was playing at the Wilson Theater. They invited my stepsister to go along. They did not invite me, but there was no way they could tell what was going on inside me, somewhere in the vicinity of my heart or liver. All I know is I was groggy in the presence of Elizabeth, who had dark hair, green eyes, a dimple on her right cheek, and the most beautiful sigh I had ever heard. And she sighed a lot.

Elizabeth never said two words to me. I just sat on the fringes, so to speak, as they all gathered around the kitchen table, talking about the coal mine strike in Illinois, Prohibition, and about somebody's new Ford sedan. Elizabeth and my stepsister Gladys giggled a lot as they bent their heads together and talked in low tones. Elizabeth also sighed. Once they both looked up at me, and I looked down real quick. It would have pleased me much if Elizabeth had sighed at that point, but she and Gladys just giggled.

And then Elizabeth's father asked if my stepmother and Papa would like to go with them to see the show, but they declined. They said it was all right if Gladys went, and so Gladys and Elizabeth and her parents went outside and piled into their Ford and drove off.

Well, I decided I was going to see that show, too, and I went to my room and discovered, to my horror, that I didn't have enough money to buy a ticket. But there was a dollar there that I owed the Grit people, and I took that.

34

I knew it wasn't honest, but I planned to pay it back, and, besides, where love is concerned, sometimes you have to bend the rules. *Blossom Time* was a popular operetta, and by the time I got to the theater, it was almost sold out. My dollar purchased me a seat in the last row, balcony, next to the projection booth, and as far away from the stage as you could get and still claim to be inside the theater.

So I ended up seeing a half a show—and a rather boring show at that, I thought—while Elizabeth with the dimple, who was unconsciously responsible for my being there, sat downstairs in the center aisle, totally unaware that I was in the theater, or even on the same planet for that matter.

As soon as the show was about over, I hopped out of there and hurried downstairs. At least, I figured, I could get to ride home with them. Which I did.

"Why didn't you say something?" Elizabeth's mother asked. "You could have ridden in with us and sat with us." The very thought of sitting right next to Elizabeth gave me goose bumps, not to mention the very thought of having someone buy my ticket.

Later that night, I experienced a sharp pang of remorse over the "borrowed" money, and I decided I wasn't in love with Elizabeth, after all. I further decided I was never going to fall in love, because it makes a man's life too complicated.

Ted, who was working in Dr. Blauvelt's jewelry store, told me he heard that Felder Waters, the owner of another watch-making store, was looking for some part-time help. I showed up at Waters' jewelry store down on Tarboro Street the next day right after school. Mr. Waters was a young, handsome man with dark hair, clean-shaven, and always with a cigarette.

"You work every afternoon after school until six o'clock," he told me. "You will sweep the floor, clean the windows and show-cases, run errands, and polish the silver, glassware, and jewelry. The salary is fifty cents a week."

"Yes, sir," I said.

"Do you want the job?" he asked.

"Yes, sir," I said.

"Well, there is one thing," he said. "You can't work here looking like that. You will have to get a haircut."

"But I don't have any money," I said.

So he handed me fifteen cents to get a haircut, which I did. I figured he would take that out of my first week's salary, but he didn't. You see, that was back in the days before everybody had all the rights they have today, including the right to look like a bum when you come to work.

I didn't mind the sweeping and cleaning and polishing and running errands. What I did mind was having to stand on the corner of Nash and Tarboro, a busy intersection, playing nurse-maid to the Waters' baby. You see, the jewelry store was upstairs, on the second floor, so every time Mrs. Waters came down to visit her husband, I was sent out to watch over the baby, who lay in a baby carriage. I kept looking up and down Nash Street to make sure one of the Dew boys or any of my other smart-aleck friends wasn't coming along. If they had been, I probably would have crawled into the buggy with the baby. It's funny. I didn't mind being razzed about Miss Bass. But then again, I wasn't in love with infant Waters.

I don't remember how it came about, but a little while later I got a job in a larger, more prominent jewelry store, owned by a man named W. J. Burden and located a couple of blocks from the Waters' store. Mr. Burden was a tall, thin, nervous man, with gray hair and glasses. Mrs. Burden belonged to that familiar class of wife later epitomized in Joseph Kramm's play titled *The Shrike*—for the predatory bird that impales its victims on thorns before tearing them apart. When I first reported for the job, Mrs. Burden was in the process of impaling poor Mr. Burden. She was straightening out his faulty thinking regarding the proper display of some new watches. She seldom paused for breath, while Mr. Burden nodded passively.

And yet perhaps I am being unfair to Mrs. Burden. Mr. Burden was very stiff and dispassionate, as though he had been washed and starched before being left out to dry. A "very cool customer" he seemed to me. The two of them seemed more like competitors in some sort of a deadly game, than man and wife.

And then there was their son, Clifford. In Mrs. Burden and Clifford, you might say my boss was "over-Burdened."

Clifford was everything a father hopes for in his enemy's sons: Lazy, callous, a drinker and womanizer, a man whose approach to life was totally self-centered and materialistic. There seemed to be an endless parade of over-painted, giggling females in and out of the store, all of them worth more when they went out than when they came in, thanks to the generous heart of Clifford.

One of my jobs, as it had been with Waters , was to clean the jewelry, a relatively simple matter of boiling it in a mixture of Ivory soap and baking soda. Then you would dip them in alcohol and dry them in cork grindings. Those diamonds really sparkled. Diamonds would sparkle; opals, I found out, would not. You do not put opals in boiling water. You don't even take a warm bath wearing an opal. I can tell you what happens when you put an opal ring into a pot of boiling water: All the color fades from the gem and the owner's face. When Mr. Burden showed the woman what happened to her ring, I thought she was going to explode.

So did Mr. Burden, who was quick to assure her the store would take full responsibility. While Mr. Burden attempted to calm the woman, who kept shrieking, "My ring! My ring! My precious ring! You've murdered it!", I remained hidden in my work area in the back room. The woman later returned with her husband and picked out a replacement, one that I am sure was worth more than the original. But I was not fired, nor did I have to help pay for my mistake. I did not even receive a severe reprimand. Mr. Burden was a very soft-spoken man, the result, perhaps, of the countless encounters with the not-so-soft-spoken Mrs. Burden.

For son Clifford, work was a drag, and he avoided it as much as possible. He asked me to go fishing with him, but I soon learned when he asked me to go fishing what he really meant was that *he* was going fishing. I was there to have all the fun—digging for worms, rowing the boat, bailing water, and stringing the fish that Clifford caught. Still, it was better than polishing silver, and I always went.

It was through the senior Mr. Burden that I had my only experience with the Boy Scouts. The Scouts put on a drive every summer to send kids to camp, and Mr. Burden always contributed. This time he arranged for me to go to the camp, an area of woods and streams near the little town of Bath, on the Pamlico River in eastern North Carolina. It had been Blackbeard's headquarters, the place where the pirate had all his boats repaired and tarred, and of course there was millions of dollars worth of buried treasure there. There still is, presumably, because to my knowledge nobody has ever found any, but that is not because they haven't tried.

It was a fun-filled two weeks. We swam and rowed boats and learned how to tie knots, and I even got to fish; and we learned how to start fires without matches. We went on overnight hikes, marching through the wilderness in the middle of the night, with the older boys always trying to scare the little kids with tales of ghosts and pirates and the like.

I remember one moonlit night after we had made camp, a boy from Raleigh named Wally told of a man who long ago was drunk and was thrown from a horse near where we stood. The man was so angry, he started to beat the horse unmercifully, and the horse stomped him to death.

"Hey," another boy said, a little later, "look over here!"

"What is it? What is it?" we called.

"Here are the hoofprints where the horse stomped the man."

Sure enough, there in that clearing, with the moon shining down like a spotlight and the wind stirring the pines, you could see those hoofprints as plain as day. If you looked real hard, as one boy pointed out, you could see splashes of red in the grass and dirt—blood! I had trouble sleeping that night, and I am sure I was not the only one.

But after I returned to work at the jewelry store, something happened that did a better job of keeping me awake than hoofprints.

Jonah and I were in the back room where the cleaning and repairing was done. Jonah, a black man, became a friend and helpmate. He had attended Tuskegee Institute and was the first educated Negro I had ever known. At the store he was janitor and general handyman, adjusting to his work in a dignified fashion. To break the calm, in stormed Mrs. Burden. I always dreaded seeing or hearing her come into the shop, for I knew it wouldn't be long before she would be all over poor Mr. Burden, her shrill voice impaling him on thorns.

Mr. Burden was at his usual station when there were no customers, bent over a stand-up desk in the rear of the main store, from where he had a view of the entire shop, including the work area to his left and rear.

I could hear Mrs. Burden's voice, but I tried concentrating on the silver plate I was cleaning. Once in a while, I could hear the low, deliberate responses of Mr. Burden. But I managed not to hear what they were saying. That plate never had such a cleaning.

Then I looked up to see Mr. Burden take off his glasses, put them down on his desk, and for a brief moment, he just stared at Mrs. Burden, a chilling stare that actually caused her to wince and induced in her the strange phenomenon of silence. Then Mr. Burden, his eyes continuously fixed on Mrs. Burden, reached inside a drawer and pulled out a nickel-plated revolver. He pointed the gun at his chest. I heard the sharp report of the gun. I heard Mrs. Burden scream, and I saw Mr. Burden slump forward. Some unknown force took hold of me. I dropped the silver plate and bolted. Nobody could have gotten out of that store faster than I did. That's what I thought. As I flew through the front door, I almost knocked down Jonah, who was already outside. We both just looked at each other.

Miraculously, Mr. Burden did not die. His watch chain, stretched across the front of his vest, impeded the bullet sufficiently. He was out of action for a while, but he lived. That time. A few years later, after I had left his employ, I heard that Mr. Burden finally succeeded in ending what must have seemed to him a miserable and pointless existence.

What a tragedy! I have no way of knowing the depths of hopelessness that apparently drove Mr. Burden to his final desperate act. I do not understand it. I even wonder if Mr. Burden understood it.

After Mr. Burden's first serious attempt at solving his marital problem, he was out of action for a while, and his son took over the jewelry store. I continued to work there, but even at my tender age, I could see the business could not possibly make it under that kind of management. For one thing, the store was understaffed quite a lot, while Clifford tended to his other more important enterprises—boating and fishing and spending considerable time in the red light district.

I spent time down there, too, at Clifford's instruction to get worms for fishing. Right across the street from the row of houses of pleasure, under the railroad loading platform, was a veritable minefield of large earthworms. Clifford would send me down there in late morning, and those women would be sitting out on their front porches fanning themselves, whether it was hot or not. It was very embarrassing the way they carried on.

"Hello, little darling, c'mon over here, and I'll make you forget all about fishing."

"Now, Gracie, he's too young for you—but he's just right for me."

"Now, you put those nasty, nasty worms down, honey, and come over here right now."

And they would all laugh and I would dig my worms and get out of there as fast as possible.

Later, Clifford realized he wasn't getting enough business at the store, and he hired a man to take over as chief watchmaker and general assistant. Imagine my surprise when the new employee turned out to be Mr. Waters. I don't know what happened to Mr. Waters' jewelry store. Of course, it was not a real good location, being upstairs and all, and it wasn't very big, so I guess it just didn't make it.

Well, the Burden jewelry store finally did collapse. Clifford then opened a newsstand in the Briggs Hotel on Main Street and hired me to help out. I worked there every afternoon and evening, selling cigars, cigarettes, notions, and other things.

I hadn't been working there very long when the desk clerk came over and said, "Mr. Burden wants you to take him up two packs of cigarettes. He's in room 36."

I knocked on the door of room 36, and I heard Clifford tell me to come in. I opened the door and my jaw dropped. Right there in front of me was Mr. Clifford Burden in bed with a woman. Clifford's naked, hairy torso stuck up out of the bedclothes, while the woman held the sheet around her neck and grinned at me.

There were bottles and glasses on the dresser, and the place reeked of alcohol and cigarettes.

"Just bring 'em here, kid," Clifford said.

I handed him the cigarettes and left. From then on I was expected to render such direct service, for Mr. Burden spent a lot of time having parties in room 36. I was learning early what went on upstairs!

40

As you can tell, I did not particularly like working for Clifford Burden, and as soon as another opportunity presented itself, I did not hesitate. Imagine my elation when I was offered a job at the World Theater.

6

THE WORLD THEATER was one of 4,000 new theaters constructed between 1914 and 1922, when moving pictures invaded the minds and hearts of all America. The fascination of people for pictures that moved was clearly shown before the turn of the century, when Thomas Edison was turning out in his East Orange (New Jersey) studio, brief films of trained bears and monkeys and Japanese·dancers that people flocked to see in kinetoscope parlors.

By the time I arrived for my brief and inauspicious career in the movie industry, film making already had matured from the crude novelty of the 1890s to a sophisticated art form. There are those who believe that quality movies came along after the advent of sound in 1927, but that is far from the case. *Quo Vadis?*, an Italian spectacular featuring ornate sets and dramatic scenes of lions eating Christians, played to capacity crowds in the Astor Theater in New York for twenty-two weeks in 1913. *The Last Days of Pompeii, Anthony and Cleopatra,* and *Les Miserables* were other highly acclaimed pictures of the silent period. But the movie that did more than any other to establish the industry as a medium capable of eloquent drama, was D. W. Griffith's *The Birth of a Nation*, adapted from Thomas Dixon's novel, *The Ku Klux Klan,* and produced in 1915.

Seven years later, when I went to work at the World, *The Birth of a Nation* was still playing to packed audiences.

Of course, the World was not New York City's Strand, with its seating capacity of 3,300, or Sidney Grauman's Egyptian Theater on Hollywood Boulevard, where twenty-eight perfumed usherettes dressed in Egyptian costumes led the patrons to their seats. No, the World was small, smelly, and stuffy. Wall fans and a big blower tried to keep the air moving. In dealing with temperatures, the World appropriately enough resorted to theatrics, using amber wall lights in winter to make the people "feel" warmer, and green lights in summer to make them "feel" cooler. One of my many jobs there was changing the light bulbs, while another—the one I liked best—was to select the rolls of music and keep the player-piano-organ operating.

But for this twelve-year old, the World was theater—second-run theater—but theater nonetheless.

Now I was a little closer to the stars I had been admiring for several years. I took pride in the fact that Charlie Chaplin, wide-eyed Jackie Coogan, curly-haired Mary Pickford, the adorable Lillian Gish, and I all were in the same business. We had different jobs, of course. They acted in the films, and I worked in the theater where the films they acted in were shown. I was the usher, bill-poster, ticket-taker, sometime janitor and, as already mentioned, temperature control engineer and music coordinator.

They made hundreds of thousands of dollars a year; I made seventy-five cents a week.

Sometimes I made more.

For example, there was the time, shortly after my arrival, when the World was featuring *The Birth of a Nation*, second run. The price of admission at the theater was usually a flat ten cents, and in large letters on the marquee it was proclaimed that you could "See the World for a Dime." For *The Birth of a Nation*, the price was raised to a quarter. Still, not everybody in the world that wanted to—not even everybody in Wilson that wanted to—could get inside the World to the see *The Birth of a Nation*, at any price. It had only 250 seats, which was usually ample for William S. Hart and the Max Sennett comedies, but for something like *The Birth of a Nation*, we could have doubled the capacity and still have had people clamoring to get in.

So, the nights we showed the film that was already hailed as a classic, we had them standing in the back and in the aisles. Keep in mind that *Gone With the Wind* (1939) was not the first long movie. *The Birth of a Nation* was three-and-a-half hours long, which is a long time for anyone to stand in a movie house.

The hustler in me came to the fore. I went out back into the alley behind the stores and picked up as many sturdy cardboard boxes and wooden crates that I could find and sold them as seats. I ran out of boxes before I ran out of customers and earned a couple of weeks' wages in a few minutes.

I was fascinated, not only by the dramas unfolding on the screen, but by the technological principles making them possible. I spent a lot of time in the projection booth, a cramped, hot, smelly place laden with carbon dust from the arc lights. One of my jobs was to help the projectionist rewind the film and patch it when it broke or burned, which it did with frustrating frequency. In those days, film was all celluloid, as flammable as gunpowder.

I learned to my surprise that the film did not run continuously, but was affixed to a sprocket, which allowed it to pause briefly between frames, giving the illusion of one moving picture instead of a series of separate pictures. The underlying principle behind this magic was originally set down in the second century by a Greek mathematician and philosopher named Ptolemy, who discovered that the human eye retains an image on the retina for almost a tenth of a second after the source of the image has changed or disappeared.

I bought myself a second-hand projector and couldn't wait to try it out. I dropped by the movie theater one afternoon after school (the theater didn't open on weekdays until six) and found a strip of about thirty feet of film in the trash can. It was from an old Charlie Chaplin movie. I was scurrying home to show it when I ran into Paulie, who was hobbling down Nash Street, all hunched over, dragging his club foot with the aid of his cane and, as usual, wearing a black coat, shirt, tie, and a derby hat. Everybody knew Paulie.

"Hey, Paulie," I said, "look what I got." I showed him the film strip.

"It's movie film," he said. "I know what that is."

"Yeah," I said. "I'm going to show it."

"In the movie theater?" Paulie said.

"No, at home. I got a projector. I want to see how it works. Why don't you come along?"

Paulie agreed to come. While he was seriously handicapped physically and had epilepsy to boot, Paulie was moderately intelligent and personable.

44

When we got home, we went into my bedroom and I put the film in the projector, pulled down the shades, and began to turn the crank. We saw a flicker of Charlie Chaplin scurrying across the wall when the film jammed, blistered, and caught fire. Smoke shot out of the projector, and I thought Paulie was going to die.

"I got to get out of here. I got to get out of here," he said, and hurried out the door.

I ran out after him and soon discovered it was not the smoking film that caused him to panic. He was having an epileptic seizure. I saw his hands leap out and his legs crumble as he went toppling down the steps from the back porch onto the ground. It was then my turn to panic, for I did not have the slightest idea of what to do. Fortunately, my stepmother came out, and she did know what to do. I do not remember exactly what she did, but one thing I do remember—the embarrassment, the naked shame of Paulie. I have never forgotten that. It helped me acquire a measure of understanding about the feelings of people who are different, or who are made to feel different, and in later life helped me understand to a degree the frustrations and sorrows produced by the unthinking discrimination many of us are prone to indulge in.

People who know me today—my wife, Anne, among them—have learned to tolerate my peculiarities, among them extravagance in the matter of clothes. Ever since I have had enough money, I have spent more on clothes than is necessary, the result of never having had enough in the way of a decent wardrobe in my younger years. It seems I was always wearing hand-me-downs, and I always felt embarrassed around the other boys whose wardrobes were a bit fancier. And I could not wait to get out of short pants. I will always remember the Sunday I put on my first long suit and took a trip to Raleigh with a boy named George Brooks. George lived with his mother—his parents were divorced—and he had a generous allowance from his father, who was rather well-to-do. It was George's idea to take the train trip to Raleigh. Well, I didn't feel like I could afford the price of the ticket, so George and I made a fifty-fifty arrangement. George supplied the money, and I supplied a relative to visit and eat off of—my brother Charlie, who was married and living in Raleigh.

I decided that this was the appropriate time to wear my

"new" suit with the long pants. It was only new to me, of course, having first been the property of my brother Ted. I had it cut down to size and acquired a hat somewhere and had it cleaned and blocked. This new finery rested in my closet for a few weeks, awaiting the right time. The trip to Raleigh seemed the perfect occasion for the coming out of I.L. Morton.

Saturday night was bath night in our house, and on this particular occasion, I took longer than usual. Not that it mattered. I was the last one to move into the big washtub in the combination living-room–bedroom, and by the time I got to it, the water wasn't exactly Ivory-fresh. However, it served the purpose.

The modern generations who have always enjoyed the luxury of hot running water have no idea what it was like to take turns in a wooden tub with the hot water carried by someone (the mother in most homes, including ours) from the stove in a kettle.

And towels weren't the soft fluffy things that caress the body today, but hard pieces of cloth. And when you're the last man up, the towels have been well used. While the water gets dirtier and dirtier, the towels get wetter and wetter. To this day, I refuse to use even a slightly damp towel.

But by the time I was finished that Saturday night, I figured I was as clean as fresh snow, and I awoke Sunday morning, feeling like a bride on her wedding day.

I arose quite early and slowly decked myself out in my new finery. I remember thinking that the suit was still a bit large. I was only thirteen and still quite short. The suit, which was green-ish-brown in color, sort of sagged all over.

But as I looked in the mirror, I gave it a tug here and there and was very gratified at the results. What I saw looking back at me was a handsome young man, sort of a Douglas Fairbanks in the making. That is, until I put on the hat. Much to my horror, it fell down over my eyes and ears. Never at a loss for a solution to a problem, I found an old *Daily Times*, tore out some pages, crumpled them up, and stuffed them inside the hat.

I stood back and gazed into the mirror. I had nothing to worry about. I was a picture of splendor.

When I met George at the station, I felt a little sorry for him. You see, George was quite tall—more than a foot taller than I was—and he was still wearing short pants, short pants with black

46

stockings. He looked—I reluctantly concluded—like a goon.

As we walked across the railroad station toward the ticket window, I noticed out of the corner of my eyes that people were staring. A feeling of pride swelled up within me. I adjusted my hat jauntily, being careful to keep the financial page of the *Times* stuffed inside, and strode with confidence to the window. I straightened my tie, and as George purchased our children's half-fare tickets, I allowed myself a look at two young women standing near the door to the platform. I caught them actually grinning at me. I gave them just a trace of a smile in return.

As we boarded the train, the conductor stared at us and then shook his head, causing me to feel even sorrier for George.

There were a lot of stares and a number of snickers during the ninety-minute ride to Raleigh, and by the time we arrived there, a feeling of doubt began to erode my confidence. I heard one reference to "side show," and overheard a man telling some-one, "They must have traded clothes."

After arriving in Raleigh, we decided to take a streetcar to my brother's, but never having been on a streetcar before, we didn't know you had to walk out to the tracks before one would stop. We stood on the corner trying to figure out how to get the streetcar to stop when suddenly the doors of a nearby church opened and people came pouring out. There must have been about 200 young girls—my age and older—who walked right by us, and I can still hear their taunts ringing in my ears.

"Ain't he cute?"

"Look at him . . . look at that little man in the big, big suit, ain't he cute?"

My neck and ears were on fire.

We finally gave up trying to get a streetcar to stop, and I went into a drugstore and called Charlie, who told us to stay put and he would pick us up in his car.

Charlie pulled up to the corner, and we climbed in. I intro-duced him to George, and then, before pulling away from the curb, Charlie gave me a long, long look. Finally, he said, "You know, I.L., if you would spit, there wouldn't be anything left under that hat."

In those days I was leading a full life. I went to school, and after school I had to work for my father—tending the garden, looking after the cow, the chickens, and the hogs, helping Papa with park maintenance, landscaping, cleaning out septic tanks, or whatever. And then five nights a week, and afternoons and nights on Saturdays, I worked at the theater.

It was a tough schedule, but Miss Rogers, my algebra teacher, helped to ease it somewhat. She caused me to quit school. In fact, her name would be in the *Guinness Book of World Records* if they acknowledged the category of "The Teacher With the Most Students to Quit Because of." After a couple of months in her class, my brother Ted had quit school, and he warned me: "Whatever you do, don't get Miss Rogers."

Well, I got Miss Rogers, and she got me, and it was a case of mutual nonadmiration from the start. On the very first day, she ascertained that I was Ted Morton's brother and commented, "Well, I hope you're not as bad as he was."

Miss Rogers was short and fat and had flaming red hair and tiny green eyes that peered out of a red, fat face. She was as mean as a cottonmouth.

"Why don't you have your homework done?" she snapped at me that fateful day.

"I just didn't have time to do it," I said. I figured that was a most reasonable explanation. Miss Rogers did not.

"Well, you are staying after school and getting it done, and what's more, I am going to give you a good thrashing just to teach you a lesson. You're worse than that brother of yours."

I gathered up my books and headed for the door.

"Where do you think you're going?" she hissed.

"I quit," I said and kept on going.

In those days they didn't have laws compelling kids to go to school whether they wanted to or not. Parents were in charge of their kids in those days, and most parents, I suppose, made sure their kids got as much education as possible.

After I left the school building, I found my father at a house on Raleigh Road transplanting some trees.

"What are you doing here?" he asked.

"I quit school," I said.

My father showed grave concern. "Grab a shovel," he said.

So I didn't have to go to school any more and read all those books and do homework and put up with Miss Rogers. Instead,

I spent my days working in septic tanks, transplanting trees, helping to maintain the ballpark, and looking after chickens and hogs—and, of course, working in the World Theater.

My brother Ted, who left home some months before to take a job with a jewelry and optical store in Raleigh, was the one who would be upset about my leaving school. He was always talking about the value of an education and told me that not having a high school diploma kept him from working as an optometrist. He had learned the profession, but could not obtain a license.

When Ted was home for a weekend, he found out about my quitting school, and he gave me a dressing down that would have even won the approval of Miss Rogers. I mention this because I am sure Ted was most influential in causing me to resume my education later.

I continued to work at the World, where I remained caught up in the great adventures, the romance, and the tears that unfolded on the screen. Once in a while there would be some real-life dramatics, like the Saturday afternoon we were showing a Hoot Gibson western. Imagine everyone's surprise when, over the sound of the piano-organ, came the repeated cracks of gunfire. But it wasn't old Hoot making that noise; it was a very tipsy gentleman who decided to shoot up his office with a .38 caliber Smith and Wesson revolver. His office was directly above the theater, and when the shooting started, the theater patrons rushed outside. Sound movies were still three or four years in the future.

Another drama in real life at that time featured a pretty little brunette whose first name was Elizabeth and who was a frequent patron at the theater. I remember one time I took her ticket and she smiled at me; I had trouble sleeping that night.

She was very young—sweet sixteen at the most—and every time I saw her I wanted to be suddenly eighteen years old.

And then, all at once, Elizabeth, who came from a prominent North Carolina family, was the talk of the town. She had been hitch-hiking into town one evening—she said—when a man picked her up and then raped her. The man was arrested and put in jail. Elizabeth's grandfather paid a visit to the man in his cell and shot him dead. The grandfather was acquitted of any wrong-doing on the grounds of temporary insanity but there were many

49

who wondered if the accused man was really guilty. The matter, of course, was beyond proving one way or another.

Perhaps that is why I liked the movies so much. When the picture ended, all the questions were answered, all the pieces were in place. And in those days, of course, the wrongdoers paid for their crimes and the good were rewarded.

By September of 1924, something inside me told me to move on again. There was within me a restlessness, an impatience to grow into manhood, to find my way, to go on to newer things. I decided to leave home and take up residence for a while with Otis and Elsie in Raleigh.

When I said my good-byes to my co-workers at the theater, I told the manager, Jack Price, how much I appreciated his giving me the job.

"You are a good worker," he told me. "You can work for me anytime."

Few people have ever said anything that meant more to me than those few words from Jack Price. I learned a valuable lesson there, and years later, when I went into business and had people working for me, I always made it a policy to let them know how I appreciated their work. It is amazing to me that so many bosses do not appreciate the value in that kind of verbal pat on the back—I mean, of course, when such expression of appreciation is deserved.

The reaction I received from Papa and my stepmother was exactly what I expected. They assented without even questioning it. Otis and Elsie drove up in their new Ford touring car to pick me up on a rainy Sunday morning. I had already said my good-byes to Aunt Annie and my sister Mary, and I remember standing on the porch, the late summer rain pouring down, a rumbling of thunder coming from the east, just standing there, Papa just looking at me, not knowing really what to say. Finally, he reached out his hand, and I took it.

"Good-bye, I.L. And you pay a mind to your brother and to Elsie, you hear?"

"Yes, Papa. Good-bye. Good-bye, Mama."

My stepmother nodded.

I ran out and got into the car. I had a lump in my throat. I knew they did too. As Otis turned the bend at Nash Road, I stole one look backward, catching just a glimpse of Papa and my stepmother standing behind a screen of rain on the small porch, and I somehow knew I would never return, that at the age of fourteen my childhood was behind me; I did not know what lay ahead, but I was unafraid and anxious to get on with it.

7

FOR THE NEXT SEVEN OR EIGHT YEARS, or until I broke out of small-town North Carolina and became a college student in Washington, D.C., I seemed to be always on the go, shifting from one place to another, and always working, working, working. And always close to the theater, drawn there not by any compulsion to be on the stage, but by some strange need to be at the foot of the stage or behind the stage, having a part, no matter how small or indirect, in the grand action taking place out front.

Of course, if work turned you aside, then you had no business staying under the same roof with Otis and Elsie Morton.

By this time, Otis was working for a large produce house, selling to hotels and restaurants, and Elsie had a bakery stall at the market, where she sold cakes, pies, cookies, and such on Saturday morning. She baked during the week and all day Friday.

Besides holding down a job at the theater, helping Otis make his rounds at five o'clock in the morning, and going to school—yes, I went back to school; that was part of the deal—I did a few things around the house, such as taking care of the grass, carrying in the coal, running errands, and doing whatever else was asked of me. I also did a little studying. What money I made outside I turned over to Elsie and was given a dollar a week for my very own. That was sufficient.

I remember the preacher saying in church one Sunday that the Lord loves a cheerful giver. Well, I think he loves a cheerful worker. I believe that if I had been exposed to complaining workers as a child, I would have ended up being like a lot of people I have seen—trudging through life doing the least amount of work possible and constantly griping because other people seem to get the breaks.

52

Otis and Elsie were both cheerful, outgoing people. And they passed that onto their children, as well. Minnie, who was born at the time I left them to go live with Aunt Matt and Uncle Kib, was now six, and her sister Vivian was five. Their brother Manley was about four. The two little girls were my chief helpers in the household chores. Or was it the other way around?

Life with Otis and Elsie was busy, but quite pleasant. The happy chirping of the little girls and the active antics of little Manley brightened up the household. Setting on a shelf in my den today is a little white and orange ceramic camel, one of those trinkets with an open back to put things in, which was given to me by Manley for Christmas.

We all went to the Methodist church on Sunday, and dinner at the Pooles was still a frequent, though not weekly, Sunday event. Charley Poole was still there, now close to twenty, still chawing, smoking, and cussing, and still not much on higher education.

One of the first things I did after arriving in Raleigh was to drop by the Capitol Theater. I had already met Mr. Rosser, the manager. His brother-in-law, Mr. Stevenson, of Henderson, North Carolina, the theater's owner, also owned the World Theater in Wilson.

"Jack Price told me you would be heading this way," Mr. Rosser said. "When can you start to work?"

The Capitol was a lot newer than the World. It had 800 seats and the usual player piano. It was not first class, not a palace, but I felt I was moving up.

Besides Mr. Rosser, a rather fidgety man who wore glasses and was meticulous about his appearance, there was the attractive cashier who dubbed me "Jack," and Mr. Rosser's son, who would come in on Saturdays to help usher.

I also helped put up the posters at night. We had four films a week—Monday–Tuesday, Wednesday, Thursday–Friday, and Saturday. Never on Sunday. In those days, movie houses were not open on Sundays.

I remember dropping by the theater one day after school to see a group of men wrestling with a large pipe organ from a truck. Mr. Rosser was there, necktie in place and suit coat buttoned, more or less supervising.

"A new organ?" I said.

"Yes," Mr. Rosser said. "And I have hired an organist to play it, Fred McCauley. We expect to have it all ready to go for Friday night's film."

Friday night's movie was *The Enchanted Cottage*, a splendid vehicle for some fine organ music, starring Richard Barthelmess as a wounded World War I veteran whose face had been disfigured, and May McAvoy, who (in the film) was almost as ugly as he was. Their love transforms them both into beautiful people in the eyes of each other. (The movie was later remade for World War II audiences, starring Robert Young and Dorothy McGuire.)

I met the new organist just before the show started Friday night, and we became fast friends. Fred McCauley was a young, handsome man who drove a convertible, wore nicely-tailored clothes, and was never ill-at-ease, even among members of the opposite sex. He reminded me of the great male movie stars of the day, Richard Barthelmess, John Gilbert, Douglas Fairbanks, and I could hardly wait to be just like him. Fred and I became good friends, and when I decided to leave home and go on my own, he helped make the decision easier by assuring me financial support if I ever needed it. Afterwards, he even signed my school report cards and counselled me on my education. He was another one of the many people who guided me at important turning points in my life.

He invited me to sit at the console with him in my idle moments, and I did. It was a real thrill to watch him follow the cue sheets, his eyes darting up to the screen and back to the music while his long, tapered fingers flowed up and down and over the keyboards, filling the screen with the music that seemed to be an integral part of the action, as it was. The right music creates a mood, enhances the action, and helps to carry the story, almost without being noticed, for it never intrudes. It is just there. It is there naturally. Think of "Tara," the nostalgic theme of *Gone With the Wind*, or the haunting harmonica strains of "Red River Valley," which seemed such a natural accompaniment to the travails of the Joads in *The Grapes of Wrath*.

For silent films, music was even more important. And thus the theater musicians were just as much a part of the cast as the actors.

During the day, I went to school. Everything was so busy in those days, and I made many friends.

I was in a hurry. Always in a hurry. And yet, I was a friendly, outgoing lad, always joking, seldom serious.

On occasion, I would move out of Otis' house and spend a little time with my other brother, Charlie, and his wife, Maude. Even though they were both still in their very early 20s at the time, they had already developed a life-style that would vary very little for the rest of their lives. They had no children. They both worked—Maude was a telephone operator— and they had a dog, a little bulldog. They were not boat-rockers or wave-makers. They were quiet, hard-working people who lived by a set routine.

While Otis was a happy scrambler—moving from one job to a better one, an outgoing live wire with the soul of an entrepreneur, Charlie was more sedate, happy in his own way with a set job to do. When I went to live with them, Charlie was a brakeman for the old Norfolk-Southern Railroad, which went from Raleigh to Wilson, Goldsboro, Newport, Morehead City, and Beaufort. It was a job that Charlie had held for years and continued to hold until the railroad went under during the Great Depression. Then Charlie got a job as a bus driver for the Raleigh bus company, and he held that for a long time until he stopped driving and was put in charge of the lost and found department, where he remained until he retired.

And while Otis and Elsie thought the busier I was, the better, Charlie and Maude thought I was *too* busy. They were more concerned with my progress in school.

So, it was particularly inappropriate that I picked a time when I was living with them to perform my only act of truancy. But then, Maude's younger brother, Paul, was partially responsible. Paul and I were both attending Hugh Morson High School at the time and were on our way there one morning when he came up with the grand idea:

"Let's skip school today," he said.

"Good idea," I said.

It was not a good idea. If you are going to skip school, you should have a good reason and some kind of plan—like going fishing or visiting a friend or something. Because if you have no good reason to skip school, you will more than likely spend the day as we did—trying to find something to do.

We wound up going to a public park that had a few dull animals, like some goats and deer and pigs, nothing anybody

55

would really want to look at. After about four hours of wandering around, we kept telling each other how much fun we were having and how much better it was than sitting in a dumb classroom.

That night, Charlie asked me if I had a good day.

I said, "Sure."

"How was school?" he asked.

"Fine," I said.

"How do you know it was fine?" he asked.

"What do you mean?" I countered while my knees grew weak and my stomach turned.

He told me what he meant. "Miss Jones called. She wondered if you were sick."

"Well, I really don't feel too good right now," I said.

Except for some extra makeup work at school, I never received any real punishment. Charlie knew I had been punished enough. For the honest man, dishonesty inflicts its own punishment, and shame cuts far deeper than a whip.

It was shortly after that incident that I went back to Otis and Elsie's, and then a little later I decided to move out on my own. While Otis understood—he had been on his own since Mama died when he was seventeen—Elsie was very upset.

"You're only sixteen," she said. "You'll never finish school. You will never do any good. You won't amount to anything."

This, of course, was the maternal instinct found in all natural and surrogate mothers, and while Elsie's apprehension proved to be unfounded, it was comforting to know she was concerned.

Living in rooming houses gave me a sense of maturity and independence, though between working two jobs and going to school, I really didn't spend much time there. In addition to my theater job, I had a job with Otis' produce company, checking outgoing shipments from six to eight-thirty A.M. I earned a total of eleven dollars a week, not a kingly sum, but sufficient for my needs.

For a time I shared a room with two other young men, one a heavyset barber who loved to eat, and who was always bringing in food to cook in a frying pan over canned heat. It seemed like a good idea until one day we were frying country ham and eggs and smoke filled the house, bringing the landlady to our door with fire in her eyes. We left there shortly after that.

But each time I moved—and in between times—Elsie came around to inspect the premises. And each time she left shaking her head in despair.

For my part, I was on top of the world, filled with good cheer and optimism. Just a few months after going out on my own, I was offered an usher's job at the State Theater, a brand new house erected by Paramount. The World Theater in Wilson, where I started my theater career, was practically a slum dwelling compared to the State, and the Capitol didn't fare too much better by comparison.

Here was luxury. Grandeur. The grand, ornate lobby opened onto a foyer under a high circular ceiling that overlooked second-floor offices and a large balcony. The aisles were laid with deep carpeting, the seats were richly upholstered in beige-orange tones, and up front was a gigantic stage and a large orchestra pit.

The State featured live music, with an eighteen-man orchestra playing music to accompany the feature pictures. Here the organ was used only for the short subjects.

Not only did the State feature first-run pictures, it also staged Broadway shows, musicals, and even an occasional opera. I saw my first Ziegfield Follies there and also my first opera, *The Vagabond King*, for which we had to wear tuxedos to escort the patrons to their reserved seats. All seats were reserved for that one.

I was given free passes for all the shows. I did not waste them. They were well placed with my teachers, and I made sure they got good seats.

I ate dinner and sometimes a late snack in a cafeteria next to the theater, and it was there one evening while looking over the desserts that I spied as nice a dish as I have ever seen, a vivacious brown-haired lovely who smiled back at me from the other side of the counter. The strains of "My Blue Heaven," as sung by Gene Austin, were dancing through my head (the popular record was being played constantly in the drugstore across the street) as I nervously introduced myself and asked her her name.

"Della," she said.

Yes, she said, she would come up to the theater when she got off.

While in many respects I was rather worldly for my age, it did not extend into the area of courtship and romance, where I remained, while not shy or awkward, certainly unsophisticated.

Della and I would meet at the theater. I would sit with her when I had no duties to perform and then I would walk her home.

In my mind, things were progressing nicely. While I didn't have much to offer a girl like Della at the time, I felt I was on my way. In time I would have a good position in some phase of the entertainment business. I would sport a convertible, like Mr. McCauley, and I would be able to take my girl out in style.

One night, while I was waiting for Della to appear, I walked up the aisle to see her standing near the door. She was early. She touched my arm. "I.L.," she said. "I can't see you tonight."

"Tomorrow night?" I said.

"No. Not tomorrow night either." Then she turned and walked outside. I watched with a sinking feeling as she got into a convertible car. It wasn't my convertible, of course. It turned out to belong to a shoe clerk.

When I told Elsie about the end of my romance (she had met Della once or twice), she seemed quite relieved.

As for me, I was heartbroken for a day or two. I was too full of life, too optimistic to remain down for long. And it was shortly after that that Mr. Enloe, the theater manager, called me in to tell me I had been promoted to head usher with a two dollar increase in salary to eight dollars a week.

But on a spring day in 1928, I was given another offer I couldn't turn down. Mr. Rosser, my previous boss at the Capitol Theater, decided to strike out on his own. He purchased movie houses in Hamlet and Aberdeen, North Carolina, and in Rock Hill, South Carolina, and asked if I would be interested in managing the one in Hamlet.

Imagine! Not quite eighteen years old and being named manager of an 850 seat theater. That was heady stuff, and while it meant quitting school again, I did not hesitate.

I was soon on my way to the town of Hamlet, North Carolina, ninety miles south-southwest of Raleigh, and seventy miles east of Charlotte, to assume my role as a rising theater executive and leading member of the community.

8

I LEFT RALEIGH FLYING HIGH on that great intoxicant, success, and rode to Hamlet on a bus without a backward glance. Well, that is not exactly true. There were no *regretful* backward glances. But as I rode through the small picturesque towns of Sanford, Tramway, and Lemon Springs, through the lush Sandhills area of Southern Pines and Pinehurst, along the fall line dividing the flat coastal plain and the gently rolling, rising terrain of the Piedmont Plateau, I looked back on my life with a feeling of pride. I was fully aware that the young man who sat on the bus was a far different person than the short, gawky, ill-dressed buffoon who rode the train from Wilson to Raleigh with George Brooks. Here now was a young man who had sprung up in the last couple of years to close to six feet in height, who was slender but not painfully thin, who was dressed well, if not expensively.

A month away from my eighteenth birthday, I found myself assuming a position normally filled by mature men, a position that was considered by townspeople on the same level as the police chief, the fire chief, and the high-school principal.

And yet, fortunately, I did not become victim to the vanity, the smart-aleckness that could easily have marked a youth in my position. I owed that to my humble background and, more importantly, to the people who had guided me—my mother and father and stepmother, Otis and Elsie, the Pooles, Charlie and Maude, and yes, even to the almost-forgotten Rileys, and Aunt Matt and Uncle Kib, not to mention the men and women I had worked for and were taught by.

At eighteen, I knew the meaning of work and responsibility, and I was quite at home in the world of adults. So, when I took over as manager of the Carolina Theater in Hamlet, I was qualified.

My first order of business, however, was to find a place to live. I do not remember who recommended it, if anyone, but I found a great home-style boarding house—if home means one young man surrounded by seven or eight unrelated female school-teachers ranging in age from twenty to middle years. Whereas all were nice to me, my interest centered on the twenty-year-old, Miss Grubbs, Dorothy to everyone, who was cute and lively and who paid a lot attention to me—like when I was sick with the flu. She was very popular and dated a lot, but during the week I was confined to my bed, she would stop in to cheer me up or to "tell" me good night. A couple of times she rubbed my chest with Vicks Vaporub—a popular curative of the times. That was one favor I would liked to have returned, but all we did was to joke about it, still the age of innocence, or better, cowardice. To this day, I never see or hear of Vaporub without my thoughts running back to the lovely Miss Grubbs. She really made me want to go back to school!

Today one could make a smutty television comedy series of that situation, but in those days, for most young people, sex was something caused by marriage. And it never occurred to me to conduct myself with anything but decorum with my fellow boarders.

Mrs. Mellineaux, a handsome and very proper widow, ran an excellent boarding house, clean and bright, and the meals, served on a large table in the dining room, were excellent. Even Mrs. Poole would have approved.

I was able to walk from the boarding house to the Carolina Theater, several blocks distant. The Carolina Theater was an old house, seating 850. It had been built—as all theaters were until more recent times—for live shows. It was a large theater for the size of the town, with an expansive stage, complete with dressing rooms below. But films had long ago pushed vaudeville and other live shows off the stage of small towns, and so the dressing rooms below were just so much unused space.

That was pointed out to me on my first morning in the theater by the janitor, a skinny black man with horn-rimmed glasses named Calvin White.

"They nice rooms," Calvin said.

"Yes," I said. I was sitting in my office off the lobby floor and wondering what the janitor was leading up to.

"A person could even live in 'em. Be right comfortable, too." Calvin White stuffed tobacco into a corncob pipe. "Mind if I light up, Mr. Morton?"

"No, go right ahead," I said.

He struck a match and took a couple of puffs. Soon the aroma of smoking maple syrup filled the room. "Be just me and my wife. She could help out a lot, too, with the cleaning and all."

I inspected the downstairs. There was a bath and several dressing rooms. I made my first executive decision. I told Calvin he and his wife could live downstairs.

Louise White was a buxom woman a shade darker than her husband and several shades larger. But she was a good-natured woman and a hard worker, as was her husband.

However, it wasn't long before I had to impose on them two restrictions:

1) No cooking of cabbage or any other dishes known to have widespread broadcasting capability, except on Sunday, and,

2) No fighting during picture showing hours.

There was one time, during the showing of a silent movie, when some of the patrons no doubt thought we had installed sound, what with Louise and Calvin engaging in a verbal battle below. The first indication I had that something was amiss was the increasingly louder strains of the organ. I could hear, not only the organ, but the vocal accompaniment—the deep contralto screams of Louise and the higher-pitched staccato responses of her husband. Try as he might, the organist could not drown them out.

I rushed downstairs, pounded on their door (it was not difficult to ascertain where they were). Calvin opened the door. He was wearing a sheepish grin. Louise stood with arms folded, looking toward the ceiling. "I tried to tell him," she said. "I tried to tell him."

I told them that if they waited for the theater to close they could scream at each other all night, but not during the shows.

But real movie sound was not far away. "Vitaphone," the magical name copyrighted by Warner Brothers, seemed to tell it all. In the wake of the success of *The Jazz Singer*, the first feature sound film, with seemingly spontaneous dialogue and ad-libbing, movie houses throughout the country were clamoring to get the necessary equipment manufactured by Western Electric, the undisputed leader in the field. They could not fill the orders fast enough.

Just 100 miles away, in Charlotte, *The Jazz Singer* was still playing at Warner Brothers Broadway Theater, one of the four original sound-equipped theaters in the country, and I knew it was time I saw and heard for myself this new wonder in entertainment. I was not disappointed.

Nothing, absolutely nothing, that has happened since—not television, not a jet airplane, not even the historic, dramatic landing on the moon—has produced the cultural shock of this movie. There was Al Jolson actually talking down to the audience: "Wait a minute! Wait a minute! You ain't heard nothin' yet!" And there was Jolson singing, "Toot, Toot, Tootsie, Good-bye," and five other songs; and Bobby Gordon as the young Jolson singing two songs; and there was Jolson actually engaging in conversation with his mother, played by Eugenie Besseler. I sat there enthralled. I no longer wondered why the entire nation seemed to have gone bananas over this new technological miracle. I also knew that the Carolina Theater in Hamlet was going to have to get sound.

Mr. Rosser had seen *The Jazz Singer* and agreed we needed to get sound. But Western Electric was out of the question at this time. It was terribly expensive, and there was about a year's waiting time. So, we decided to put in one of the less expensive systems. There were a number of these with different brand names, but all were known in the business by the unflattering epithet of "Funnyphones."

In those days all movie sound was recorded on disc records and played on a turntable attached to, and synchronized with, the film speed. The record turned 33 1/3 r.p.m., while the film ran at a speed of 90 feet per minute. If a film had to be cut and spliced to remove damaged sections, it was now necessary to replace the damaged film with the exact amount of blank film. Still, the sound and film were known to get out of synch. Scratched records were another problem. And if a theater installed "funnyphones" instead of a quality system, the problems were multiplied.

Later, of course, came photoelectric cells and the recording of sound on the edge of the film. It was called "Movietone" and was developed and used by Fox Films, later to become Twentieth Century-Fox.

In those early days of talkies, they were turning out movies in two versions—silent and sound. The difference in cost was so substantial that most movie houses bought some of each. At the Carolina Theater we could make a profit on a gross of $400 a week if we used silent films.

But I was hooked on sound—so hooked, in fact, that I decided to create some of my own for the silent version of *Lilac Time*, a World War I story starring Gary Cooper and Colleen Moore. (The movie, incidentally, introduced one of the hit songs of the time, "Jeannine, I Dream of Lilac Time.")

Mr. Rosser opted for the silent version, so I asked the organist to strip down the organ and tighten the drums, enabling him to make sounds of firing machine guns. Encouraged by the results, I obtained ten-foot strips of tin roofing, put handles on them, hung them backstage, and when they were rattled they sounded like thunder or the rumblings of big guns. Shooting guns with blanks into barrels simulated cannon fire. But my real stroke of genius was my sound effects for the caissons rolling over the cobblestone streets while Colleen Moore called to Gary Cooper to get his attention. In the silent film, of course, the noise was implied by the camera work, the gestures of the stars, and the titles. I obtained a bunch of horseshoes, nailed them to wooden blocks, and had kids beat the horseshoes on concrete blocks—all backstage and unseen by the audience. I advertised the film in posters and handbills as having "sound effects!" The result *was* sensational. I will always remember standing in the back of the theater and hearing a child saying: "Daddy, listen to the horses."

News of the simulated sound spread, and for three more nights we packed them in.

Because Mr. Rosser guaranteed me a commission on any gross above the $400 break-even point, I earned an extra twenty-eight dollars that week. That was the most money I had ever made in a week in my life.

My salary was eighteen dollars a week. We had shows every evening except Sundays, with matinees on Wednesdays and Saturdays, when we would close down for dinner and reopen at seven o'clock.

To supplement my eighteen dollars a week salary as manager

of the Carolina Theater, I took on other activities, such as selling sheet music in the lobby of the theater after the movie that featured special music. I also sold made-to-measure suits and displayed my samples in the theater office, which opened onto the lobby. Both of these ventures were rather short-lived.

I would see Mr. Rosser about once a week. He had to preside over his other two theaters—in Aberdeen, fifteen miles away where he lived, and in Rock Hill, South Carolina—seventy-five miles away.

While Mr. Rosser was in charge of buying the films, I ran everything else at the Carolina. We had a projectionist, organist, cashier, and ticket taker, and, of course, the janitor and his wife. I had to make sure everything went well; I had to check constantly to see that the place was clean. I personally put out the posters in front and hired several kids from my Sunday school class to distribute handbills door-to-door, the same kids I used as "sound technicians." Yes. I taught a Sunday school class at the Methodist Church. Everybody must have wondered why all the kids wanted to come to my class. It wasn't that they were religiously inspired. The truth is I gave them free passes to the theater if their attendance was perfect.

Oddly, one of the best friends I made in Hamlet was a Catholic priest, Father Termer, who ran the little Catholic church.

In those days there was kind of a "barter system" working in small towns. I gave out theater passes to certain people, and I was given service in return. I paid no medical or dental bills, had my hair cut, my clothes cleaned and pressed, and my shoes soled and heeled gratis and, as a result, I was as well turned out, as though I really made money.

Of course, I also tendered the courtesy of the theater to certain officials, such as the mayor, the police chief, fire chief, and school principals, and to members of the clergy. That is how I met Father Termer, a pleasant, gray-haired man with a sharp nose and glasses.

He came to the theater one night to inquire if the pass that had been extended by my predecessor was still good. I assured him it was.

Father Termer took an interest in me and invited me to his home for Sunday dinner. Soon, I was a regular there, along with two or three other young men.

I would go to the Methodist church Sunday morning, then drop over to the Catholic church and sit in the back listening to the strange, but somehow beautiful, Latin intonations.

Father Termer lived in the rectory beside the church. His housekeeper, a stout Irish widow with white hair and a ready laugh, was an excellent cook, and I used to look forward to those Sunday dinners.

But the more memorable aspects of those afternoons was not the roast lamb with the mint jelly, or the roast pork and sauerkraut (the housekeeper had been married to a man of German descent), or the home-baked, hot apple pie. No, the most memorable thing was the stimulating conversation that followed. Father would give me a cigar, because he loved the aroma but did not smoke.

These were not just "bull sessions." They were educational. In his quiet way, Father Termer was trying to instill in us a deeper appreciation for God and religion and education, but always in a general, nonsectarian way.

Father Termer encouraged me to return to school. Visions of gloomy forecasts about my future came back to haunt me. Yes, I told myself, I would have to finish high school at least.

I was truly an enigma. The "business Jack Morton" was old for his years, somewhat mature and responsible, holding down a managerial position and doing it well, while the "social Jack Morton" was immature, naive, innocent to a fault, and highly unskilled in even the basic functions of social intercourse.

I didn't even know how to dance. For an eighteen-year-old boy not to know how to do the black bottom, the shimmy, or the Charleston, let alone the waltz or fox-trot, in those dance-crazed days was an indication of some kind of retardation.

And so, when I was invited to a dance at the home of Mary Lamb, one of Hamlet's more popular young ladies, I went into a panic.

"What am I going to do?" I asked Jimmy Williamson, whose father was my predecessor at the Carolina Theater, but who now managed a theater in Southern Pines. Jimmy and I had become friends early after my arrival in Hamlet. He was very lively, and you could tell by looking at him that he could dance your shoes off you.

"Take a couple of lessons," Jimmy suggested.

Jimmy insisted on taking me over to the new Arthur Murray

Studio. This was on a Thursday, and the dance at Mary Lamb's was Saturday. I had another lesson Friday—a total of two.

Those were heady days, the late 1920s. The motor car had come into its own, the airplane was winning worldwide acceptance, and modern technology was working miracles in the communications and entertainment world.

The whole country seemed to be dancing, singing, or listening to rotating discs—Ruth Etting; Paul Whiteman; Rudy Vallee; Clif "Ukelele Ike" Edwards; the Rhythm Boys, featuring Bing Crosby; Russ Columbo; Kate Smith; Harry Richman, and more became nationally known headliners.

Dance bands sprang up like poppies in Flanders. *Variety* estimated that in the mid-1920s there were as many as 60,000 dance bands in the United States. The better ones could be heard on radio and on records and seen and heard in the new sound movies. Besides Whiteman, there was Ted Lewis, Vincent Lopez, Ben Bernie, Red Nichols, Fred Waring, Duke Ellington, and many, many more, all producing music to be accompanied by the lively stepping of millions of feet. As F. Scott Fitzgerald put it: "People danced in a champagne haze on the rooftops of the world."

I think it is understandable why I had reached the age of eighteen without ever having danced. I was too busy and had little social life.

I was looking forward to the dance at Mary Lamb's with a strange mixture of eagerness and total panic. Fortunately, I thought, I had to work and could not get to the dance until late. But if I thought I was going to escape making a spectacle of myself, Jimmy Williamson was there to straighten me out.

"You have to dance with the hostess," he told me.

"Why?" I asked.

" 'Cause you have to. It's expected. Even if you don't dance with anyone else, you have to dance with the hostess."

"Did you?" I asked, hoping I would trap him.

"Sure," he said. "Three times. Go ahead. It won't kill you."

Mary Lamb lived in one of those large, white colonial houses. There must have been twenty couples elbow to elbow and hip to hip, dancing to the great hits of the day played on the Lambs' new Victorola-Radiola Combination—"Baby Face," "Breezin' Along with the Breeze," "Charmaine," " 'Deed I Do," and others.

Mary was attractive, with brown hair, rather quiet, as I recall, more popular among the adults. She had what you might call "group popularity"; all the boys liked Mary, but she wasn't the one they wanted to back into a quiet corner.

Maybe that made it easier for me to finally ask her to dance.

Having had two days of lessons, I wasn't exactly a dancing fool. In fact, I was very stiff and formal, holding her at length, trying to keep from stepping on her while I kept my eyes fastened on the great crystal chandelier overhead. In fact, I counted those crystals, four at a time.

I started going to dances after that with Jimmy Williamson and another boy named Odum, who worked on the railroad. There were dances all over the place—in people's houses, and public dances in the clubhouse at the lake in Rockingham, about six miles away. Somebody would hire an orchestra, sell tickets, and you would have a dance. For the dances way out in Rockingham, I always managed to get a ride with Jimmy, or Odum, or someone.

It was about this time that I began to date Liz Hardy. I had met her, of course, first at Mary Lamb's, but she seemed about as attainable to me as Clara Bow. She was a vivacious blonde, with big blue eyes, a lot of curves, and a great smile. She had one of those bubbling personalities. In short, she was the one all the boys wanted to back into a quiet corner, and I think a lot of them probably did. So, with the pick of all the young men in town, you can imagine my amazement when she began showing an interest in me one night at the theater.

She was coming out of the theater with another girl, and I was in the lobby. She stood there for a second. "Hi," she said.

I gulped and said "hi" back.

She introduced me to her friend and then said she was having a bridge party at her house the following Sunday night and would I like to come.

"You do play bridge, don't you," she asked.

"Of course, of course," I said.

I knew less about bridge than I did about dancing, but I wasn't going to allow that technicality stop me from having a date with Liz Hardy.

But the next day I suddenly realized the horrible predicament

I put myself in. I knew I needed some quick lessons in bridge. And they had to be basic lessons, because I had never played cards, except Old Maid and Rook when I was a child.

But Ronnie, the cashier, was a bridge player, and she put me through the paces for three straight days. She was a bridge drill instructor. Two dance lessons won't make you Fred Astaire, and three days of bridge instruction won't turn you into Goren. But I guess I got through. At any rate, my romance with Liz blossomed.

When I say "my romance blossomed," I probably don't mean the same thing that someone else would mean by those words. Actually, it was the same kind of idyllic romance I had with Della. Liz would come to the theater in the evening, and the two of us would sit together and watch the great figures on the screen—John Gilbert, Douglas Fairbanks, John and Lionel Barrymore, Clara Bow, Dolores Del Rio, Dolores Costello, Norma Shearer, Joan Crawford—and then I would walk her back to her home, and sometimes we would sit on the porch talking small talk. At least that's about all I'm ready to admit. I have always had romance in my soul, but unfortunately—or perhaps fortunately—I controlled some natural responses to some tempting situations. I've never decided if it was romance or timidity.

Meanwhile, I was always looking for ways to improve things at the theater. I was very disappointed in the Funnyphone. The sound was always getting out of synch, and I spent a lot of time trying to fix that and a lot of time in the projection booth helping Jack Davis, the projectionist, splice in blank film to keep the thing in synch as much as possible.

So, I was greatly relieved and excited when Mr. Rosser told me on one of his visits to Hamlet that he had ordered Western Electric to be installed. I could hardly contain myself.

"Great!" I shouted. "I'll get an advertising campaign started. Man, we will really pack 'em in."

"Hold your horses," Mr. Rosser said. "I just ordered it. It takes awhile to get it. They say next June at the earliest."

That was almost a year away, but it was still something to think about.

Meanwhile, we kept things humming at the Carolina, alternating sound movies with silents and showing such crowd pullers as Clara Bow in *Ladies of the Mob* and *Red-Head*; Mary Astor in *Three-Ring Marriage*; *Romano*, starring Dolores Del Rio; Richard Barthelmew in *The Little Shepherd of Kingdom Come*; and George O'Brien in *Honor Bound*.

A word or two more about the times. America during the 1920s was a three-ring circus, as the smartest, most flippant generation to come along until the one that followed it flung itself into life with amazing abandonment. It was the day of the flapper, the hip flask, and the flivver, a time of grand optimism and incredible cynicism, a time of Bunyonesque heroes, ranging from a reticent flyer named Lindbergh, to a brash, roundish, home-run hitter named Ruth; from an all-American, golden-boy Marine named Tunney, to a hedonistic, alcoholic writer named Fitzgerald.

It was a time when the spectacular and the bizarre competed with each other for the adulation of the crowds. Shortly after I arrived in Hamlet, two Australian and two American flyers, attempting a flight from San Francisco to Hawaii, became lost for a time, found themselves, and landed in Honolulu after a flight of twenty-four hours and twenty-five minutes. For most Americans in those days, Hawaii was as far away as the moon.

Meanwhile, other daredevils attracted attention by sitting on flagpoles. One, named Shipwreck Kelly, made a successful career out of it, causing amateurs to spring up all over. A fifteen-year-old Baltimore boy sat on top of a twenty-two-foot pole in his backyard, and for that dubious accomplishment was hailed by the city major as possessing "grit and stamina" that showed "the old pioneer spirit of early America." That is what he said.

It was a time of fads, games, and hijinks. Mah-Jongg, a Chinese game played with dice and dominoes, swept the nation. Crossword puzzles became so popular that the Baltimore and Ohio Railroad placed dictionaries on their trains. College teams competed in tournaments, and one university—the University of Kentucky—even offered a course in crossword puzzles. The dean described them as "educational, scientific, instructive, and mentally stimulative." That's what he said.

Contract bridge, yo-yo's, roller skating, rocking-chair derbies, and dance marathons all got in their licks. One man in Minnesota was acclaimed for setting the world's record for bobbing up and down in water—1,843 times.

This was the era later dubbed the "Golden Age of Sports"—and it truly was. It was the day of Bobby Jones, Knute Rockne, Big Bill Tilden, Ruth and Gehrig, Red Grange, and, of course, the unbeatable Tunney.

It was the time, too, that the nation was beginning to suspect that Prohibition, the "great experiment," was creating more problems that it was curing. At a meeting of the American Bar Association in Seattle, a number of spokesmen assailed syndicated crime and corruption in public offices and laid the blame directly at the bootlegging industry.

It was a time for smoking cigarettes and driving big, fast cars, a time of unprecedented and eternal prosperity, a time for living and loving life. "America," F. Scott Fitzgerald wrote, "was going on the greatest, gaudiest spree in history."

This, of course, was public America. Down below that swirling madness, mainstream America worked and lived, loved, married, and had children. Most of them did not get drunk in speakeasies or stand on the wings of airplanes.

I suppose I belonged somewhere between, one foot planted in one of the circus rings, the other on solid, sober ground. The excitement I felt then I still feel now, for it was self-generated. I did not need alcoholic stimulants to make me feel good. I always felt good; therefore, I rarely drank.

And though I was not an active participant in the more flamboyant pursuits of the great gaudy spree, I was part of the times and I was fully aware of them.

By late summer of 1928, I, too, was fascinated with the political drama unfolding as a Catholic Democrat from the East Side of New York was locking horns with a longtime government administrator and engineer from California over the highest elective office in the country.

While my background was rural Southern Baptist-Methodist, I had never really been subjected to religious bigotry. For one thing, I hardly knew any Catholics until I met Father Termer. But the religious undertones in that election could not be denied. There were all kinds of reports and rumors floating around, including one that had Al Smith making a secret deal with the Pope to have a tunnel built between the Treasury, a couple of blocks from the White House, or more logically from the Bureau of Engraving and Printing, also nearby, to Catholic University, a couple of miles across town.

Still, the dapper Democrat was tremendously popular, with crowds almost trampling each other to get close to him during his campaign trips. And a couple of days before the election, New Yorkers put on a ticker-tape parade that rivaled in size and enthusiasm the one that hailed Lindbergh on his return from Paris the previous year.

Interest in the election was keen everywhere. In Washington, plans were made to keep people informed on the progress of the election by means of flares fired from an airplane at ten o'clock on election night. Red flares would mean Hoover was leading, and green flares would mean Smith was ahead. The *Washington Star* made arrangements with the coast artillery to signal the results with two 800 million candlepower antiaircraft searchlights—a steady sweep if Smith had the lead, and a blinking sweep if Hoover led. Sweeps would be made every two minutes starting at ten o'clock.

I read about those plans and wondered what I could do to tie in the theater to the elections. I suddenly hit on it. I contacted the local Western Union office, which would be getting returns continuously, and made arrangements, for the price of fifty dollars, to have a boy come to the theater every thirty minutes with the latest results. I then stepped onstage, signaled for the movie to be halted and the lights turned on, and announced the latest results. Oddly enough, Smith led throughout the evening until well after the theater had closed. Hoover finally took a slight lead at two in the morning.

It was the defection of the onetime solid Democratic South that cost Smith dearly, with North Carolina, Florida, Tennessee, and Virginia all shifting to the Republican side. Not that Hoover really needed them. It was a landslide defeat for the Democratic candidate, and the last time a Catholic would make a serious challenge for the White House until John F. Kennedy's successful bid in 1960.

That election was significant for me personally. It aroused my interest in politics and pointed up once more my lack of knowledge in this and other areas. That realization, along with the subtle influence of Father Termer and the recurring recollections

71

of Elsie's dismal sighs, and finally, the encouragement of Mr. Rosser, himself, combined to bring me to a point of decision. I decided to go back to Raleigh and get my high-school diploma.

I cannot help but continue to mention the great good fortune I have had in my life in the matter of the people who have influenced me. Take Mr. Rosser, for example. Basically he was a small-town businessman whose major concern was the profitability and progress of his small chain of theaters. If all he cared about was making money, having me take a leave of absence for a few months would not have been in his best interests at all. I now knew enough about managing the theater so that it went smoothly. He was going to have to hire some temporary help and spend more time there himself. And yet he insisted I go back to school.

"Jack," he said, "nothing is more important than your education. Get your diploma. Your job will be here when you get back."

And so, at the end of January 1929, I packed my few belongings, said my good-byes—Mrs. Mellineaux assured me my room would be waiting for me on my return—and went back to Raleigh, anxious to get my diploma, but a little nervous over what kind of reception I would get from the teachers and the students. I need not have worried.

9

I HAVE JUST RETURNED from Los Angeles, where I produced one of the most rewarding shows of my career and am now relaxing in my den in my comfortable Northwest Washington home, my old high school annual in my lap. I smile down at the dark green cover with the gold-embossed label. "The Oak Leaf 1929, Hugh Morson High School."

That, too, was quite an accomplishment.

And yet, if you will forgive an old man's note of pride, that accomplishment of more than fifty years ago and the one of more recent vintage are directly related. Both were fashioned from the resolve that has been my trademark since watching my father plant a tree, carve out a baseball diamond, or sink a well.

"I.L.," he would say, "never do nothin' halfway. If it's worth doin' at all, do it right."

If I were to tell the average person that I put on a show at the American Trucking Associations' 1982 convention banquet headlining two musicians—a piano player and a violinist—the response would be: "You *only* had a piano player and a violinist?"

And my reply would be: "No. I did not only have a piano player and a violinist, I had talent, ability, drama, and beauty. It is quality, not quantity or variety that counts.

The pianist was Roger Williams, a tremendous talent; the violinist was a very fine artist who specializes in country music, named Jana Jae.

Originally, Vaughn Bonham, who handles ATA conventions, wanted another top star in addition to Williams. I thought I had come up with one. Helen Reddy was all set to perform, but called just a couple of weeks before the convention to say she wanted

73

to cancel to take a six-week engagement in Europe. I couldn't blame her.

Actually, I considered that development a blessing. Not that Helen Reddy is not a great performer. But the mix, Helen Reddy and Roger Williams, was not to my total liking. For one thing, Roger gives the kind of performance that needs time for developing; for another thing, it is an artistry that would suffer not only because of the shortened time span, but also because it would be in competition with an equally super but uncomplementary performance.

So, we ended up with a show built around Roger Williams and supported by Jana Jae and a twenty-five-piece orchestra. It was a great show. I judge a show by the audience reaction. And in all my years in this business, I do not recall a greater response than that one. This was quality entertainment. There were no comedians; not really a belly laugh in the whole show. And again, there is nothing wrong with a comedy show. I have put on hundreds of them, featuring such headliners as Bob Hope, Jack Benny, Red Skelton, and Alan King. But there was something about this show, with the grand piano of Roger Williams, complemented by the violin of Miss Jae, that produced an overall effect that enraptured 1,500 people seated in the California Ballroom of the Los Angeles Bonaventure Hotel and left me feeling like I did fifty-five years before when Charles E. Wessinger, Hugh Morson's principal, handed me my diploma, shook my hand, and said, "Congratulations, I.L., if anyone deserves this piece of paper, you do."

I now open the school annual, and there is the likeness of Mr. Wessinger, a clean-shaven, handsome man with kind eyes, looking back at me, a half-smile on his lips, and beneath the oval photograph, still looking as fresh as the day he inscribed them, are the lines: "With best wishes to I.L., may you have a successful and wonderful life. Chalmers E. Wessinger."

Nostalgia takes hold of me as I leaf through the book, peering at those long-ago familiar faces and savoring once again the sentiments inscribed in the margins:

"Don't forget our good times in 7th period, Arabel."—Arabel Cox.

"I.L., you're a riot—Keep on rioting!! Louise."—Louise Bridges.

"I.L., I hope you always have as many friends as you have now, Allen."—Allen Rogers.

"I.L., you sure were fine to loan me your typewriter, and I will always remember it, Edna:"—Edna Womble.

"Hope you become a famous Humorist. You could do it very successfully. Lots o' luck, Demerit."—Dorothy Merritt.

(A famous humorist . . . in the back, in the feature section of the annual, is a list of predictions for the graduates, and beside the name of I.L. Morton is the forecast that he will be Will Rogers II. That was not in the cards. It was my lot—and a happy and fulfilling one it has been—to stand in the shadows, playing the anonymous role of organizer, producer, never a star, but working closely with the stars.)

"Jack, we are very happy to have seen you come back and do the work you have done. We hope you will do the same in the future, Tommy."—Thomas Jones.

Yes, Tommy, I came back and did the work. But I was not alone.

First, there was Otis and Elsie, who welcomed me back like a member of the family. I was amazed at how the children had grown. Minerva was eleven now, Vivian, ten, Manley was almost nine. Manley asked me if I still had the little white camel he had given me for Christmas a few years before. I assured him I still had it.

Then there was Mr. Enloe, the manager of the State Theater. I stopped by to see him, and after shaking my hand, he said, "When can you start to work?"

And finally, there were the teachers, who seemed almost as ecstatic as Elsie over my return to school. Speaking of teachers, I again had a favorite—Miss Gilmore, my French teacher. We struck it off good and fast. Her classes were the brightest part of my school day, and I learned French even while my thoughts were often roaming elsewhere. I recall taking a trip with her. She knew I wanted to visit Hamlet and invited me to go along since she had to go through Hamlet on her way to her home in Ruby, South Carolina. I got all excited about being with her—and a free ride, too—but I cooled a bit when she brought along the Latin teacher. I never knew if this was her protection or just accommodating another passenger. Between the two of them, my education broadened a bit because I couldn't help learning something in such a situation. Later, she would lend me her car, which I used dating other girls. Today, I can't imagine such a relationship, but I'm certain she was just a wonderful young lady trying to help a struggling student. She autographed my school annual: "To I.L., 'Mon Chauffer,' " but later added "Mechant," which translates into "bad child!"

Another of my favorites was Miss Alexander, my typing teacher, who taught me a useful skill. She also nourished my musical ambitions by letting me select the music to which we typed. The music was reproduced by a portable record player that I had to keep cranking so it wouldn't run down. The tempo had to be maintained. Different tempos dictated the various speeds at which we typed. I doubt if such primitive methods are used today, but they were standard practice then. Miss Alexander was a lovely woman, but no romance blossomed between us. If it had, I may never have graduated!

For my part, I felt it was something I had to do; a job to get done. I worked at the theater evenings and Saturday, but managed to work in a few dates with a girl in one of my classes named Dorothy McGee. She was a lovely girl, but I was really being true to Liz. I had no idea whether Liz was being true to me.

Graduation night was warm, and I do not remember too much about it except for the feeling of elation as Mr. Wessinger handed me my diploma and there, near the front of the rows of chairs, were Charlie and Maude, and Elsie and Otis. Elsie was smiling, but once I caught her dabbing at her eyes with a handkerchief.

The next day I said my good-byes—it seems I was always saying good-bye—and was on the bus back to Hamlet.

After getting resettled into my old room at Mrs. Mellineaux's and checking into the theater, I called on Liz. My feelings about

76

Liz are difficult to remember, let alone describe. As I said, she was one of the prettiest girls in town and fun to be with, and I guess I had envisioned a growing relationship for a long time to come. Any notions like that were quickly squelched by her announcement that she was moving away to Charlotte.

"Oh, no, all the way to Charlotte?" I said.

"Yes," she said. Her father was being transferred.

Still, whatever depression I might have felt over that development was dispelled the next day when I arrived at the theater. I found Mr. Rosser there with a man who had the appearance and demeanor of a Santa Claus, with a flowing mustache, but no beard. Mr. Rosser introduced me to Benjamin Ralston, a top engineer with Western Electric, the man who would supervise the installation of Western Electric's sound in the Carolina Theater.

"Nice to meet you, Mr. Ralston," I said, extending my hand.

Mr. Ralston smiled and took my hand in a firm grip. "It's nice to meet you, Mort. And I want you to call me Uncle Benny. All my friends do."

"And you call me Jack, Uncle Benny. All my friends do." Uncle Benny nodded. But he always called me Mort.

Uncle Benny was a joy to be around. He was in tune with the great gaudy spree, in that he loved big, fast cars, hot chili, liquor, and airplanes. In fact, he owned an airplane, a low-winged monoplane that he kept on a dirt landing strip in Charlotte. He had two big cars, an Auburn and a Dusenberg. I got to drive them both, particularly when Uncle Benny had been imbibing.

It took two weeks to install the new sound system, but Uncle Benny drove down frequently after that to check on the system and just to keep in touch. We became friends, and later his kindness greatly affected my life.

It was late in the summer of 1929 that I got my first view of a really major city. Odum, the boy who worked on the railroad as a brakeman, asked me if I wanted to hitchhike to Philadelphia with him. He said he had some real good friends in both Washington and Philadelphia and it wouldn't cost us any money.

We left Saturday morning and made it to Washington that night. As we moved out of Alexandria in a big Packard we had hitched a ride with in Richmond, I got my first view of Washington, and it took my breath away. We had a magnificent panoramic view of a thousand jeweled lights and that tremendous capitol dome, lighted up like a wedding cake in the east, and to the west the towering, majestic Washington Monument.

The man who owned the Packard didn't say more than two words the entire trip. He left us off at Twelfth Street and Pennsylvania Avenue Northwest, near the old Post Office Building. A couple of blocks down the avenue, we made our way up a flight of black iron steps to a row house and rang the bell. Odum's friend, who worked as a soda jerk, fixed us up with a room. Well, "fixing us up" is not exactly what he did. We ended up paying two dollars a piece for a room that I thought would be free. That reduced my total assets to twenty dollars.

Sunday we got as far as Aberdeen, Maryland, and then stood there on the highway most of the day trying to hitch a ride. We finally got a lift on a horse truck, and by the time we made it to Philadelphia, a cold, steady rain was falling. Odum's other friend lived near the Navy Yard, but we couldn't find his house. Finally a police car spotted us, and the next thing I knew we were being searched and then told to open our suitcases. I was soaking wet and shivering with cold, and then on top of that, to have the police shining their flashlights in my face and questioning me like I was a fugitive from a road gang, was almost too much. They were finally satisfied we weren't part of the Capone gang, and Odum and I ended up in the YMCA next to a printing plant. We hit the road early next morning.

The trip was almost a total disaster.

The only saving thing about it was that while in Washington I had a chance to look at the grand movie theaters on F Street—the Fox (later called the Capitol) and the Palace. I was fascinated with the grandeur of those lighted marquees and impressive art work outside and the spacious lobbies inside. Compared to these movie mansions, the Carolina seemed almost like a shack.

But once I returned to Hamlet, the Carolina looked pretty good.

I was always looking for ways to liven things up, so I began to present local talent on the stage. It wasn't long before ambitious and doting mothers were bringing their children down to perform. We had dancers and singers, reciters of poetry, and musicians of all kinds. For the most part these performances were well received. However, I will never forget the night a little girl, a very talented tap dancer, ran sobbing from the stage. It was a traumatic experience for her and for me, one of the most embarrassing moments in all my years in entertainment. Moreover, it was not the girl's fault. The blame belonged squarely on the accompanying pianist, who flubbed the music, destroying the girl's rhythm. Backstage, I tried to comfort the girl as best I could.

I learned a cardinal show-business rule that night, one that is unfortunately violated all too frequently: You never back up a performer with anything but the best—whether it be acoustics, introductory material, visual aids, or most importantly, musical accompaniment. An inadequate musical accompaniment can ruin an otherwise excellent act.

In the fall of 1929, cracks began to show in the nation's economy, but few wanted to pay attention.

On the evening of October 24, the Associated Press reported from New York:

NEW YORK, October 29—A stock market panic appeared to have been checked early this afternoon, as leading bankers issued reassurances, and prices of many leading stocks, after declining ten dollars to forty dollars a share, rebounded sharply.

The following day, front pages through the nation carried this AP dispatch:

WASHINGTON, October 30—Official Washington kept a watchful eye on Wall Street today, and expressed the optimistic, if unofficial, opinion that the disastrous slump in security prices need have no depressing effect on the general business structure of the nation.

The view was advanced in many quarters that the stock market was in no way a reflection of any factor in the business world and that the latter is at present upon such a sound economic basis that there should be no fear of a general recession.

When government officials say there is no danger of war, dig yourself a foxhole. But I figured that while J.P. Morgan and the Rockefellers and Astors might have something to worry about,

I sure didn't. I had no stock in anything, and the moving picture business was doing well.

Clara Bow, Jack Holt, Fay Wray, Gloria Swanson, Ken Maynard, Joan Crawford, the Barrymores, and all the others were drawing people into movie houses in unprecedented numbers. And now, with our Western Electric system, we were showing the best movies with the best equipment.

But my sense of security was soon shattered.

The beginnings of what was to be known as the Great Depression stole into North Carolina almost overnight. Mr. Rosser lost his theaters in Aberdeen and Rock Hill and moved to Hamlet. In typical Rosser fashion—he would protect appearances at all costs—he rented one of the biggest houses in town and asked me to move in with him and his family, to help pay for it. I left Mrs. Mellineaux's, where I was quite comfortable and paid only five dollars a week, and moved in with the Rossers, where I was not comfortable and paid nine dollars a week—half my salary. Mr. Rosser then put his wife to work in the box office and his son as ticket taker while he ran the theater, leaving me with practically nothing to do.

By Chirstmas I knew I had to get out of there. It so happened Uncle Benny was in town one day, and it didn't take him long to see what the situation was. "Mort," he said, "they are going to hire a clerk in our Charlotte office. Why don't you go for it?"

Charlotte. My first feeling was one of relief at the chance to get out of what had become an intolerable situation. My second thought was of Liz Hardy, whom I had seen only a few times since she moved to Charlotte that summer.

I took the bus up there the next day and reported to Mr. L.A. Patton on the eighth floor of the Johnson building on Tryon Street near Trade Street, in the heart of bustling Charlotte.

Mr. Patton interviewed me. The job was for day clerk (they also had a night clerk), and one of my duties, Mr. Patton said, would be to dictate letters, most of them in response to complaints or questions.

"While I'm at lunch, why don't you see what you can do with these?" he said, handing me a couple of letters. "You can dictate appropriate responses to Margaret and she'll type them up."

He then went out to lunch, leaving me with the letters and two of the bluest eyes I have ever seen, belonging to the kind Margaret Burgess. The blue eyes didn't bother me nearly as much as the letters, the contents of which I have long since forgotten. I will never forget my feeling of utter frustration as I sat there in front of Miss Burgess' desk, staring at the letters while she sat behind her desk, her steno pad and pencil poised and ready to go. She was a lot more ready than I was. I had never dictated a letter in my life.

"Now, let me see here," I said. "Don't put that down," I blurted out as she started to write. "Let's see now."

Blue-eyes smiled. "Would you like me to help you? I've taken dictation on a lot of these letters."

"I would certainly appreciate it," I replied.

Miss Burgess composed two beautiful letters and typed them up. And there in the bottom left corner was the notation, JM: :MB On his return from lunch, Mr. Patton said, "I couldn't have done better myself."

No wonder, I thought. Did I just imagine a quick, bemused exchange of glances between Mr. Patton and Miss Burgess? At any rate, I was hired—at the magnificent salary of twenty-five dollars a week. And in the two years I spent working in that office, I never was called on to dictate a single letter.

Once again it was good-bye time. I could almost see the feeling of relief in Mr. Rosser's eyes when I told him I was leaving. We shook hands. As usual, he was dressed impeccably—dark, pin-striped suit, white shirt, blue- and red-striped tie, every hair in place. He had treated me well all the way, and I told him how much I appreciated it.

"You did a good job," he said. "Good luck to you."

Two hours later I was on the bus for Charlotte.

10

I SPENT TWO YEARS IN CHARLOTTE—from January 1930 to January 1932—and little did I know that it was going to be the next-to-last stop in what I call the "milk-run phase of Jack Morton's life."

From Charlotte I headed to Washington, D.C., and what turned out to be home, home at last. I did not plan it that way; probably never gave it a moment's thought. But then, who among us actually writes a script for ourselves and follows it to the letter? All I know is that in Washington I met Anne, who gave me the stability I was probably always looking for.

As for Charlotte, it was a quick and not particularly significant period, not too much different in most respects from my life in Hamlet.

Charlotte was a lot bigger, of course, the largest city in North Carolina and known as the "Queen City of the South," though Atlanta and New Orleans might argue the point. Charlotte was a bustling city, heavily into the manufacturing of industrial chemicals, textiles, and food products, though maintaining a kind of sleepy Southern charm unknown in the great manufacturing centers to the north and northeast.

And my work, of course, was different. The supervisor, Mr. Patton, had his own office, the two salesmen each had an office, while the five or six engineers, who spent most of their time on the road, shared another office. The secretary, Miss Blue Eyes, had an office next to Mr. Patton's, which also served as my base of operations. We had a stockroom in the basement, and it was my responsibility to keep inventory and order parts as needed—speakers, vacuum tubes, gears, lubricating oils, and whatever else was needed to keep the sound systems for theaters in a wide area operating.

I was paid handsomely—twenty-five dollars a week for my job as stockboy, file clerk, and errand runner, and as the economic situation worsened, I feared that I would lose my job. They also had a clerk on at nights, mostly to take care of emergency calls, and they decided to combine the duties of the daytime job with the nighttime duties, which consisted mostly in taking calls from theaters with sound problems and getting hold of the engineer closest to the theater. Fortunately, they kept me, perhaps because of my typing skills, which the lovely Miss Alexander had taught me.

I worked from 5:00 to 11:15 P.M., Monday through Friday, and 12 noon to 11:15 P.M. on Saturdays.

For a short period of time, I had an apartment with a couple of male schoolteachers, but then I paid a visit to a cousin Helen. Helen was married to a film salesman named Cicero Alexander, but called Alex by everybody. Alex was one of those high-spirited, friendly types who never seemed to get upset. They asked me if I would like to stay with them, and I accepted. Of course, I paid a modest amount for this board and room.

Charlotte was an important film hub. Films were shipped there for distribution to theaters in a wide area. It was Alex's job to travel to theaters through part of the state, taking orders for new movies. (The going rate was fifty dollars for an average film, as much as one hundred dollars for a good one. But, if you wanted a good one, a *Ben Hur*, for example, you also had to buy the "dogs" the studio made.) Alex's job kept him on the road from Monday morning to Friday evening. For her part, Helen seemed to accept the absences in good spirit. They had a young son, Jimmy, and a child on the way when I arrived, and they were a normal, happy family.

One of the first things I did, of course, on moving to Charlotte, was to resume my relationship with Liz. But working nights did not leave me much time for romance, and it wasn't long before Liz was dating someone else on a regular basis.

The inevitable end came on a cold wintry Sunday afternoon. "I guess it's best we don't see each other anymore," Liz said. "I'm really going with someone else now."

"Okay," I said, trying to be as nonchalant as Douglas Fairbanks. "I wish you luck. What kind of work is he in?"

"Why, he's a shoe clerk," she said.

"That figures," I said.

I wondered if I was doomed to lose all my girlfriends to shoe clerks. What was it those fellows had, anyway? I had never thought of them as being particularly dashing, but then, what did I know?

Working nights, I decided I had an excellent opportunity to return to school. I enrolled at Central High School, only a block from my cousin's house, in the fall of 1930, and for the next three semesters I pursued the subjects I had avoided at Hugh Morson—math, physics, chemistry, and more French and English.

It was not easy. For one thing, I had to overcome the self-consciousness of being twenty-one years old and attending high school. I knew most of the kids in school thought I was either a teacher or just plain stupid. But my teachers were most encouraging, and I finally was able to laugh at myself a little.

As for the courses, I did well in all of them—better than I had expected—and it all proved worthwhile later when I decided to go to college.

I had a couple of other "romances" in Charlotte—one with a girl named Tibby, whose father was an executive with the telephone company. My "affair" with Tibby was as usual. No scandal or great unbridled passions. But what a dish! She had assets that would put her on camera or stage today. She displayed them with such innocent abandonment that I got a guilty feeling just being around her. Her parents treated me wonderfully, which helped dampen any impulses I had toward Tibby—so I merely nibbled at the forbidden fruit. I could never betray such a trust! Her father had a big Packard limousine and often took Tibby and me on trips. It really boosted my ego when Tibby came to pick me up. It would have been easy to succumb to such luxury, but I guess my ambition was more compelling than other temptations. The other was the exciting Beatrice, a nurse whom I met in the hospital when I had an emergency appendectomy. While under anesthesia, I had a paralytic seizure and needed to be revived with artificial respiration. The nurses referred to me as "the guy that died." I got a lot of attention—especially from Bea. We dated and had a lot of fun till I left Charlotte.

84

One could easily ask if the subject of marriage ever arose. I know I never seriously considered it at the time, because of my old-fashioned, naive, and innocent appraisal of the marriage institution, namely: "get a high-school education, a job, save enough money to build a house," all *before* marrying. How outdated such an idea is today! Also, I have always had a built-in restlessness that dictated so much in my life. It propelled me through exciting times and relationships, but best of all, it led me finally to a marvelous wife, family, and circumstances beyond my fondest dreams.

Money was always scarce in those days, and it took me a long time to pay off the surgeon's bill of about $200. Then there was the time my dentist told me I needed a gold crown for one of my teeth and it would cost twenty-five dollars. He did not do the work until he had his money, so I paid him something each week until it was all paid, and then he put on the crown.

It was in the summer of 1931 that I received news that Manley, Otis and Elsie's youngest child, drowned at a Sunday-school picnic. I remember sitting in my room, holding the little white porcelain camel that Manley had given to me that Christmas. (I still have it; it rests on the mantle in my library.) I never did learn all the details of the tragedy. Apparently, Manley, then eleven, and another boy went out in a rowboat, and Manley jumped out of the boat to go swimming.

I now have three children of my own and eight grandchildren and am far more able to appreciate the grief that Otis and Elsie had to endure than I was then. Few things in life are more painful than tragedies affecting one's children.

My boss, Mr. Patton, a graduate in electrical engineering from VPI, continued to encourage me and was always emphasizing the value of higher education. Finally, just after Christmas 1931, he called me into his office.

"Jack," he said, "there's a fine liberal arts college in Washington called George Washington University. You ought to go there."

I just looked at him. My salary had already been reduced ten percent—as had everyone else's—and now, I thought fearfully, I was being fired.

"There is an opening in our Washington office," Mr. Patton said. "Same job as you have here; same hours. If you wanted to you could go to the university during the daytime. It's yours if you want it."

It was that quick and that easy. On the night of January 27, 1932, the Pattons took me to the railroad station and put me on the train for Washington. I was wearing a lightweight suit, carried all my possessions in one suitcase and had in my pocket my life's savings of $239. Within me stirred feelings of apprehension mixed with a sense of great adventure. It seemed my life really had been planned for me after all and that I had my own guardian angels who took a special interest in me and gave me the guidance or the push I needed to keep me on track. Mr. Patton was the latest of these guardians. There is no way he could ever guess how much he influenced my life by pointing me toward Washington.

Everything that has happened to me since—meeting Anne, getting married and having a family, planting strong roots and getting to know and work with some of the greatest artists in entertainment—all had their beginnings in one man's kindness.

11

LOOKING BACK ON MY COLLEGE YEARS in Washington, I am amazed at the balancing act I managed to perform; but I did not look at it that way at the time. In fact, I thrived—I always have thrived—on being busy, and being busy to me is a full-time occupation.

Once in Washington, it wasn't long before I found myself caught up in my own three-ring circus of college life, job, and what proved to be the real beginning of my career in entertainment.

Those also happened to be some of the most exciting and meaningful years in the history of the world, the nation, and the city of Washington.

Washington has now been my home for half a century, and I have learned to love it in a way I have never loved any other place. But during these past fifty-odd years, this city, whose chief occupation is legislation, has undergone tremendous growth and change. In the days of the early- and mid-1930s, Washington was an enchanting blend of small American southern town and Parisian beauty, its white glistening monuments, its imposing government buildings and tree-lined boulevards standing in sharp contrast to its provincial grass-roots ways. Alexandria, Virginia, and Rockville, Maryland, now close-in parts of the Washington area, were so distant in those days that they were given datelines in the Washington newspapers. Silver Spring, Maryland, was then a distant town along a narrow, rural two-lane Georgia Avenue, and the Washington Airport, known as Hoover Airport, was a couple of hangars and a runway about where the Pentagon now stands. The runway intersected with a road so that ground traffic had to stop to allow aircraft to take off and land.

When I arrived, Washington and the nation were at the dawn of a new age. Franklin D. Roosevelt was waiting in the wings to go on center stage, and before he died thirteen years later, he would have inalterably changed the way the federal government operated and the way people looked on that government.

There were a number of forces or developments coming to play on our nation in those days, all of which combined to serve as a backdrop for those vital years in the life and times of Jack Morton.

First there was the Depression, which hung over the country like some poisonous smog, and while Washington escaped the ravages felt elsewhere in the country, we knew it was around.

But the major manifestation of the Depression for Washington without a doubt was the great gathering of the Bonus Marchers, which ended on such a bitter and tragic note.

That happened during my first summer in Washington, the summer of 1932, and I can still see the great black pillars of smoke rising out of the rubble left at Third Street and Pennsylvania Avenue, one of the "Bonus Expeditionary Force" encampments after troops had cleared the area and set it on fire. The troops, under command of General MacArthur, went on from there to lay waste the B.E.F.'s main camp on the Anacostia mudflats in Southeast. The 10,000 World War I veterans and their families who had come to Washington seeking payment of a war bonus were sent scurrying, leaving the rest of the nation sharply divided on the issue: Some believed the government had acted correctly in disbanding what was becoming an increasingly unruly mob, while others viewed the marchers as desperate men who had served their country in the Great War and really posed no serious problem to the law and order of the city. The government, they charged, had overreacted.

And then there was crime. It was a different kind of crime in those days, not the everyday presence that stalks all of our cities today. In fact, Washington was relatively crime free in those days; one could walk in any neighborhood at any time without fear, and a Washington policeman seldom had reason to point his gun, except on the firing range. Crime in those days was a sensational phenomenon, starring the flamboyant gangsters on the one hand, and on the other the law enforcement officers, led by the determined and efficient J. Edgar Hoover. It was the era of John Dillinger, killed by FBI agents on a Chicago street in the summer of 1934; Pretty Boy Floyd, shot dead fleeing officers on an Ohio farm; Machine Gun Kelly, wanted in Oklahoma City for the kidnaping of an Oklahoma oil magnate, wanted in Kansas City for murder, wanted in Chicago and St. Paul for robbery and murder, captured in Memphis in September 1933, put on trial thirteen days later and sentenced to life in prison three days after that. In those days, justice was swift. Joe Zangara attempted to shoot President-elect Roosevelt in Miami on February 15, 1933, killing Mayor Anton Cermak of Chicago, and a month and five days later, on March 20, was executed in the electric chair in Raiford, Florida.

What has been called the "Crime of the Century," the kidnapping and murder of the Lindbergh child, dominated the front pages of the newspapers just after my arrival in Washington.

And while sensational crime and the Depression tainted the national scene, there was nonetheless an adventurous spirit alive in the land. It was the era of the great leap forward in aviation. I remember walking down Pennsylvania Avenue on my way to work one afternoon just as a black limousine was emerging from the White House gate, in the back seat of which was a woman and a couple of men. They were animated, all of them smiling, and as the car turned right toward Sixteenth Street, I wondered who they were and what they had been doing in the White House. The next day a picture in *The Star* showed Amelia Earhart Putnam receiving a gold medal from President Hoover for being the first woman to fly solo across the Atlantic.

Other aviators, like Wiley Post and Roscoe Turner, became household names, with their record-breaking flights, and when Pan American Airways inaugurated its clipper service from San Francisco to the Hawaiian Islands and the Philippines in the twenty-five-ton super flying boat—the largest plane ever built until that time—it induced the noted aircraft designer, Igor Sikorsky, to predict giant flying boats capable of carrying seventy-five to one-hundred passengers and featuring such luxuries as "baths, dining salons, small dancing rooms and facilities for showing motion pictures." He did not think they would have swimming pools.

It was also the day of the dirigible, but while heavier-than-air aviation continued to progress even beyond Sikorsky's dreams, tragedy seemed to stalk those immense lighter-than-air ships. I can still remember reading with a kind of fascinated horror about the three navy ground crewman attempting to help dock the *Akron* at San Diego who were suddenly pulled skyward by the wind. Up and up they went, dangling from the mooring cables as the crowd screamed up at them to hang on. But two of them let go and fell to their deaths. The third sailor hung on for two hours, buffeted this way and that by the winds until he was finally pulled into the cabin, a little shaken, no doubt, but unhurt.

The *Akron* came to an untimely end in April 1933 when it crashed into the Atlantic during a severe storm, killing seventy-three of the crew and passengers. Somehow four survived.

Whenever I think of the ill-fated *Akron*—and I sometimes do when I see the Goodyear blimp floating above a stadium on television—I also remember a hot August day in 1936. I was excited about my marriage to Anne just a few weeks hence and was doing some shopping down on F Street when I noticed people looking skyward. I followed their glances and was treated to the spectacle of the largest man-made thing that had ever been seen up to that point—a huge dirigible cruising lazily across the gray-blue Washington sky, on its mighty stabilizer, white against black, a foreboding swastika, emblem of the emerging new Germany. As it crossed in front of the sun on this early Saturday afternoon, its monstrous shadow was cast upon the streets of Washington.

The ship was strangely prophetic. In August 1936, it sailed across the skies, threatening, invincible, a mighty symbol of the great power building in Germany. In May 1937, it came crashing down in flames at an American naval station in New Jersey.

The drums of war were already beating quite loudly when I arrived in Washington. I can still remember the headlines in the *Washington Post* on the morning I stepped from the train into a chill January air (and me without a proper topcoat for the Washington winter)—large ominous black type telling of the Japanese attack on Shanghai. It all seemed so far away and certainly of no consequence to my world. Later storms gathered in Europe as Adolf Hitler defied the post–World War I agreements and began to arm Germany to the teeth.

I recall there was an antiwar movement in the States, particularly among college students. At the University of Pittsburgh, students protested the selection of General MacArthur, U.S. Army Chief of Staff, as the commencement speaker, while on another occasion thousands of students went on strike throughout the country to condemn war.

But all of these worldly things were furthest from my mind that January day in 1932 when, after checking into the Harrington Hotel at eleventh and E Streets, I walked to the Western Electric offices six blocks away at Fifteenth and G, across from the treasury department and in the shadow of the Washington Monument.

Everyone seemed happy to see me. I met Mr. Applegate, the division manager, and Mr. Turner, the supervisor, and his assistant, Mr. Peterson. I met the engineers and one of the salesmen, Ed Shriver, who gave me a cigar and lit it for me. "A cigar," he said, "is a man's smoke." Every time I saw him after that, Ed Shriver insisted on giving me a cigar. There were also three or four secretaries, all rather attractive, I thought, and all very nice to me.

I left the Western Electric offices, and on Mr. Peterson's recommendation, I opened an account at the National Savings and Trust Company by depositing my life savings of $239 and then went over to George Washington University to register and spent eighty dollars of it for four courses.

The job proved to be exactly like the one I had in Charlotte: different theaters, different territories, different coworkers, but essentially I did exactly what I had done before—act as a kind of liaison between theater managers who needed help with their sound systems and our engineers who supplied that help.

Largely, it was an uneventful job, with long hours of silence, which was perfect for my needs. I used the time for studying and later to manage my growing orchestra business.

Once in a while I was called out of the office to help an engineer, like the night I found myself, to my astonishment, standing inside the White House, in the same room with President Roosevelt, Mrs. Roosevelt, and other members of the family and some friends.

I was hard at work in the office, studying for an American history exam when the phone rang and the engineer told me to bring a certain part to the White House as fast as possible. I found the part and ran practically all the way to the White House. I walked right through the gates—security was not like it is today—and explained to the doorman who I was, and he directed me upstairs, where the engineer and the First Family were waiting for me.

It was a large, heavily carpeted room with high windows covered with golden drapes. The President and the others were gathered together, seated on sofas and chairs in front of the screen, waiting for the movie to start. Here I was, playing a part in President Roosevelt's life!

On another occasion, I found myself in the great ballroom on the top floor of the Willard Hotel, helping the engineer repair a sound projector for the showing of a newsreel. This was the annual White House photographers extravaganza, and the ballroom was packed with famous diners, including the President. I stayed around the little balcony we had made into a projection booth. Just before the show started, into the projection booth walked Will Rogers, whom I recognized immediately from his movies. People today usually think of Will Rogers primarily as a cowboy performer, humorist, and newspaper columnist, but until his death in an airplane crash with Wiley Post in June 1935, he was one of the biggest money-making stars in Hollywood, along with Marie Dressler, Wallace Berry, Clark Gable, Joan Crawford, Janet Gaynor, and Joe E. Brown.

"How are you, young man?" the great Will Rogers said to me.

"Fine, thank you, Mr. Rogers," I said.

That was the extent of our conversation.

I do not really recall how I felt at the time. I suppose when I found myself so close to President Roosevelt and later Will Rogers I experienced the feelings of awe and elation that normal people feel in the presence of the famous. But, of course, since that time I have come to know and work with so many celebrities, that I have recognized they really are ordinary human beings. I also know that is something *they* wish everybody would recognize.

Perhaps the most memorable incident in my four years of working at Western Electric in Washington occurred on a Friday night in the spring of 1935.

I received a call from a Mr. Phillips, manager of the Stanton Theater in Northeast Washington. "My sound has gone out," he said. "Can you get somebody over here tonight? I've refunded everybody, but tomorrow's Saturday and I have a matinee at one o'clock."

"Sure thing," I said.

I called Arlington Brooks, the engineer on duty for the area.

"You said Stanton?" I heard him say.

"Yes, Stanton," I said.

There was quite a flap the next morning in the office. It seems that Mr. Brooks had gone to the town of Staunton (pronounced Stan-ton), 150 miles to the southwest, could find no theater looking for him, and returned to Washington. By the time Mr. Brooks had arrived in the office the next morning, the irate Mr. Phillips had already been on the phone wondering whatever happened to the engineer who was going to fix his sound system. Mr. Phillips had spent the entire night in his office at the theater and was understandably upset. Mr. Brooks got the sound fixed in plenty of time for the Saturday afternoon double feature, and I learned a valuable lesson: Always be complete and clear in your instructions and make sure the other guy understands exactly what you mean.

Our offices at Western Electric, which were on the seventh floor, offered a tremendous bird's eye view of Washington's big parades, and from that vantage point I watched the parade for Roosevelt's first inauguration, March 4, 1933, the last one held on that date before the Twentieth Amendment moved it up to January 20. We were ideally situated along the small stretch of Fifteenth Street, where the parades swung north before turning west again up Pennsylvania Avenue toward the White House.

During my first several months in Washington, I shared a room with a young man named Monroe in a house right on campus. He was from Milford, Delaware, and knew more about Delaware, the first state, than any man alive. He willingly imparted all his knowledge about Delaware without being asked. Did you know that Henry Hudson discovered the Delaware Bay and River in 1609 and that Delaware furnished two of the finest regiments to the Continental Army? I could tell you a lot more about Delaware if I had paid more attention. Still, he was a very pleasant fellow, rather quiet and studious, and we got along just fine.

But, in the fall of 1932, a fellow I took history with by the name of Dick Snow invited me to a "rush" party at the Phi Sigma Kappa fraternity house. All the fraternities were looking for people to help pay the rent on the houses, but what particularly settled it for me was the fact that Phi Sigma Kappa was looking for someone to fire the furnace and do some other chores, in exchange for a nice reduction in the rent.

I will always look back on my Phi Sig days with a real feeling of warmth (and I'm not trying to make a pun here about firing the furnace). I made a lot of good friendships there, some of which have lasted to this day. Ed MacCoy, the Phi Sig treasurer, who was a master at keeping us one jump ahead of bankruptcy was one. Dick Snow, who was the house manager, was best man at my wedding. He was a fidgety guy, always busy, and always misplacing things. There was Woodie Thomas, a Kentuckian who worked on Capitol Hill at the time. Almost everybody in the fraternity worked. Woodie, who went on to law school, became a vice-president with Trans World Airlines, specializing in congressional relations. Tom Jackson, a tall, solid individual from Washington, D.C., later became a successful Washington lawyer. Les Gates, who was editor of the *GW Hatchet*, wound up in the newspaper business as an advertising executive. Win Weitzel, who became a highly successful real-estate man specializing in commercial property, had an older brother, Frank, who served as controller general.

Anne and I kept close touch with Woodie and Beal Thomas and Win and Virginia Weitzel all these years and continued our friendship with Ed and Charlotte MacCoy until his death in 1981. He became a successful sales executive with Standard Register. Ed and Woodie were also in our wedding. Charlotte still lives in Washington, and Anne and I see her often.

I have never been in the military, but I know the camaraderie, the closeness, that comes from living and sharing with a group of men, particularly, as in my case, when the others are very much like yourself. We had one fellow, whose name was Ted, who did not have to work, an Oklahoman whose father owned a newspaper. I don't remember Ted too well, but I do recall we gave him the use of three dressers because he was the only one

94

who had enough clothes to make use of them.

I remember the first time Ted took a group of us and our dates with him to the Shoreham Hotel, where we wined and dined and danced and lived it up like rich people. Ted paid the bill with some kind of "credit" his father had. The Shoreham advertised in his father's newspaper, and instead of paying cash, they extended credits. At Ted's invitation, I helped redeem those credits on a number of other occasions, and that is where I learned the real meaning of "freeloading."

The fraternity house was a three-story red brick row house with the black iron steps so prevalent in Washington. It was located at 1822 I Street. The first floor contained a living room, dining room, kitchen, and bath. The second floor had a bath and shower and several bedrooms. The third floor, or attic, was the dormitory and everybody—about seven or eight of us—slept there in barracks fashion, dressing in the rooms below.

It was the established custom to sleep with the windows open, winter and summer. We all slept on cots with thin mattresses and flannel blankets. If everybody was there, we all froze; if anyone was not staying there on any particular night, his blanket was put to good use. I understand the custom began because someone thought it was very healthful, all that fresh air and snow and rain, and I suppose nobody wanted to be the first to yell chicken.

The floors below were usually warm in winter, thanks to a good working coal furnace in the basement and the guy who kept it going—me.

My children and lots of others have grown up with finger-controlled heat and have never experienced the wonders of shoveling coal and ashes. At least, I did not have too far to shovel the coal, because the coal company would pour it right down through a basement window in the furnace room. I became an expert at banking the fire at night so it would be relatively easy to get started again in the morning.

We had a cook, a black man named Carl, who cooked two meals at the house, breakfast and dinner (never lunch). I ate breakfast, but during the dinner hour I was always working at Western Electric.

In the winter I had to get up earlier than anyone else, and

Carl always had a steaming cup of coffee waiting for me. After I got the furnace working, we would sit in the kitchen talking and waiting for the others to rise and shine. Carl would fix breakfast and then go off to his other job—and I would go to my classes at George Washington University.

As for my schooling, though I did not distinguish myself as a scholar, I got by fairly well. And while I have not used my learning there directly, as a doctor or lawyer would—I majored in psychology and thought I wanted to get into personnel work—I have benefited immeasurably.

It was at GW that I learned about history as a living force, a dynamic ongoing relationship among nations.

I learned about art, about the relationships among shades and colors and the meaning of composition. I was taught to identify the great masters by their individual techniques and styles. One of the American artists was Durand, whose great imaginary scenes symbolic of an endless America can inspire in the same way John Ford could with his Western epics on the screen.

I learned that *Whistler's Mother* was not just a portrait of an old lady, sitting prim and proper while staring into space, but an ingenious *Arrangement in Gray and Black*—its actual title—pleasing in its design and powerful in its subtle mood of gentleness, dignity, and resignation. I learned about the Impressionists and Old Masters, such as Renoir, Degas, El Greco, Van Gogh, Vermeer, Monet, Velazquez, and many others.

Now, all of these things and more, much more, I learned at the university, and while they probably strike the truly cultured as rather elementary, to this country boy fresh from the rural South, they were truly a revelation, and the doors they opened remained opened so that I continually drew on that reservoir of knowledge to enhance my life in many, many ways. I still do.

I had for European history a virtual classroom tyrant in Dr. Lowell J. Ragatz, who pounded the lessons into us with a vigor that could not be ignored. He had us frequently visit the Library of Congress, museums, and galleries; he forced us to read a book a month; and whenever anyone asked a question, he never answered it, he directed us to where we could find the answer. "The mark of an educated person," he said, "is not knowing all the answers, but in knowing where to find them." Dr. Ragatz was a short, intimidating man with a Hitler mustache. He was a brilliant professor and knew his subject from A to Z. But I learned he also had a bit of human kindness in him. I made a "C" the first semester. Later, he was hospitalized for an emergency operation, and I visited him there. Next semester I made a "B." Kindness and psychology do pay off. The next year he married one of his students, which made me believe that my earlier "romances" with my teachers were not as farfetched as I had thought.

For American history I had the eminent Dr. Elmer Louis Keyser, who could lecture to several hundred students and have every single face riveted on him. He interspersed his lectures with an occasional humorous quip, an outrageous pun, or a little joke of some kind, and they always were unexpected—shocking, really, in their suddenness—and they would always elicit, after a second's pause, a great roar of genuine laughter.

For general psychology I had Dr. Fred A. Moss, a professor who looked like an unmade bed. A Georgian, he had worked his way through college selling Bibles. He did not care a whit about his appearance. His clothes were ill-fitting and a designer's nightmare. His hair never looked combed.

One of the big scandals of the school during my second semester was Dr. Moss' divorce. "His wife is divorcing him," someone told me, "because he keeps conducting psychological experiments on the children." Pavlov was a hot item in those days.

But despite all that, he was a very competent professor.

Life often turns on what appears to be insignificant at the time. Someone told me the government was looking for junior interviewers and the job paid twenty-seven dollars and fifty cents a week, five dollars a week more than I was making at Western Electric. I applied, barely passed the civil service exam, but I did not measure up on the ensuing interview.

I sometimes wonder how much different my life might have been had I gotten that job and went on to pursue a career in personnel management.

The more I got into psychology, the more I recognized that I had spent considerable time with one of the world's great psychologists—my father.

In American and English literature, taught by Dean Wilbur,

97

I gained an understanding of the greatness behind the well-known works in our language. I took courses in economics, sociology, philosophy, and statistics. I learned that I was not really cut out for statistics, though I passed the course through sheer determination and hard work and the patience and help of Professor Weida. In the final exam, Dr. Weida paced up and down the aisles, stopping at my desk to stare down at my paper; a smile meant that I was on the right track, a shake of the head meant the opposite. I wore out all the erasers I had!

Another worrisome course I took was in public speaking. I don't remember the professor's name, but I will never forget his technique—merciless embarrassment. We would all have to get up in front of the class and give our talks or read aloud, but the professor was right there to point out our failings. I had trouble correctly saying the words "literally illiterate," and he made me use them every day till I overcame the problem.

"Mr. Morton, your enunciation is atrocious. Let me hear those endings loud and clear."

It was most uncomfortable, but I must admit it was effective. I learned how to use the dictionary; I improved my enunciation, and I gained a better feeling for what words mean and how they should be pronounced.

In advanced psychology, taught by Dr. Thelma Hunt, we took field trips to St. Elizabeth Hospital, in Southeast Washington, the federal hospital for the mentally ill (a sprawling institution that resembled a college campus, except for the herd of brown Jersey cattle that would often line the tall iron wrought fence along Nichols Avenue and stare out at the passing traffic).

On my first visit to St. E's, we received a grand tour of the facilities, including the maximum security buildings where the patients were kept under lock and key. The doctors would lecture us. One psychiatrist talked about the hopelessness of most of the patients. We learned about maniac depression and dementia praecox, or schizophrenia. It was all fascinating and very sad.

But, while I went to George Washington University, I was not of it. There were two distinct types of students who attended college in those days, and I suppose still do. There were those whose lives were completely immersed in the university. They went to all the school dances; they participated in the bonfire football rallies; they went to all the sports events, some participating as players, cheerleaders, or managers; some worked on the school paper. The other type had their lives divided. They worked. Going to school meant one thing—going to classes. And there was only one reason for going to classes and that was to learn enough to get a diploma and a degree.

I belonged to the second category, although I was not as totally divorced from school life as some. For one thing, I belonged to a fraternity and even became active as a member of the interfraternity council; for another thing, I became very much involved in fraternity dances, because I was booking orchestras for them.

In a way, my experiences with this phase of my college life was just as much a course in psychology or American history and in many ways more important to the career I finally settled on.

12

THE TWO GREAT SOCIAL CENTERS for GW students were Quigley's Drug Store, at Twenty-first and G Streets, and the little coffee shop, one block down at G and Twentieth, where you could get a fairly decent lunch for a reasonable price, reasonable being under thirty-five cents.

I was sitting in there having lunch on a golden fall day in 1932 with two students I knew only casually, when one of the fellows invited the other young man and me to his fraternity's pledge dance a couple of weeks hence.

"They made me dance chairman," he said, "and I don't know the first thing about it. How do I go about getting a band?"

I couldn't tell him. Neither could the other guy. But a light went on somewhere in the back of my mind. There must be a lot of fraternities and sororities continually needing dance bands, I reasoned, and there must be a lot of dance bands continually looking for engagements. The trick was to match them up.

The next morning, when Carl served me my bacon and eggs, I put the question to him. "Carl, do you know any bands looking for work?"

"Oh, sure," Carl said. "I know a good one. It's all colored folks, though."

"That's all right," I said, "as long as they can play music."

"Oh, they can play, all right," Carl said.

"Fine," I said. "How do I get in touch with them?"

That afternoon I took a streetcar up to Fourteenth and U Streets to a hall the orchestra used for rehearsing. I heard them play a few numbers and then made a deal with the leader, a heavy-set man with a wide grin, named Sylvester. I would get them bookings for ten percent of the gross.

The going rate for his orchestra for a typical dance was forty-five dollars. My cut would be four dollars and fifty cents. There were eight of the musicians beside Sylvester, and they would each get four dollars, while Sylvester would get eight dollars and fifty cents.

That is not much money these days, but it was then. Tuition was only twenty dollars for three semester hours, a ride on the streetcar was five cents, and you could eat well for two dollars a day. Eggs were twenty-nine cents a dozen, a quart of milk cost ten cents, coffee was eighteen cents a pound and you could buy a nine piece living-room set for sixty-nine dollars—five dollars down and the balance on easy terms.

So, I was in business as an orchestra booking agent. But while I had an orchestra to book, I still had no clients to book with. How do you get people to book your band? I decided the best way to do it would be to invite the presidents and social chairmen of the fraternities and sororities to hear the orchestra.

The black orchestra leader told me about the Crystal Caverns Club on U Street, where they played occasionally. It was owned by a black man named "Dizzy" Vance. It was closed on Sundays. I soon learned where Dizzy lived and called on him—at all times—early Sunday morning. Unfortunately, I woke him from deep sleep and an obvious hangover. At first I thought he would throw me out, but I guess he was too dumbstruck to give an expected response. Dizzy spluttered—and stuttered when I explained I wanted to "borrow" his night club for a Sunday afternoon dance. Quickly, I explained I may be able to "sell" the idea to others, for which he could collect rental money. I guess he was willing to grant any request to get rid of me and get back to bed. He agreed. I don't recall being surprised, because my plea was so plausible—at least to me. The date was set and I got on with my promotion. Incidentally, Dizzy showed up for the dance and even had his cook prepare tea—I mean real tea! I don't believe any rentals resulted for him, but he didn't complain. He realized, perhaps, better than I, that the white college crowd wasn't quite ready to integrate U Street!

So far I was making splendid progress and it hadn't cost me a cent, except for streetcar fare. I was determined to keep it that way.

I secured lists of all the presidents and social chairman of the sororities and fraternities and sent them invitations to a free tea dance—it had to be free, of course—at the Crystal Caverns. I used the typewriter at Western Electric, as well as the office paper, envelopes, and stamps. There were no copying machines then, and I had to type a separate letter for each name on the list.

One afternoon, as I stopped in the coffee shop for lunch, as was my custom, I mentioned my plans to the woman who owned the shop, a middle-aged pleasant woman who did all her own cooking, including the baking, on the premises.

"If only I knew where I could get some refreshments," I said wistfully.

"Well, if that's all that's standing between you and Broadway," she said, "I can whip you up some cookies and cakes."

I don't know why people were always wanting to do things for me—even people I did not know very well—but that happens to be one of the lucky phenomena that has marked my life from its beginning. I don't even remember the lady's name, but I hope she knew how much I appreciated her kindness.

Oh, if only all my promotions had been as successful as that first one. They poured into the Crystal Caverns (remember, it was free and that word attracted a lot of attention in 1932), perhaps the first time that large, ornate club with the painted white stucco had ever played host to an all-white audience. Sylvester and his boys were ready, and they never sounded better. Everybody danced to such favorites of the day as "Let's Put Out the Lights and Go to Sleep," "Say It Isn't So," "Please," "All-American Girl," and "A Shanty in Old Shanty Town."

And it worked. I secured a number of bookings for the orchestra, including one from my own fraternity—to my regret.

For the most part, fraternity (and sorority) dances were held in the fraternity and sorority houses, usually on the first floor. In our house, we just moved all the furniture out of the living and dining rooms and waxed the floors.

I remember getting a little nervous about this one—after all, this was my fraternity, and I wanted everything to go right.

Unfortunately, the musicians had been drinking even before they arrived and, more unfortunately, continued. They got pretty sloppy, and the music was terrible. I sent them home before the appointed quitting time. I suffered humiliation I had never known, but actually the fraternity fellows did not condemn me.

Toward the end of the evening, only a few couples had the nerve to try to dance to that wild cacophony. That was the end of my first management venture. I paid off Sylvester and severed my relations with him and his band. The injury inflicted on my feelings was not permanent; my fraternity brothers were more amused than angered, and I went on to better things. But from that point on, I was always aware of the potential for harm in the little brown jug.

I discovered that once the word got around that I was in the business of booking bands, the bands sought me. I discovered also that musicians welcomed someone with selling and business capabilities to handle their bookings.

There were a lot of bands in the area that were doing well. One was led by a GW student and piano player named Frank Mann, who later became the mayor of Alexandria. Another was the Knapp-Davis Orchestra. Harry Knapp later was an important executive with Eastern Airlines. Louie Allen had his orchestra, but he usually did his own bookings. That's not surprising. Louie was an astute businessman and later became well known as a meteorologist. He had his own weather-forecasting business (his clients included some of the larger shipping lines) and for years was a popular TV weatherman in Washington. Louie passed on a few years ago.

My band-booking business thrived. I would sell orchestras and I would appear to make sure the orchestra was there—and ready to play—and then checked with the person in charge, collect the fee, pay the leader, who paid the other band members. Book-keeping was simple.

I often entertained dreams of learning to play an instrument and getting into the business as a performer or orchestra leader. But in saner moments, I recognized I was not Bennie Goodman. I recognized that certain abilities are innate gifts. Music is one of these. There are those of us who can appreciate the talented pianist or singer, the gifted writer, the extraordinary painter, but we cannot hope to match their performance. However, my appreciation, judgment, and taste in music, entertainment, and people have enabled me to select talent objectively, to choose artists

103

who consistently please our audience. Creative people by nature are more subjective, which is a handicap in producing shows.

My talents were on a more moderate scale and had to do with managing and promoting, going back to the days when I was just a boy in business for myself on the streets of Wilson, "riding on a smile and a shoeshine."

And so, my orchestra-booking business prospered. It placed a strain on my work at Western Electric, but fortunately, I was not too busy there. I had business cards made—"Jack Morton Orchestras," and two telephone numbers—the pay phone at the fraternity house and the Western Electric number. Fortunately, the secretaries were good about taking messages.

I also made quite a few calls from the office, which caused the phone bills to jump, and that caused Mr. Peterson to also jump. He had one of those cold, humorless personalities, but was not without a talent for sarcasm, greeting me not warmly.

"And how would you like your name?" he asked loudly enough to attract the attention of others.

"What do you mean?" I asked.

"Well, I just presume that you would like us to take the name of the company off the front door and put yours on. Would you like 'Jack Morton Orchestras,' or just 'Jack Morton'? You're getting more phone calls than the company."

Arlington Brooks stood up for me. "He's doing a good job for us," he said, "and he is working hard and going to school and all."

Mr. Peterson said Western Electric could not afford to continue to pay my "other business" phone bills and went back to his office. Looking back, I have to conclude that he was a lot warmer inside than he showed on the outside. I was never seriously threatened with dismissal, and when I left there Mr. Peterson and Mr. Applegate both gave me enthusiastic letters of recommendation.

Among the bands I was promoting was a young, enthusiastic, and talented group, mostly high-school students, who really didn't have a leader. They needed a name and, with my permission and subtle urging, started calling themselves "Jack Morton's Orchestra."

So, I finally was an orchestra leader, but I didn't do any leading. I just got credit for it.

104

They went all out, even painting their bandstand and decorating it with a large "JM." They were good. There was Fred Farnsworth on trumpet, Mel Holober on sax, and Jack White on piano, to name a few. As I said, they were young. In fact, Jack White's mother wouldn't let him out at night until I came by to pick him up.

As you might suspect, the dance business was brisk during the school year, but with summer there was no demand at all.

The musicians in most of my orchestras had full-time jobs. There were accountants, jewelers, a number of government workers, and there was even one undertaker, who played one lively clarinet. But the Jack Morton Orchestra musicians were out of school in the summer and had no jobs, and that caused another light to go on. I decided to look for summer work.

The Jack Morton Orchestra played occasionally in the Silver Grill, a nice ballroom that had been converted from a dining room in the Broadmoor Apartment-Hotel on Connecticut Avenue. I had some pictures taken of the band in that rather glamorous setting, captioned the pictures "The Jack Morton Silver Grill Orchestra" and sent them along with letters to hotels and clubs at summer resorts—in Atlantic City, Ocean City, and in the Catskills in New York State.

I received a promising response from a man who was in Florida managing a resort hotel there during the winter months. I contacted him by phone and we negotiated a deal for the orchestra to play during the summer at the Ausable Chasm Hotel in the Adirondacks.

It was a short time later, in May, when I received a telegram at the fraternity house: URGENT. CONTACT ME IMMEDIATELY. ROOM 702 AMBASSADOR HOTEL. There was a phone number, and it was signed simply, "Roberts." I called immediately.

"What kind of a business you running anyway?" he asked. "I've been trying to get hold of you all day. You're not listed in the phone book. I've been getting Western Electric and pay phones, but no Jack Morton Orchestra or booking agency. What have I got myself into?"

"Look, I'm just getting started," I said, "but the band is great. If you want to, you can hear them."

He did. It was obvious that he was a bit on edge. He had

105

hired an orchestra and couldn't find it or the booking agent of the same name.

I set up a quick audition at the fraternity house. The man was there right on schedule, a short, heavy-set, nervous man in his mid-50s.

"Okay. Okay," he said taking a chair. "Let's hear what you got."

The Jack Morton Silver Grill Orchestra, with no leader, and only a few people looking on, gave the best performance of its life, playing "Smoke Gets in Your Eyes," "Stormy Weather," and "Deep Purple." These kids did not improvise. They played arrangements with each musician following his own score. When each musician concentrates and knows his music, the effect is easy on the ears. Mr. Roberts was satisfied. In fact, we signed a two-week, renewable contract, starting the third week in June. He shook my hand, waved his cigar at the band and said, "See you next month." The price was $250 per week with rooms and meals. I made $25 per week—about the same Western Electric paid me.

When it was time for the band to open its engagement, I could not stand the idea of not being there. After all, it was my band. I talked a friend of mine, Fred Rawlings, who was a member of Sigma Phi Epsilon, and who (most importantly) had a car, to drive up to Ausable Chasm. I got Elder, the day clerk at Western Electric, to cover for me, and off we went.

I do not remember the drive up, but I will never forget the breathtaking panorama of Ausable Chasm, nestled in the great mountains with the sprawling, weather-beaten turreted hotel looking like a page out of *Grimm's Fairy Tales*.

They gave Fred and me a room in one of the auxiliary buildings where they put all the help, including waiters and musicians.

After the second night, I got the feeling the band was not working out. I guess it was something Mr. Roberts said. He said: "I don't think the band is working out."

Glenn Miller wouldn't have satisfied this guy. But he agreed to keep them on for a while, and I went back to Washington.

Two weeks later, I got word that Mr. Roberts had fired the band. The Ausable Chasm was more in tune with "society music," where there is a lot of improvising, with first one musician then

106

another taking over center stage. But it wasn't just the playing style of the band. It was also the drinking style of Kenny, the guitar player—a great musician, but unable to hold his liquor. He wasn't even twenty, but he was already on his way to getting a doctorate in drinking. Moreover, he brought a girlfriend along with him—contrary to our rules—and she also drank. And they fought all the time. At any rate, the deal was ended and we never even got all the money due us.

Things went better at Rehobeth Beach, where I next booked Jack Morton's Silver Grill Orchestra—minus the guitar player. We had picked up a musician who could also sing. At one time or another, we also featured a girl vocalist.

But, by far the most significant booking I ever made, before or since, occurred on a Saturday night in October 1933. I had a band booked for the Kappa Alpha Fraternity on Connecticut Avenue, and as was my custom, I dropped by about 11:30 to see if things were going well and to pick up the twenty-five dollar fee.

As I walked in the front door, I saw a friend from my fraternity. "Say, Jack," he said, "is that Morton girl related to you?"

"What Morton girl?" I asked.

"I think her name is Anne," he said.

I made my way back to the kitchen, where I found Kappa Alpha's social chairman, who graciously handed over the fee without my having to ask for it.

"Are you related to Anne Morton?" he asked.

"Somebody else just asked me that," I said. "I never heard of her before."

"Well, you should meet her," he said.

"Why?" I asked.

"She's quite a number," he said. "In fact, I told someone she couldn't possibly be related to you. C'mon, I'll introduce you."

As he led me across the dance floor, I saw her—at least, I thought that might be her—and I thought . . . umm umm umm! I can still remember seeing Anne Morton for the first time—a lovely, dark-haired girl with large brown eyes, a beautiful figure, wearing a white dress and some kind of sequined, beanie-like cap. She danced easily, listening attentively to her partner. I later learned that she had this unique gift of being able to give her total attention to whomever she was talking.

My friend introduced us, Morton to Morton, and we danced, and we talked a lot about Mortons. I discovered that this was the weekend of her nineteenth birthday, that she was from Columbus, Georgia, and was attending an art school in Washington.

I thought she was the most beautiful girl I had ever seen. Now, fifty years later, I still think so.

13

Until I met Anne, my relationships with girls were more casual than anything else, not only innocent, but lacking in any real commitment on the part of either. Had not Della and Liz fallen victims to the mysterious charms of shoe clerks, somebody else would certainly have come along. As for Bea, while I did take a couple of trips to Charlotte during my first months in Washington and saw her on those occasions, that relationship was a natural victim to time and distance.

But Anne was different. From the very beginning, I knew she was special, and I viewed her with both desire and apprehension. In her presence, I was alternately filled with elation and despair, confidence in my capacity to win her over in time, and total dread that I could never measure up to her expectations.

Anne was from that Southern genteel society that I was able to view only from a distance, a fascinating but foreign land of stately homes, maids and cooks and chauffeurs, where even breakfast was served on tables adorned with fresh-cut flowers and white linen.

There was also a sensibleness about Anne that made her immune to superfluous charm and cautious in her relationships. I learned later that after we met that first night and she had given me permission to call her, she asked a friend who knew me all about me. I passed muster.

But that was only the first step. Though we dated, I could not claim her as "my girl." Anne was pursued by lots of boys, and she wasn't about to settle down to just one. Her suitors no doubt included men of fine character with far more to offer than I. I knew from the beginning that if our relationship even had a chance of progressing into something meaningful, it would require time, lots of time, and a great deal of patience on my part.

Not only that; I could not have monopolized Anne even if she had been willing. Going to school days and working nights while attempting to build a business on the side, left me very little time for courting.

Still, we managed to see each other, mostly on Sunday during the beginning, with an occasional weeknight when I was able to get Terrell Elder, the day clerk at Western Electric, to work for me.

When I first met Anne, she was living at the King-Smith School for young ladies off Dupont Circle on New Hampshire Avenue. At first I thought she went to school there, but later discovered she was attending the Felix Mahoney National School of Fine and Applied Art a few blocks from King-Smith at Rhode Island Avenue and M Street.

"My grandmother's influence," she told me. "There are only a few of us who live at King-Smith, but do not go to school there. I wanted to come up here to study art, but my parents would not hear of my living in a rooming house."

The Mortons of Columbus, Georgia, had every reason to feel their daughter would be safe at King-Smith, where practically any kind of pleasure was equated with sin. It was so stuffy, so devoid of humor, that Anne and I would laugh about it.

That got me to thinking. King-Smith could use a good laugh. One night, as I was cleaning out the storeroom and taking inventory at Western Electric, I found myself with a boxful of useless hardware—nuts and bolts, screws and vacuum tubes, pieces of pipe, strands of wire, parts for speakers, brackets, springs, and other gems that were obsolete and of no value to Western Electric, or to anyone else for that matter. I sealed the box and had it delivered to Anne at King-Smith.

"I got your present," she told me later. "I took it into the sitting room and I spread all the nice things on the floor. All the girls were intrigued, but Mr. King-Smith considered the whole thing unladylike and my Saturday afternoon swimming privileges have been taken away."

Shortly after that, with her parents' approval of course, Anne moved into the Kappa Delta Sorority House, at 1756 K Street,

110

which I thought was just fantastic, inasmuch as my fraternity house was just around the corner, on I Street.

At my urging, Anne began dropping occasionally by my office, where I would be busy pursuing my studies or drumming up orchestra business. Sometimes I did some work for Western Electric. On some nights after I got off from work, I would walk around to Anne's house for a short visit, or we would go to the corner of Eighteenth and K to a little Greek restaurant, where we would have something to eat.

Occasionally, in the fall, I would take her to a GW football game, where we would see the famous Tuffy Leemans, the curly-haired dynamo of the Colonials' backfield, churn up and down Griffith Stadium.

In the spring there were trips to the Glen Echo Amusement Park, several miles out MacArthur Boulevard in the Maryland countryside, not far from where the Cabin John Bridge now stands. In those days, you would take the streetcar—an open summer car—to the park. We would get on board on M Street in Georgetown, and in a few minutes the car would be clickety-clacking its swaying way, and we would be overcome by the pungent smell of honeysuckle. "Smell that honeysuckle," Anne would say. "It reminds me of home." It was a fun ride. If you ever watch people on a public conveyance, they all seem to have a blank, withdrawn look about them, kind of sad or worrisome. Not on this streetcar, where everybody was laughing and joking, and occasionally a few would break out in song.

Anne was always smiling or laughing, her lively brown eyes sparkling in delight. She seemed to enjoy every minute of life, and I enjoyed every moment I was with her.

Still, there was the occasional despair I experienced, for I knew I was in love. I would be overcome with waves of hopelessness, particularly when I allowed myself to dwell on our diverse backgrounds. And there was one occasion when I feared for a few moments that I had shot myself down in flames.

I took Anne to a restaurant on Connecticut Avenue, a rather expensive place for my pocketbook, and discovered to my great pleasure that the menu included broiled pig's feet. Where I came from, pig's feet were considered a delicacy, but I lost sight of the fact that Anne did not come from where I came from.

111

"I think I will order them."

"Please don't," Anne said. "I can't stand the idea. If you do order them, I'm leaving."

I did not eat pig's feet that night, and to this day, I do not eat them with Anne.

That night I ordered something far less exotic, but my disappointment soon vanished when, as the waiter placed my steak in front of me, Anne reached over and clasped my hand and said, "Thank you."

I think that this was the moment I realized that this young lady with the grand sense of humor and exquisite poise really had me completely under her spell.

I gave Anne her ring, for which I paid twenty-five dollars, just before Christmas 1935, and she went home for the holidays. "Mama"—as I now called Anne's mother—phoned me the day after Anne left to invite me down for Christmas. I sat in a day coach all night Sunday, changed trains in Atlanta and arrived in Columbus late Monday morning, Christmas Eve.

Anne was waiting for me in a chauffeur-driven Cadillac. George, the chauffeur, took my bag and held open the back door. I was not used to all that luxury and wondered if the car would change into a pumpkin.

But I was not in the Morton home five minutes when I knew I had been accepted by a wonderful family.

The Morton home was a beauty—a white Victorian house with a large porch across an expansive front, located in downtown Columbus on the Court House Square. Inside it was splendid, with large rooms with high ceilings and fine furnishings.

The family consisted of Anne's mother, a petite woman with black hair and Anne's eyes; her father, a man of medium height, a little stout, baldheaded, and blessed with an outgoing personality; Anne's younger sister, Louise, who had the same brunette loveliness as her mother and sister; Anne's brother, Dan, a teen-aged schoolboy at the time, a copper-haired handsome lad with bright blue eyes and a ready grin. And finally, there was Anne's grandmother, a regal woman who was not able to get around much as a result of being struck by a luggage wagon at the railroad station at Warm Springs. The accident had broken her hip, but not her spirit. She could make it around the house and from the house to the car with the aid of crutches. She was a woman of indominable spirit.

While Grandmother and I got along fine, she was most concerned about her granddaughter's marrying anyone who would take her away from Columbus. This concern was so great that I actually looked into some job opportunities in Columbus, but finally decided, with Anne's complete assent, that we would be better off on our own in Washington.

Anne's maternal grandfather had passed on, as well as both grandparents on her father's side. From what I gathered, Anne's maternal grandfather was the kind of man I could relate to, a hard-working businessman who would not take an unfair advantage, but who was always aware of opportunity. He had been a food broker, dealing in such staples as sugar, flour, grain, and feed, and he was able to leap far ahead of his competitors by making full use of the telephone and telegraph. In fact, so many wires were going out of and into his warehouse that Western Union built a small office next door to take care of his needs.

Anne's father was in the insurance business, primarily, but was also associated with his brother in the real-estate business. The brother was a longtime city manager of Columbus. Anne's father was one of those genuinely happy individuals who made friends easily and was known throughout the Columbus area as "Mister Billy."

As I got to know the city better, I could understand Anne's feelings for it. It was a lovely town in those days. Anne used to say Columbus had two things it was really famous for—its proximity to forbidden Phoenix City, Alabama, across the river, a den of iniquity complete with gangsters, prostitutes, and illegal liquor, and its proximity to Fort Benning, Georgia, which became the largest infantry training center in the world.

I found myself making the trip to Columbus frequently. It was always a dirty trip—worse in summer than winter—and I found it necessary to take a few minutes off in Atlanta to take a shower. You could get soap and a towel and shower facilities for twenty-five cents in the station. After a good scrubbing, I would board the next train for Columbus—a trip of about three hours—also sooty, but not nearly as long.

One of those trips to Columbus was different. At George

113

Washington University I had become friends with an attractive, interesting girl named Dorothy, whose home was in Mississippi. (Later she became chairman of the Democratic National Committee.) On one occasion, we discovered we were both taking the same trip as far as Atlanta (she was to stay on the train to Mississippi), and I was looking forward to the companionship.

I met Dorothy at Union Station, in Washington. Her sister and brother-in-law, Lee and Gerry Walwork, were there, and we enjoyed a little conversation before the train arrived. As Dorothy and I began to board the train, her sister and brother-in-law began to pelt the two of us with rice! As we moved into the coach, the passengers were smiling broadly at us. Some of them were no doubt sorry that we were spending our honeymoon night in a day coach. I wanted to straighten things out, to tell them, "Hey, this is the wrong man, the wrong woman, and the wrong honeymoon!" But it was just too complicated to explain.

By the time we arrived in Atlanta, our fellow passengers must have concluded we were the coldest honeymoon couple in the world. We didn't even hold hands. They may have been even more surprised when I got off the train in Atlanta and left "my bride" to continue alone to Mississippi.

Those were happy days, though, and I was soon caught up in the whirlwind of Columbus life as Anne had lived it. Anne had a lot of friends, and we were constantly on the go, with picnics, swimming parties, club dances, and the like. There were also family activities, camping and fishing with Mr. Billy and Mrs. Morton.

Everyone there seemed to have a "country place," and the Mortons belonged to some kind of a fishing club at Box Springs, about fifteen or twenty miles from Columbus. The family and friends would spend the night there occasionally, and during the day we would swim, take out the rowboat, fish, eat, drink, and talk.

Occasionally, there would be fishing trips to Apalachicola, Florida, on the Gulf. I made one such trip with three or four new male friends, who told me I hadn't lived until I went fishing on the Gulf. That was really living! We spent one whole night driving to the place. It rained the whole time we were there. The other guys had too much to drink and spent the whole day hanging over the rail. I was the only landlubber in the crowd and I did all the fishing, and I don't even like to fish.

We visited a lot of people, including frequent trips to the Foleys, next door, where the widowed "Cousin Della" made quite a fuss over me, and there were many stops at a lovely old Southern home down on Broad Street, where four of Anne's great-aunts lived. The aunts also had a house at Warm Springs, where a long time ago Anne's cousin found the warm spring waters a balm for his crippled limbs, the result of a polio attack in the Philippines. Anne's aunts were influential in getting Governor Roosevelt of New York to try the soothing waters. When he became President, Roosevelt invited them for a visit to the White House.

While I was made to feel quite at home by all of Anne's family and friends, I still was somewhat awed by what was to me a new way of life. I would think of my background, of my poorly educated, poverty-ridden father, and wonder if Anne would not be far better off with a young gentleman from her own class. Fortunately, these feelings would not last.

Back in Washington, Anne, being the proper young lady she was, told me we should go to North Carolina to meet my family. I was hoping to avoid it. But, one afternoon, I knew there was nothing to do but face up to it. I had picked up Anne at the sorority house, and we walked down Seventeenth Street, along with a lot of other people, to witness a sight no one had seen before or since, to my knowledge—water everywhere. This was the great Eastern Flood of 1936. K Street to Twentieth was totally under water. All of Hains Point was under water, with only the tree tops and the roof of the tea house visible from the air. A couple of days before, 1500 men—army, navy, and volunteers—had turned out to stack sand bags behind the "temporary" World War I navy and munitions buildings while an anxious city was relatively safe. The raging Potomac swirled just under Chain Bridge, twenty-six feet higher than normal. The bridge was not expected to survive, and with it would go the entire Arlington county water supply, which then was carried from Washington over a main attached to the bridge. Fortunately, the bridge held.

There was an air of excitement in Washington, which was fortunately spared the death and destruction that marked the flood elsewhere. As we gazed at the strange sight of a river flowing

115

where there was once a street, Anne turned to me and asked again about Wilson, causing a kind of a churning flood within me. Finally, I said, "Yes. We'll go soon."

It is difficult for me to explain my feelings during that trip to Wilson. Was I ashamed of my own family because they were poor? Was I ashamed, not of them, but of me because I was not a cultured gentleman from a fine home? I do not think it was that. What it was, I believe, was stark, unadorned fear, fear of losing Anne. I knew there would never be another like her. I loved her and wanted her, and now I was afraid she would take a look at where I came from and would finally see the real Jack Morton.

We advertised for a ride to North Carolina and were lucky to find someone who would not only drive us down, but also back. We stayed with Aunt Annie. Her daughter, Charlie Gray, who once tried to teach me piano, had married and moved away. Aunt Annie was as gracious as ever, and while she was far from wealthy, her home was clean and comfortable. My sister Mary was still living with her.

My father and stepmother had moved away from town out to the country, and after getting directions from Aunt Annie, Anne and I rode out there in a borrowed car, on a hot, humid afternoon. I was perspiring profusely when we made the turn up a rutted, dirt road, but I believe I could have been sweating had it been December and I had the windows down.

It was worse than I had anticipated.

The house was a yellow frame dwelling with not even a front porch, just a stoop in front of the door—a simple little farm house, so typical of the poor, rural South, a little like the images from *Tobacco Road*.

Papa and my stepmother were most happy to see us and most gracious; but the situation was tense. Anne was her usual smiling, pleasant self, but though she never mentioned it, I sensed that she was wishing she could call on her fairy godmother for an instant change in wardrobe. She wore a becoming outfit, a dark red dress with a thin lace blouse, a family heirloom, and she was beautiful, far too exquisite for this plain house with the plain, worn furnishings.

We stayed for a little while, making small talk and eating a cake my stepmother had baked for the occasion and drinking coffee. We finally left, and I felt like I had just been tried for some crime and still was awaiting the jury's verdict.

I need not have worried, of course.

"I liked your father," Anne said. "There is something about him that is really grand."

I broke down.

We were sitting in the car in front of Aunt Annie's, and there I was in front of my girl, the woman I was going to marry, crying like a baby.

And then I told her about my life, and I began to recount the years in Wilson and Raleigh, the early years with the Rileys, Otis and Elsie, Charlie and Maude, the short time with Aunt Matt and Uncle Kibb, and the following years with Papa and my step-mother. Foolishly, I had taken one aspect out of my childhood, the poverty, and allowed my pride to turn it all into something ugly. It wasn't ugly. There had always been enough to eat and enough to wear and a place to sleep and, bygawd, over and above everything else, there was love there. And I had my share of that.

I told her about my jobs, shining shoes and working in the jewelry stores. I even told her about how I had to watch the Waters' baby and about poor old Mr. Burden and about the jobs in the movie theaters and how wonderful everyone had been, always encouraging me to get my education, to go on to better things.

"I was ashamed to let you see my childhood," I told Anne.

She put her arms around me and placed her cheek against mine. "You know something, Jack Morton," she said, "you and I are going to do just fine together. But please, don't order pig's feet, okay?"

117

14

THE 115TH COMMENCEMENT EXERCISES for George Washington University were held at Constitution Hall on the warm, showery night of June 11, 1936. Dr. Marvin, president of the school, awarded us our diplomas and gave a rousing speech attacking the New Deal and warning that the federal government could not possibly be a cure-all for the nation's ailments. I did not really agree with him, for, as my last undertaking at the university, I had written my final paper emphasizing the complete opposite. I had even gone to Capitol Hill and spoken with Senator Huey Long about the need for a great deal of social reform, including all kinds of legislation to ensure the working man his rightful compensation. I even studied the Townsend Plan. My youthful view of the issue has been tempered somewhat by the years of experience on the other side of the table.

But politics and social change were far from my mind that evening, even as Dr. Marvin spoke.

I had reached another crossroads in my life, and nothing could have dampened my spirits. Sitting in the audience was the lovely Anne Morton; my life opened up before me, sweetly challenging. As I rose, along with my fellow graduates, to receive my diploma, I was filled with a great sense of pride. I had done it. I was the first member of the Morton family of North Carolina since Uncle Clem to graduate from college.

After the graduation, Anne and I went up to the roof garden of the Roger Smith Hotel and danced under the stars.

Later, as I lay in my bed in the dormitory, I thought of all the people who had helped make this night possible, not only Papa and Ted, and Otis and Elsie, and Charlie and Maude, and all the others who were family or guardians, but also people outside the family who took a special interest in me, people like Jack Price at the World Theater in Wilson, who told me I could work for him any time; Father Termer; Mr. Rosser; Uncle Bennie Ralston—all who continually urged me on to higher education; Mr. Patton and all the people I worked under at Western Electric; all the kind teachers during high school and college years. All of those people, whether they knew it or not, played a role in Jack Morton's college education.

But my last thoughts before drifting off to sleep were of Anne and of the wedding we were to have in September.

That was some wedding.

I don't mean just the ceremony and the reception. I mean all the days leading up to the wedding. It was an enchanting time.

You have to remember that Columbus was not a big city in those days—a population of about 45,000 (compared to 165,000 today)—and Anne and her family were part of the Columbus society, and so I found myself caught up in a social whirlwind that left me limp but happy. I was more than just caught up in it; I was a leading player, a co-star.

We still have those clippings, yellowed with age, folded and kept all these years by Anne in a small cardboard carton from Kirvins—"Distinctive ready-to-wear accessories, 1150 Broadway, Columbus, Georgia." We have long since forgotten what came in the box; a gift, perhaps, most assuredly something small and lacy and feminine.

I can best describe that exhilarating time by quoting directly from the *Columbus Ledger-Enquirer* and the *Columbus Record*. Social events in those days were covered by the press with an earnestness and eye for detail that might seem a bit grandiose in today's world.

Our engagement was officially announced in the *Ledger-Enquirer* with an eight-column banner across the front page of the society section:

BEAUTIFUL BRIDE-ELECT HOLDS
SOCIETY'S INTEREST TODAY

Engagement of Miss Anne Morton and Irving L. Morton, Jr.,
Holds Interest of Society in the South

Of social interest throughout the South is the announcement made today by Mr. and Mrs. William G. Morton of the engagement of their daughter, Anne Barschall, and Irving Leonidas Morton, Jr., of Washington, D.C., formerly of Wilson, N.C.

Miss Morton is a member of a distinguished southern family. Her mother, the former Fannie Joseph, is the daughter of Mrs. Annie Barschall Joseph, whose name the bride-elect bears, and the late Dan Joseph. On her paternal side, the bride-elect is the grand-daughter of the late Mr. and Mrs. Charles Morton, of Pamplin, Va.

Miss Morton attended school at Ward-Belmont and Wesleyan College and was graduated in June from the National School of Fine and Applied Arts in Washington, D.C., where she had been studying commercial design for the past three years. She is a young girl of striking beauty and charm and is a popular member of the younger social set.

Mr. Morton is the son of Irving Leonidas Morton, of Wilson, N.C., and the late Gertrude Alice Riggs Morton, of Cataret County, N.C. Mr. Morton was graduated in June from George Washington University in Washington, D.C., where he was a member of the Phi Sigma Kappa social fraternity.

The marriage of Miss Morton and Mr. Morton will be a social event of outstanding interest in the early fall.

I arrived in Columbus for this important event in my life on Wednesday, six days before the wedding:

OUT-OF-TOWN GUESTS ARRIVE
FOR MORTON-MORTON WEDDING

Out-of-town guests are arriving for the wedding of Miss Anne Barschall Morton to Irving Leonidas Morton, Jr., which will be a brilliant event of Tuesday evening, taking place at eight o'clock at the First Presbyterian Church, followed by a reception at the home of the bride's grandmother, Mrs. Dan Joseph, and parents, Mr. and Mrs. William G. Morton.

Among the first arrivals was the groom, Wednesday evening.

Miss Charlotte Maidlow, of Washington, D.C., and Miss Lois Fisk, of Wichita Falls, Texas, arrive Sunday and will be the guests of Miss Sarah Slate on Sherwood Avenue. Miss Fisk and Miss Morton were roommates in Washington, D.C., last year.

Richard Snow, of Boston, and Washington, D.C., who will serve as best man, arrives today. Others to arrive at the same time will be Russell Payne of Washington and Gaynor Britt, of Austin, Texas, and Washington, D.C.

Arriving Sunday will be Woodrow Thomas, of Dover, Ky., and Washington, D.C., and Edgar MacCoy, of Washington, D.C.; James Thomas, of Portland, Oregon, and Washington, D.C.; and Fred Rawlings, of Washington, D.C.

Henry Hartmann, of New York City, and his friend, John Larder, of New York, will arrive Monday, and will be the guests of George Burrus, III.

My favorite affair was the rehearsal dinner given by Louise and Dan at the Night Owl, a lodge-like club that was available for parties. The clip from the *Columbus Record* sets the scene:

DINNER PARTY MONDAY NIGHT
HONORS MISS ANNE MORTON AND
MR. MORTON PRECEDING REHEARSAL

Miss Anne Morton and Irving L. Morton, whose marriage will be solemnized tonight, were the honored guests at a dinner party given on Monday night at the Night Owl. The hosts for the party, which preceded the rehearsal for the marriage of the honorees, were Miss Louise Morton and Dan Morton.

White and green was the color note emphasized. The table was laid with damask and centered with crystal bowls holding white snapdragons, lilies and gypsophelia. White tapers and bride and groom place cards completed the appointments.

Miss Morton was beautiful, wearing a gown of ice-blue crepe with a corsage of gardenias.

Miss Louise Morton was very lovely, wearing an evening dress of white crepe.

I was very impressed with Anne's brother. Only sixteen, he was already a quiet, poised, self-assured young man. I can still see him, standing beside his sister Louise, greeting the guests as they came through the door, a handsome, reddish-haired lad dressed in formal attire and looking every inch at home in it.

As I climbed into bed, I once again felt like pinching myself. No person ever before had the good fortune that had befallen me. I was particularly pleased that three of my best friends from college were willing and able to take part in this big event in my life.

My best man, Dick Snow, was a dark-haired, nervous young man, an excellent student, and the one chiefly responsible for getting me into Phi Sigma Kappa. Woodie Thomas was a handsome young man, a good mixer and completely caught up in the fascination of politics. Through his college years, he had operated an elevator at the Capitol, and before he graduated, he knew just about everybody on the Hill.

But I guess I was actually closer to Ed MacCoy than anyone else, even though Mac did not live in the fraternity house, but stayed at his parents' home in Takoma Park, Maryland. As house manager and treasurer, Mac spent some time at the fraternity house, and we got to be close friends.

Anne and I often double dated with Mac and his girlfriend, Charlotte. Mac had a car (it might have belonged to his parents) and the four of us would go out, sometimes riding aimlessly to Mount Vernon or Fort Dupont Park. They married a year or two after Anne and I did.

On the night of the rehearsal dinner, I couldn't get to sleep. So, I lay there trying to remember my lines. You would have thought I was appearing in a Shakespearean drama the next evening before a packed theater. Finally, I began to doze off, and suddenly somebody was knocking on the door. Mac and Woodie, my roomies for the night, were playing knock-knock, a silly game that was popular at the time and has had recurring periods of popularity since. I told them to "knock it off" so I could get to sleep.

The First Presbyterian Church was a pretty, buff structure with an impressive spire, typical of the nineteenth and early twentieth century Protestant churches in the American South. Its tower housed what was regarded as the town clock, which struck out its mighty chimes every hour. That clock figured prominently in the Morton-Morton wedding, for the bride, a stickler for punctuality (I have never known her to be late for anything), ordered the organist to strike the first note in the Lohengrin bridal chorus in perfect synchronization with the first chime from the tower clock in its eight o'clock peal.

I mention this because the brevity of the service was to me amazing. It still is. It was a lovely ceremony, to be sure, and no bride in history was more radiant that the soon-to-be Mrs. Morton.

But when you consider the months of preparation; the designing and arduous production of the wedding gowns; the endless lunches, parties, dances, and dinners; the collection of people from far and wide; the investments made by the bride's family and well-wishers; the reams of publicity in the newspapers—when you consider all of this and then consider that the bride and groom were in the bride's home, two blocks from the church, at 8:08 P.M., then you have cause to wonder why the groom was in such a sweat over messing up the ceremony.

Well, I insist I had more than one thing to worry about.

First, I couldn't remember my lines, as meager as they were, though I managed to stumble through.

And second, I was afraid Dick Snow wouldn't remember anything, including the ring. Dick had a reputation for forgetting things, so I had my brother Ted furnish me with a second (duplicate) wedding ring. As it turned out, Dick remembered the ring.

Well, it may have been only eight minutes, but it was the start of a lifetime, and it was a gorgeous eight minutes, perhaps the most meaningful minutes of my entire seventy-plus years.

The reception was tremendous, with a continuous flow of people in and out. There was the exploding lights of the cameras for the wedding pictures, and good food and punch, which was stimulated somewhat by some good bourbon Mr. Billy had stashed away in the pantry.

And the presents. There were some from my side—the people at Western Electric, members of my family, and friends—but most of them were from Anne's family and legion of friends. There was a lot of silver, some family treasures—and these were lost forever when our home was broken into just a few years ago.

And there was the car. Anne's grandmother, the irrepressable Mrs. Joseph, presented us with a brand new 1936 Pontiac sedan, priced at $950. It was the first car either of us had ever owned, and we were naturally thrilled. We were also naturally frightened out of our wits that some of the more reckless and imaginative guests—like those wild-eyed drinkers I went on the fishing trip with—would attempt to doctor up the car to give us something special to remember.

Anne's brother Dan solved that for us. He hid the car before the ceremony. Earlier that day, Dan drove the car to a predetermined spot six or seven miles out of town on the road to Atlanta. After the reception, he drove us to the car and we were on our way.

By the time we made the rendezvous with Dan, the groom was on the verge of collapse. I can get out of breath now just thinking about those hectic days and weeks before and up to the wedding. So, Anne drove the ninety-five miles from Atlanta to Columbus, the first of many sacrifices she was to make on my behalf over the next forty-odd years. And, typical of the thoughtfulness that is just as natural to her as her smile, she awakened me just before we got into Atlanta to allow me to salvage my macho pride by driving up to Piedmont Hotel.

We spent one night in Atlanta and then drove to Lake Lure, N.C., a man-made lake not for from Asheville. I congratulated myself for having had the foresight to make reservations, and then uncongratulated myself when we discovered that we could have walked in unannounced and had our pick of rooms, because the hotel was practically empty, which incidentally did not bother us.

I had heard or read since that honeymoons for some couples are a great disappointment and a trying time. Ours was not. For me, at least, it was the continuation of a dream come true. It was only for a few days, but it was the kind of lovely, lazy, loving retreat that set the stage for a long and happy union.

We went back to Washington the following Sunday. We had an apartment secured, a one-bedroom apartment at Hamilton Street, N.W., at forty-eight dollars a month. It was not going to be ready for our occupancy for another week, but I was able to borrow an apartment for that week from friends—Lee and Jerry—the same couple who threw rice at her sister and me at the station. Their kindness in letting us use their apartment more than made up for the embarrassment of their practical joke.

15

As a LOW-PAID CLERK and orchestra booking agent, I was not exactly setting the world afire, or even my small part of it, a fact that made me feel a bit uneasy. After all, I was now a married man, a husband, a breadwinner, with responsibilities. And the orchestra business was both marginal and seasonal.

I booked orchestras for fraternities, sororities, state societies, and government departments (which were big on sponsoring dances), only a few of which held dances in the summer.

As this point, early in 1937, I lost faith in the music business and allowed a former GW classmate talk me into trying my hand at selling refrigeration equipment.

My career at General Electric was both undistinguished and short.

I remember bidding farewell at Western Electric, where everyone, including Mr. Peterson, wished me well. Ed Shriver even offered me a cigar and predicted I would set records in sales at G.E.

I set no records. I did make a few sales. But it was not my kind of job. I sold to commercial places—meat markets, grocery stores, and warehouses. I received $200 a month against commissions, but some of my commission money was always being eroded by my inability to measure and calculate, so that I was consistently short on my estimates for installation costs.

About this time, GE came out with a new refrigerator with a fan that circulated the air. It was the forerunner of the frostless refrigerator. I remember calling on a Mr. Anthony, the owner of a restaurant on L Street that specialized in steaks and chops. He was interested, but he wanted to see one that was already func-

125

tioning and keeping fair-sized quantities of meat fresh for reasonable periods of time. My supervisor came to the rescue.

"We recently sold one to the Seventh-Day Adventists in Takoma Park," he said. "Take him out there."

The Seventh-Day Adventists had extensive facilities in suburban Takoma Park, including a university (Columbia Union College) and a hospital, both of which are still operating today. The new refrigerator was in the hospital, and the administrator was quite congenial, taking me and Mr. Anthony back to the kitchen and allowing us to inspect it closely. Mr. Anthony peered inside at length and then turned to the administrator.

"Where's the meat?" he asked. "How come I don't see any steaks and chops in there?" It wasn't funny then, but I think about the recent hamburger commercial about "where's the beef?" Surprising how the same words have a different impact under different circumstances.

"We're Seventh-Day Adventists," the man said. "We don't eat meat." That was a new part of my religious education!

I still made the sale and earned a good commission, but I got more kicks from making a lot less money booking a small dance band into a fraternity house.

There was also the constant frustration of trying to convince naturally skeptical businessmen that the frozen food industry had a future and the exasperation of trying to conduct a sales campaign while the customer was conducting his own sales with his customers. It was not unusual for me to wait behind some woman who couldn't make up her mind whether she wanted chicken legs or chicken wings, before I could give my sales pitch for an item costing several thousand dollars.

I have nothing against refrigerators or frozen-food cabinets. I own two refrigerators and a freezer myself. But after sixteen months in that job, I had reached a new low. Never before, or since, not even when I was selling holy pictures and Rosebud Salve door-to-door as a boy, have I felt so depressed over a job. I was ready to cash it in anyway, but the final impetus came from a man named Walter Rhinehart, who had been the class president at GW. I ran into Walter one evening, and he told me something that I believe holds true for virtually everybody: "If you are unhappy in your job, find another one, because you will never be a success in it."

126

Anne, of course, had long since detected my unhappiness, and when I approached her with the idea of going back to what I really wanted to do—the music-booking business—she never hesitated, even though we were eating regularly, paying the rent, and were expecting our first child in three months. And so, we sat down one night and made what I called our "disaster contingency plan." I would go into the music-booking business full-steam ahead. In three months, Anne would be going home anyway to be with her mother for the birth of her first child. If I wasn't making enough to support us, she would remain home, we would sell or store our furniture, and I would move back into the fraternity house until I started earning a respectable living in the music business or something else I could tolerate.

Anne's parents put their unqualified support behind our plan, and I have always been grateful for their confidence and trust and been delighted that it turned out not to have been misplaced.

So, in October 1938, after a sixteen-month absence, I was back in show business, this time to stay. Without so much as a backward glance at the world of refrigeration, I rolled up my sleeves and dove into the music business. Mine was an eighteen-hour day of re-establishing old contacts by phone and in person; visiting the social chairmen of the fraternities and sororities; beating on the doors of private schools, state societies, and government departments, and calling on band leaders. I had no trouble picking up where I had left off.

I needed an office, so we moved the dinette table into the living room, bought a secondhand desk and put that in the dinette, and I was a full-time entrepreneur. I called my business "Jack Morton Enterprises" and had business cards and stationery printed.

That was an exciting, happy time. I was willing—and most importantly, Anne was willing—to put it all on the line. And I was back out there in the blue riding on a smile and a shoeshine. I never looked back.

Somehow, I made contact with Fred Moss in New York, the Music Corporation of America's man in charge of managing the big bands, and I made a deal to line up dates for the MCA clients for five percent commission. In those days, you could hire Sammy Kaye, Glen Gray, Glen Miller, or the Dorsey Brothers for about

$500, so we are not talking about big bucks. Still, it all added up.

Booking the big bands was only a small part of my business. Mostly, I was busy matching local orchestras with organizations wanting to put on a dance. I found plenty of bands looking for dates and enough organizations looking for bands.

During November I landed two or three jobs and in the December-Christmas–New Year's whirl, I wound up making a whopping $400 in commissions—which was about twice what I was making selling ice boxes, even when I was measuring accurately. It was a very merry Christmas at the Morton house.

A lot of those bands became regular clients of mine, and so did a number of the hotels, which needed someone like me to book dances into their ballrooms. While most of the dance-sponsoring groups usually dealt directly with the hotels, there were still a number of them that left the facilities to me, giving me an extra small commission from the hotel or club.

The most popular ballroom in Washington in those days was at the Willard Hotel. Dances also were held at the Mayflower, the Raleigh, and, farther out on Connecticut Avenue, the Wardman Park (now the Washington Sheraton), and the Shoreham. The Shoreham did not have a large ballroom in those days, but the Blue Room, a more intimate cabaret-type room, was used for private dances. Out on Sixteenth Street, there was the "2400," and also the Roosevelt. The Washington Hotel had a large ballroom, but it was in the basement and was not very popular. Occasionally, someone would book a dance at a country club, but in those days of relatively few automobiles and relatively poor roads, the country clubs were considered too inaccessible by most dance sponsors.

So, I built up a small but dependable clientele, and it soon became apparent that the disaster contingency plan would not be needed. In the beginning, though, we would do anything respectable to earn an honest dollar. I remember at one point Anne used her creative talents to make little paper decorations to place around the tables, instead of flowers.

In addition to the MCA big-band bookings, Fred Moss would occasionally ask me to line up dates for bands whose itineraries would bring them close to Washington with one or two open dates. These bookings, always during the slow part of the week, helped the bands with their travel expenses. Like everybody else in those days, they also were hustling for a buck. So, I started promoting dances on my own.

On those occasions, I had to keep a close watch on my costs, which included the rental of the ballroom, ticket-takers, and advertising (usually posters that I would put up around fraternity and sorority houses, government offices, etc.). Tickets usually went for a dollar, plus ten cents tax, and most of the time I made a few bucks.

But not always.

On one occasion, I booked in Hal Kemp, and it was a flop. The dance was during the middle of the week in the basement ballroom at the Washington Hotel, and I didn't take in enough money to pay Kemp his modest fee. I must say he was a real gentleman about it. I paid him part of it then and the rest later.

On another occasion, on a Wednesday evening in February, I booked Shep Fields into the Raleigh, and it was a disaster. In lining that one up, I just hadn't paid enough attention to the calendar. It was Ash Wednesday. Again, I had to make arrangements to pay off the leader in the future and got another lesson in religion. Namely, don't promote dances on Ash Wednesday!

But there were a lot of successes, too, that more than offset the occasional bomb. I remember one time I promoted a dance featuring Tommy Dorsey and his orchestra; at the time his recordings of "Song of India" and "Marie" were sweeping the country. We packed them into the Willard Hotel Ballroom that night. The Dorsey band got $600, and my profit was about the same.

It is difficult to explain the feelings of excitement and elation I experienced in those days. Perhaps some of it was based on my gambling instinct, though I have done very little conventional gambling. But each promotion was a gamble of sorts, and when we hit the jackpot, as with the Dorsey promotion, there was a tremendous feeling of accomplishment. Of course, the entire venture was a gamble. Anne and I had planned for the worst and, lo and behold, it was all turning out better than our fondest dreams.

But the biggest thrill was actually being there and watching the production that I had helped fashion, listening to the music and watching the happy couples crowd the dance floor and knowing I had a hand in bringing it all together. For this was show business, too, live and exciting, and I was part of it. I belonged.

My family life also bloomed. Billy was born on January 28, 1939, in Columbus. I was there, of course, but could stay for only a few days because my business was at the critical stage between takeoff and cruising. When Anne returned with our new addition a few weeks later, she was accompanied by her mother. Mama stayed on for a few weeks, sleeping on the living-room sofa while we kept Billy's crib in our room.

It wasn't long after that that Anne's grandmother told us that she was bequeathing Anne $4,000 in her will and was going to give it to her now. "You can use it now," she said. "And besides, I am not planning to leave any time soon."

That generous gift enabled us to realize one of our dreams early—a home of our own. By the time we started to look for a house, I had an additional $1,500 to add to the $4,000—a sizable down payment.

We naturally looked in the Northwest section. We never even considered any other area. For one thing, both Anne and I had lived exclusively in the Northwest section since our respective arrivals in Washington. For another, Northwest was the action center, and I did not want to be too far away from the hotels and nightclubs—the milieu, so to speak, of my business.

It may surprise a lot of people to know that it was not intended for Washington to grow to the west as it did. The Capitol building, which marks the center of the city and the meeting point of its four sections, was deliberately designed to face the East, the expected direction of growth. But business, the "downtown" area, grew to the west.

Of course, we did not want to be in the midst of downtown, and we concentrated our search in the newly developing sections out Massachusetts Avenue, finally settling on an area called West Gate, fifty-four blocks northwest of the Capitol. One builder was putting up four houses facing Massachusetts Avenue, selling in the $14,000–$16,000 range. Those were precarious times in the real estate and home building business, and this builder was barely staying one step ahead of bankruptcy. We got our house, at 5411 Massachusetts Avenue, for a couple of thousand dollars off the list price because it wasn't quite finished and the builder

130

had hit bottom. We bought it for only $11,500 and finished it ourselves, putting in the driveway, front walk, and the landscaping. It was a nice house, with a full basement, garage, three bedrooms, living room, dining room, kitchen, screened-in back porch, and a den, which I used for my office.

Naturally, we invited good friends to see our new home, and sometimes they wanted to dance or play foolish games—all of which made me nervous because I was afraid they would wreck the place. After one such long night, I decided we should have a recreation room where our friends could romp without destroying the family heirlooms. I ordered materials and spent every spare hour transforming the basement into an inviting playroom with a tiled floor, a real bar, and attractive appointments. Because of my inexperience, it was a frustrating, dragged-out job, but at long last it was finished. The last thing I had to do was hang the door and fit the hardware. Very late on the final night, I called for Anne to come view my masterpiece. She studied it, complimented me, hesitated and asked, "Aren't the widest door panels supposed to be at the bottom?" I had hung the door upside down! I knew this would haunt me if I didn't change it, so I did it all over. The next Saturday—always the big party night—our friends had a ball! I sat and watched, nursing a punctured big toe that happened when I stepped on a nail—my last "act" just before the grand opening. The sympathy—laced with bourbon—helped, but it was a poor substitute for dancing.

I have never liked debt—particularly large debt. We had a twenty-five-year, $7,000 mortgage at four and one half percent interest, and the payments were forty-four dollars a month. Every time I had a spare forty-four dollars, I made an extra payment. Thanks to my booming music business, I paid it off in about three years.

Advertising helped. I started to advertise extensively, including an ad in the telephone directory's Yellow Pages, announcing twenty-four-hour service. You'd be surprised how many calls I got at odd hours of the night and morning from people representing groups wanting to put on a dance. But that was an inconvenience I was willing to put up with in exchange for watching the business grow.

If there is a need out there for a service, if you can provide it and are willing to work hard at it, your business cannot help but grow. It wasn't long after moving into our new house that I found I needed secretarial help, and so I hired a neighbor woman who was looking for something to do two or three days a week.

Keep in mind, my business was strictly dance business, and my clients were chiefly organizations wanting to put on dances and the myriad orchestras wanting to supply the music. But there was plenty of business, and things never looked brighter.

During the '30s, Washington boasted an impressive list of social events by the elite. The music most in demand for these affairs was supplied by Meyer Davis and Sidney—the society orchestras of Washington. Jack Morton's music was unknown to such party givers, and I constantly aspired to be accepted and share in the limelight and publicity given to these sparkling events. I got my break by persistence and an unexpected source—namely, the teenagers who regularly danced to my bands at their schools. When some of these arrived at the debutante age and asked for my music, it created a dilemma among the parents and social arbiters. The youngsters just didn't like the same music with which their parents had grown up. Consequently, I began to achieve some success in the society circles, but two in particular gave me the greatest satisfaction. The first was the famous Evelyn Walsh McLean, who usually set the pace for all others. She favored me with occasional parties, but was bewildered because I did not lead the orchestra. Nevertheless, she was kind and helpful, always taking the time to talk with me about her fabulous life and the present.

The other charming and wonderful lady was Marjorie Merriwether Post, who, when I met her, was the wife of Joseph Davies, the former ambassador to Russia. I recall the time Mrs. Davies' secretary asked me to come see her, which I happily did. She explained that Mrs. Davies' daughter requested my music, and since Mrs. Davies had never heard of me, wanted to be sure I was real and acceptable. The first party for which my orchestra played was at "Tregaron," the Davies' famous home. The ambassador and Mrs. Davies gave me the grand tour of their home, but the most impressive bit was seeing their collection of the Faberge jewels and art creations, acquired by the ambassador while in Russia.

I felt I had reached the top when I provided music at the Pan American Union for a visiting South American president at which President and Mrs. Truman were the honored guests. I had to agree to lead the orchestra for this affair, and that was my one and only such engagement. It was a nervy experience, but it must have been a success, because we played till 4:00 A.M.

Then I was fortunate to get an engagement at the White House when the Voice of Firestone program was produced there for President and Mrs. Eisenhower. Those were heady times for me—playing for Washington society and getting to meet and talk to the President!

On my thirty-first birthday, June 6, 1941, I was given a special present, with the birth of our daughter, Mary Lou, in Washington's Doctors Hospital, on the site where our office is now located.

Six months later, I was still riding on a shoeshine and a smile when Jack King, one of my band leaders, came by to see me on a wintry early Sunday afternoon. Jack had played two or three jobs for me during the previous week, and I had not been able to make contact with him. So, he came by to settle up the money matters. I had spent the morning quietly reading the papers and working in the office, so I was totally unprepared for Jack's greeting when I opened the front door.

"Did you hear about the Japs' bombing of Pearl Harbor?"

I hadn't. Neither Anne nor I had the radio on that day, and we did not know a thing about it. Until that minute, we didn't even know where Pearl Harbor was.

War has a way of intruding into personal lives, and though I did not serve in the armed forces, the war changed the direction of my business. The dance business as I had known it was on the way out.

16

THE WAR TRANSFORMED WASHINGTON, and it was never to be the same again. Looking back, it seems like a sudden metamorphosis. One day Washington was the same as it always had been—a pleasant, rather slow-moving town, a little on the sleepy Southern side, with small-town, early-to-bed ways. The next day it was a bustling metropolis, its streets crowded, uniforms everywhere, and everywhere people moving quickly, as though speed was somehow related to survival.

No one could escape the war fever, and I suppose every man under fifty had the itch to grab a gun, or at least to get involved in some way with the war effort. I had mixed feelings. I love my country and would fight for her even at my age today, but I also had the responsibilities of a wife and two small children.

For a brief time, I tried to push those responsibilities aside. Again, I happened to run into my friend, Walter Rhinehart, the man who finally convinced me to get out of the refrigeration-selling business. Walter was coming out of a downtown restaurant one afternoon, looking splendid in his navy lieutenant's blue and gold uniform.

"Nothing to it," he said. "The navy is looking for officers. If you have a college degree, that is all you need, provided you can pass the physical. Why don't you apply?"

I thought it was a splendid idea. Anne did not. She thought of it as being something less than splendid and a little more than stupid. She was not against my going if it really came down to that and I had to go, but meanwhile, she wanted me home where my first responsibilities lay.

It wasn't easy to be under forty and a civilian during wartime.

134

Of course, I had to report to the draft board and was classified 4F anyway, because of an ulcer I never even knew I had. I was called up on three different occasions, and all I can remember is standing around naked with a lot of other naked men, feeling extremely foolish. The potential draftees met at the B&O station in Silver Spring and from there were taken by a uniformed soldier to the induction center in Baltimore. On my third trip, however, they put me in charge. I guess they figured they could use their military men for something better and I had the experience. It was my only command during the war.

The draft board instructed me to take a job in some industry related to the war effort. I wound up with a job at the Capital Transit Company. I guess streetcars and buses were considered essential to the war effort, but I did not feel like Audie Murphy running around investigating minor traffic accidents. That was my job, at the princely sum of thirty dollars a week. I was given an automobile and gasoline, and while I abided by all the rules and did a creditable job, I did not allow it to interfere with my music business, which actually took what was ultimately a turn for the better during the war years.

I had the accident-investigation job for less than a year, but that was long enough to impress me with the necessity of avoiding any kind of contact between my automobile and streetcars and buses. The transit company was all for assuming responsibility for accidents, so long as the other guy did the assuming. I had cases where the streetcar conductor or bus driver admitted the fault was his, but my supervisors never accepted that. My job was just to turn in the reports. Theirs, apparently, was to take every measure possible to see that Capital Transit didn't have to pay.

I remember on one occasion the streetcar's brakes failed and the streetcar plowed into a stopped car. Simple, open-and-shut case, right? Wrong.

"He shouldn't have been there," my superior said.

"Look," I said, "it wasn't the automobile driver's fault. Our conductor even admits that. It's right there on my report."

"Well, you make out the reports, Morton; we'll make the judgments," he said.

I fought with them often. A lot of times, they wound up

135

paying, but not until they did everything possible to wear the poor victim down.

I was also very active during the war years with the Junior Chamber of Commerce and managed to serve as an air-raid warden as well. How I managed to do all this and still advance my business, even I don't understand. I didn't spend a lot of time at home, that's for sure.

I had joined the Jaycees in 1939. During the war years, the organization had two primary purposes—to keep its membership in the face of depletion by the military (the age for membership was 21–36) and to aid in the war effort. Keeping up the membership was difficult, and by the time the war was coming to a close, the Jaycees was a civic organization for 4F's and men with dependents.

In 1943, I was named membership chairman, a real challenge, while the following year I served as president, and for a stretch I was in charge of getting prominent speakers for our weekly luncheons at the Annapolis Hotel.

The natural-born salesman in me came to the fore as membership chairman. I initiated the idea of having companies sponsor memberships for their employees. I also organized our members into three recruiting teams—red, white, and blue. Each team had a "bombing" target—Berlin, Tokyo, or Rome. The more members a squadron recruited, the closer it got to its target, and results were displayed on a large board every week at the hotel.

By vigorous recruiting, we managed to keep our ranks respectable, but we lost a lot of members to the service. I was proud of the fact that so many of our group volunteered, instead of waiting for the draft, and many were given commissions.

One of our more successful projects was a series of War Bond selling rallies. We put up booths on busy street corners, distributed posters and enlisted the aid of entertainment personalities. I remember on one occasion I had the pleasure of working beside Loretta Young, one of the great Hollywood stars, whose career spanned a decade and later included a successful weekly television show. Miss Young spent three days in Washington, drew fantastic crowds, and we sold a lot of War Bonds. Loretta was a delight to be with—sharing her beauty and cheerful personality with us all. The USO was another war activity in which we all participated—helping service people have some fun and relaxation.

The Jaycees also developed a program in cooperation with the navy in which we sponsored LST ships and provided the crews with magazines, newspapers, records, and record players. The LST (Landing Ship Tank) was the Kaiser-built ship that was used to transport men, tanks, and other supplies to the beaches during invasions. It was a sleek, barren, efficient vessel with little of the refinements you would find on larger vessels, and thus our project was particularly welcome. Jaycee chapters throughout the country sponsored ships, and on one occasion the commander of our LST was in Washington to attend one of our luncheons to tell us how much our efforts were appreciated by his crew. The Jaycees received a special commendation from the navy for that project.

My favorite job for the organization was lining up speakers for our weekly luncheons. We had a number of impressive speakers, including Carlos Romulo, ambassador from the Philippines and later secretary general to the United Nations; General Hershey, selective service director; the British Ambassador Lord Halifax; Chicago Tribune columnist Walter Trohan; Congressman and later Senator Jennings Randolph of West Virginia; Senator Happy Chandler from Kentucky, later the major league baseball commissioner; and Mrs. Roosevelt.

I will never forget the time I had the honor of introducing the First Lady to a packed room at the Annapolis. I rose at the podium and said:

"Gentlemen . . . we are indeed fortunate and honored to have with us today one of the most popular First Ladies in our history. . . . a woman who has made her own mark on national and international affairs . . . a woman who has proved to be gracious and unstinting with her time and efforts for worthy causes. It gives me great pleasure to introduce to you America's First Lady—Mrs. Eleanor Roosevelt!"

And with that I turned to face the still-seated Mrs. Roosevelt and knocked over her water glass into her lap.

Talk about a grand moment going suddenly sour! Talk about humiliation! I wanted to hide under the table.

I blustered. I apologized. I hardly noticed that what had be-

137

gun as a roaring applause had diminished to something between a sigh and a gasp and then to stunned silence.

But Mrs. Roosevelt was up to the occasion. Without blinking her eyes, she quickly brushed her dress with a napkin, stood before the microphone, smiled at me, and said:

"Mr. Morton, I want to apologize to you for not drinking my water."

That brought down the house. Mrs. Roosevelt went on to give an excellent talk and afterwards reassured me that all was forgiven. She even came to another of our luncheons.

Upon retiring as president of the Washington Jaycees, I was elected to the board of directors of the national Jaycees and served with the national president, Henry Kearns. Henry went on to high government positions, serving as assistant secretary of Commerce in the Eisenhower administration and later as chairman and president of the Import/Export Bank in the Nixon administration. Henry and his wife, Marge, have become wonderful life-long friends.

My experiences as an air-raid warden are hardly worth mentioning except for the fact that they do reflect the mood of wartime Washington. There was a serious apprehension over a possible bombing attack by the Germans, and air-raid warnings, some announced in advance and others sprung on the public suddenly, became a part of life. As an air-raid warden, I patrolled a section of just under a mile along Massachusetts Avenue west of Westmoreland Circle. When the air-raid sirens went off at night, houses were to be blacked out and motorists were to pull over to the curb and extinguish their lights. We carried flashlights for the purpose of signalling erring motorists to follow the rules. We also knocked on the doors of houses that were not observing the blackout, and while we had the authority to call the police, I never found it necessary.

But, it was as an air-raid warden that I suffered my only war injury. In the darkness, I fell into a culvert, skinning my shins and seriously hurting my dignity. I did not apply for a Purple Heart. I did lament losing the cigar I was smoking, plus breaking the extra one in my pocket.

Our third and last child, Diane, was born during the war, on March 12, 1944. But the joy of having a new baby in the house was tempered by the sad news that Dan, Anne's "baby brother," had been killed fighting for his country at Saint-Lô.

Anne corresponded with Dan regularly, and when he went overseas, she was struck with an awful apprehension, so much so that when a client would call me late at night, she would be stricken with fear. She made a point to ask her mother never to call late at night, no matter what the reason.

Dan was a fine young man. He was graduated from Virginia Military Institute in 1941 and entered the army as a second lieutenant. He participated in the North Africa and Sicily invasions and was part of General Patton's Second Armored Division, which stormed the beaches at Normandy. He had married his high school sweetheart—the only girl he ever cared for—and was at the start of what promised to be a beautiful life when he was struck down on 28 July 1944.

His death brought home to me the painful fact that the war dead are not names and numbers, but real persons, young people for the most part, whose passing brings great pain to their loved ones.

Dan now rests in France, along with thousands of his comrades. They paid the ultimate price so that Jack Morton could be free to pursue his happiness in his own way.

And, of course, my pursuit was always in the direction of the show, the dance, entertainment. It surprises me now, as I look back, that with everything else I was involved in during the war and with the tapering off of club dances, my chosen career nevertheless continued to prosper.

As the demand for bands for dances diminished, the demand for entertainment for nightclubs and hotels increased. I continued to hustle. Even throughout my stint with Capital Transit, I carried a pocketful of nickels to make phone calls throughout the day.

During the war years, it seems, everybody wanted to "go out." There was plenty of work for everybody, plenty of money and an excitement in the air. Add to that the influx of servicemen, and the streets of America's cities were alive at night with crowds of people looking for a good time.

I managed to get contracts at half a dozen or so downtown clubs. Depending on the type of club or the entertainment desired, I would book anything from a solo pianist to a large dance band with boy and girl vocalists.

Of course, there was always the problem of keeping the

dance bands intact, for they were in a constant race to keep up with the draft. Because of this, at one particular time I was a victim—or I should say casualty—of the draft. Musicians were being taken by the services on a daily basis, which left me with one of the worst orchestras for a very important occasion; namely, the night at Bolling Field Officers Club that was chosen to introduce to the staff—including General and Mrs. Hap Arnold—the new air force song. This selection had won a nationwide contest, and the evening was especially planned by Mrs. Arnold to let the air force people hear their new "anthem."

The number is best when played by a large orchestra and, unfortunately, we had only four musicians. To make things really bad, none of them could read a note. It was humiliating beyond description, and my explanation about all the musicians being drafted fell on deaf ears. I believe the club entertainment chairman was shipped off to some foreign front, and I was never invited back. Every time I hear the air force song, it brings back vivid memories of that dismal night.

My biggest contract and one that proved invaluable later, was with the new Statler Hotel. The gleaming white structure at Sixteenth and K streets opened in January 1943 after a delay caused by a fire. Every music and entertainment agent in town was after the Statler account, and I really didn't believe I had much chance, but decided to give it a try.

The key to the Statler account was a tall, reserved man named Fred Kenny, who was the hotel's general manager and a difficult person to corner. I knew him by sight and happened to see him and his wife dining one evening in the Shoreham's Blue Room. I finally arranged an interview—in the men's room. I just followed him there, introduced myself and told him exactly what was on my mind.

"Are your musicians union?" he asked, washing his hands.

"No sir, they are not."

"Well, that is the first thing you have to do. If I hired non-union musicians, every union that does business with the hotel would be on my neck, and there are a lot of them. Put your musicians into the union. That doesn't mean you'll get the contract, but you won't get it without that, and you'll have trouble landing other big contracts as well."

140

At least I had my foot in the door.

The next day, I dropped by Local 161 of the American Federation of Musicians at Sixteenth and L streets, right across the street from the Statler, and increased the membership by more than 100—every musician I had under contract. At that point, they were doing more business in Washington than all the union musicians combined. But I also knew—and I knew they would agree—that for any kind of a secure future they would have to be union. I had to personally join to be able to represent the union musicians.

But to join the union one is supposed to be able to play an instrument. I don't play a note. Many believe Jack Morton is a band leader—a musician—because my name has been, and still is, associated with orchestras.

I'll never forget the interview and "test" with Local 161 President Paul Schwartz.

"Jack, what instrument do you play?"

"Paul, I don't play any instrument, I'm not a . . . ."

"Wait a minute, Jack, I didn't hear you right. You must play something; didn't you ever play anything?"

"Well, a long time ago, when I was just a kid, I did have a drum, which I played a lot, but not very well."

"That's it, that's great—you're a drummer! Just sign right here, welcome to Local 161, and congratulations! Here is your membership card and our rule book."

I've been explaining this bizarre situation for forty years.

I got to know Mr. Kenny a little better by dropping in on him occasionally and letting him know I was still interested in the account. He said he would keep me in mind. On one of those occasions, I invited him and his wife to our place for dinner, and he accepted, much to my happy surprise! In the selling business—whether you are selling shoe shines, refrigerators, or entertainment—you have to sell yourself. And you also have to know your potential customers or clients. And that is also true for the purchaser. I knew Mr. Kenny was not the type of man to bring into his hotel, even on a contract basis, somebody he knew little about. When he accepted my invitation, I knew he was interested in getting to know me a little better and that meant, of course, he might be interested in hiring me. I was right. I got

141

the contract. None of this could have been accomplished without the loving help from Anne. Mr. and Mrs. Kenny—like everyone else—responded to her warm personality and ladylike qualities. Today, fifty years later, Anne is Mrs. Kenny's best friend.

Mr. Kenny joined a long list of the people I regard as my patrons—men and women who have been inordinately kind and helpful to me.

With my work at the hotel, I got to know Mr. Kenny much better. He was not nearly as reserved as I first thought. But he had the self-assurance and the prudence of the successful businessman. He was a man of integrity and respected that quality in others.

Later in 1944, Mr. Kenny was partially paralyzed by a stroke. I visited him regularly, and when he was able to walk reasonably well, I would often stop at the hotel and take him to lunch with me at the University Club, which I had joined at that time. He died in 1945, and I went to New York for the funeral. His son, Austin Kenny, incidentally, is the head of the Washington Convention Bureau and, like his father, is a personable and successful businessman.

In addition to supplying musicians for special occasions at the hotel—dances, dinners, luncheons, etc.—I was asked to put a string quartet in the Embassy Room for lunch, on a regular basis, six days a week. The total cost to the hotel was $225 a week, and I netted ten percent of that.

Soon after, I landed the Roger Smith and Willard Hotel as well, and was already booking music and entertainment at the 400 Club on F Street, the Mayfair Club, the Neptune Room, the Trade Winds, Treasure Island, and a half dozen or so other clubs and restaurants.

Do not let me mislead you. This was not big time. The big time was still around the corner.

Take the Embassy Room. I booked a small, virtually unknown local group in there for lunchtime. At night, the Embassy Room was transformed into a gala supper club, featuring some of the biggest names in music, including Xavier Cugat and Guy Lombardo, who were at the peaks of their careers and regular performers there. Big name entertainment was regular fare.

I began to take prospective clients to the Embassy Room for

dinner. Because of my relationship with the hotel, whenever I arrived—alone, with Anne, or with others—I was given the red-carpet treatment. But more importantly, I was not just a diner; I was a student. I learned something about music and musicians and entertainment. I also met people who were influential in the entertainment business and proved most helpful to me in building my business. Besides knowledge and contacts, I gained in sophistication and poise and was preparing myself, even though I was unaware of it, for another change in the direction of my career.

For the end of the war signaled a change in the direction of the entire country. Men came home, families were reunited and families started, jobs picked up, educations pursued, and careers launched. America went to work. But it was a different America, a forward-looking, fast-moving, ambitious America, anxious to make up for lost time. New technologies burst forth; business boomed. Television, which whetted peoples' taste for variety acts, brought a new dimension to the American at home. It also helped my business. The automobile and the launching of new interstate highway system put American families on the move as they had never been before. The commercial airliner, given such a great impetus during the war, put business on the move as well.

It was shortly after the end of the war that the business convention as we know it today came into its own. Before World War II, hotels were built to accommodate the individual guest. But starting in the 1940s, they began to build hotels to accommodate thousands of guests, hundreds coming together at one time for one purpose. Meeting rooms as big as theaters became a part of the hotel architect's blueprints. Sound systems, facilities for audio-visual presentations, and large banquet rooms with theater-like stages for entertainment are now standard features of the modern hotel and convention center.

Standing in the wings, so to speak, were the associations, both trade and professional, which were coming alive and enjoying real and visible growth. In the early 1900s, there were only a small number of these associations, but by the mid-40s they had grown to nearly 2,000 active groups. The number has approximately tripled in the years since.

As the war wore down, I became increasingly aware of these

143

associations, some of which had large budgets and full-time staffs, and others which were smaller but growing. I began to sense the opportunities in the expanding convention business.

More and more of these organizations (some headquartered in Washington, and others in other cities, though a great number of those out-of-town groups have since moved to the nation's capital) began to hold meetings in Washington and were in the market for entertainment, particularly for their final night banquet.

I was fortunate enough to pick up a number of those accounts.

In the beginning, the shows were quite modest by today's standards. I used local talent. There were two or three good singers in town; also, an excellent magic act featuring a very talented sleight-of-hand artist named Harry Baker and his assistant, Dolly Snow, who also worked with him in his downtown magic shop.

We could put on a three-act show, plus a piano player, for $125, with twenty-five dollars going to us. I say "we" and "us" because right after the war ended, I expanded. To my staff of secretary, I added a part-time bookeeper and then a man named Stan Brown, whose band had worked for me. Then came Fred Perry, home from the war. Both Brown and Perry are still working with Jack Morton Productions.

Late in 1945, I moved my office out of my home and into a three-room office on the ground floor of Stoneleigh Court, a one-time fashionable apartment house at Connecticut and L. It was still mostly an apartment house, but under a slow conversion to commercial use. With wartime rent controls in effect, the building owners could not evict any of the tenants. But if an apartment was vacated voluntarily, it was immediately converted to business use. I managed to get one such suite—three large rooms and a bath—all for $150 per month.

The business was prospering, what with our hotels and clubs, and even though the nightclub business was on the wane, the new convention business was coming alive. So, I decided to make my move in style. I hired an up-and-coming interior designer and decorator named Ethel Pilson Warren. Except for one desk and a chair, I brought nothing from home. I put in all new furniture. With new carpeting, drapes, venetian blinds, and electrical fixtures, all chosen and arranged tastefully by Mrs. Warren, the new office was indeed a milestone for the Morton Enterprises.

144

17

AS I MADE THE TRANSITION from a booking agent for nightclubs, a job I didn't particularly like, to producer of shows for conventions, I became acutely aware of my need for more knowledge about the kind of talent that was available, where it was, and how much it cost. Most of it, I knew, was in New York, the entertainment mecca of the world.

So, I began to take trips regularly to New York, where I would make the rounds of the clubs—the Latin Quarter, Billy Rose's Diamond Horseshoe, the Copacabana, the Blue Angel, the Little Club, and others—and, of course, the Palace Theater. The Palace was a font of entertainment, "eight acts" every show. And while I couldn't spend all my time in the Palace Theater, I did the next best thing. I made a deal with an usher there to send me the weekly programs, with notations of audience reactions to the acts. I emphasized I was interested in the audience reaction, not his personal appraisal. I paid him two dollars a week, and before long, I was building up a comprehensive file on singers, dancers, magicians, jugglers, comedians, and other acts.

On one of my trips, I met Al Rock, who was producing the same kind of shows in New York that I was in Washington. In the early going, I depended a great deal on Al to line up acts for me, for which I paid him a commission.

It got to the point, and it did not take long, before I was familiar with the talent and the prices and was able to line up shows for a wide range of clients. Yet I kept the number of acts I dealt with regularly to a small number. Even today, putting on shows starring some of the biggest names in entertainment in cities throughout the country, we do not rely on a great number of artists. But we must be knowledgeable about all of them.

One of the nicest experiences has been to watch virtual unknowns blossom into stardom. I used to book Bob Newhart for $200 and George Gobel for $250. Others who worked for me for a small fraction of the fees they command today included Johnny Carson, Rowan and Martin, the Osmonds, the Lennon Sisters, Rich Little, and Fred Travalena, who worked for me for $100; a highly skilled impressionist, he now commands $10,000 an appearance.

So, we were doing all right, putting on shows for various conventions, while continuing to supply music for a few hotels and nightclubs when, on an early winter day in 1947, Ed Doty was to make a suggestion that would prove to be a major turning point for the business.

Ed was sales manager of the Statler, a likeable son of Ireland.

"Jack," Ed said, "you should go see the American Trucking Associations and talk to Ray Atherton. ATA's a pretty big trade association, and they are going to have their convention here next October. They might be looking for someone to help with the entertainment."

Ray Atherton, ATA's top administrative executive, was a mild-mannered, no-nonsense man who had a reputation for making quick, and mostly correct, decisions. He invited me into his second floor corner office and offered me a firm handshake.

I later discovered I was the third producer to see him that week, and I am glad I did not know that at the time. Instead, I was able to put on what I considered an air of confidence, even though Mr. Atherton could tell I still had a lot to learn about my business. But I got the job.

Years later, I asked him why. "Ray," I said, "why did you hire me for that convention job back in 1948?"

"Jack," he said, "I knew damned well you didn't know what you were talking about, but I was sure you were honest, and you would learn enough to do it right by the time of our meeting. Also, you didn't tell me how to run my convention."

I will never forget my first ATA convention. ATA split its convention that year between the Statler and the Mayflower, and we had a show to do in both places. Al Rock helped me line up

146

four good acts. I also provided two ten-piece orchestras. The total price to ATA was $2,500.

The acts were the Vikings, a five-man singing group; Prince Hara, who raised pickpocketing to a fine art; a French comedian who later showed up as a regular character on the TV series, "Hogan's Heroes"; and a harmonica player named Alan Schackner. Schackner was an unknown, but very talented musician, and I suggested he change his name to Alan Black. He did, and went on to build a very successful career as an entertainer, teacher, writer of books on playing the harmonica, and provider of background music for a lot of commercials. We still put him in every show we can, because he is superb.

We started the show at the Mayflower thirty minutes earlier than at the Statler. As each act finished at the Mayflower, we quickly shuttled it over to the Statler. Mr. Atherton, God bless him, loved the show.

"How did you make out?" he asked as we walked down the hall.

"What do you mean?" I asked.

"You know damned well what I mean. Did you make any money?"

"Not much," I said, "because I had overtime on both orchestras."

"Would an extra $500 help?"

"Well, that would be the difference between losing money and making it."

"Okay, Jack. When you send your bill, put an extra $500 down and mark it 'overtime.' On second thought, you'd better make it $475, because George Minnick, our treasurer, will catch $500, but won't question $475."

And thus began a happy and rewarding relationship with the trucking association that has lasted thirty-six years to this day. Ray Atherton is gone now, having passed away a few years ago. But I have found the other leaders at ATA to be cut from the same cloth; exceptionally bright men, men of integrity and honesty and good humor.

By opening the gate to ATA, Ray Atherton also opened the gate for me to other associations and companies. Subsequently, I found myself producing convention shows for many others, such as Super Market Institute; Cooperative Food Distributers; National Association of Chain Drug Stores; National Automobile Dealers, Ford, General Motors; International Harvester; Soft Drink Association; Banking Groups; Insurance Companies; Medical Meetings; National Association of Food Chains; Mortage Bankers, etc.

As these grew and their entertainment budgets increased, I found myself dealing with the big names of the business: Bob Hope, Jack Benny, George Burns, Red Skelton, Ray Bolger, Lawrence Welk, Enzo Pinza, Xavier Cugat, Herb Shriner, Alan King, and others.

But the launching pad was ATA. Immediately after my ATA debut in Washington, Ray Atherton informed me I had the job for next year in Boston. Again, it was a doubleheader, with the show playing first at the Copley Plaza and then at the Statler. I also picked up some other jobs at the same convention for trucking industry supplier groups, like Ford Motor Company, Goodyear Tire & Rubber, Mack Trucks, and one or two others.

At the 1950 ATA Convention in Los Angeles, there was the same problem of limited capacity. Hotel building had not yet caught up with convention demand. So once again, we used two hotels, the Statler and the Biltmore. I lined up the Sportsmen, the male quartet that was a regular on the Jack Benny Show; Luxor Gali Gali, the great magician from Egypt; a sensational violinist, Maria Neglia; and Bob Williams and Red Dust.

I remember that Maria Neglia played "The Hot Canary," a new number at the time, a most difficult score that required some unorthodox violin playing. It later became a standard number of practically every violin soloist in the country.

I was quick to pick up Gali Gali for the show because I had seen him perform at the Hotel Pierre in New York a few years before. In fact, I was the audience stooge. Once up on the stage, I found myself harboring a number of baby chicks. Gali Gali kept pulling them out of my pockets, the back of my collar, from my sleeves, and from behind my ear. And then, as I was walking back to my seat, to a healthy applause, Gali Gali called me back.

"You still have one more chick," he said.

"Where?" I asked.

148

"I cannot tell you; it is too, too embarrassing, sir. Please shake your pants."

I shook my trouser legs and, sure enough, a baby chick came out of the bottom.

It was a tremendous act and Gali Gali repeated it in Los Angeles; this time, the audience participant was the president of a large Midwest trucking company.

But the big hit of the show was Bob Williams and Red Dust, and that gave me great personal satisfaction, because Ray Atherton had been so skeptical.

When I arrived in Los Angeles, my show was all set. But Alice Faber, the agent with whom I was working, said, "Jack, there's a great act who just happens to be available Wednesday night for your show."

She described the act as a man with a dog that ignored commands and was hilariously funny. I found Ray Atherton and told him I would like to add Bob Williams and Red Dust to the show.

"Who is Bob Williams and Red Dust?" he asked me when I presented him with the suggestion of adding an act.

"A man and a dog," I said. "Red Dust is a brown and white spaniel."

"A dog, eh." Mr. Atherton was not enamored with dog acts. "What does this dog do?"

"Well, he doesn't do anything," I said, "well not anything right."

"Doesn't he do anything?"

"It's not like it sounds," I said. "Bob Williams tells the dog to do something and the dog doesn't do it."

"The guy next door to me has a dog just like that!" Atherton said. "I never thought of him as a vaudeville star. Tell me, what is this dog act going to cost?"

"Twelve hundred and fifty dollars," I said.

"Well, if you think so, let's do it."

I am happy to report that Bob Williams and Red Dust were a sensation. It wasn't that Red Dust did nothing when ordered to do something. He did just the opposite of what he was told. The audience roared with laughter, and I noticed Mr. Atherton was laughing and applauding with the rest of them.

My business was prospering so well by early 1950 that Anne and I decided to build a new home. We signed a contract with W.C. & A.N. Miller Company to put up a modern brick home in fashionable Spring Valley, on Loughboro Road.

Two weeks after we signed the contract, the Korean War started, which put a crimp on the home-building business, but also served to inflate the market, with the result that we got a better price for our old house.

Anne designed our new home, and her ideas were accepted by the Miller architect. It all won the full approval of Mr. Miller, who happened to like the same things.

It has been a beautiful home. It still is. After a year there, I transformed the back-lot wilderness into a garden, and over the years we have developed that into a satisfying showplace of camellias, azaleas, rhododendrons, and other plants. My only hobby has been gardening, a talent I inherited from my father.

Our home sits up behind an old brick wall, back off the street. There our children grew and blossomed, and it is still "home" to them; they come frequently, bringing their children with them.

Anne and I have been most fortunate with our children. We have seen and known parents, honorable, loving, determined to see their children grow up to be responsible, happy adults, only to suffer that especially bitter grief brought on by errant offspring. And in every case I have ever known or heard about, the parents beat themselves with the eternal question: "Where did *we* go wrong?" Chances are they did not go wrong at all. You can provide both love and care, economic and emotional security, and do your darndest day in and day out, and still they will go their own way; develop in their own fashion, for better or for worse.

So, we count our three blessings—Billy, Mary Lou, and Diane, who have given us nothing but joy and happiness and pride.

But, as a parent of growing children, you worry, you fret, you wonder at times if you are doing all you should. I know I worried at times about being a part-time father, since my work kept me away from home so much.

I remember wondering if we should send our daughters to private school. They were doing well in the public schools, Mary Lou at Alice Deal Junior High, and Diane at Horace Mann Elementary, when one incident made up my mind fot me.

Mary Lou had gone to a party at a schoolmate's home, and at about 9 or 10 o'clock, she called and asked me to come and get her. I drove over there and found Mary Lou sitting on the front porch, alone and upset.

"I don't want to be here," she said. "They're all in there drinking."

I just whisked Mary Lou out of there and the next day began to look at the available private schools in the area. I had furnished music to many of them, so I knew a little about them already. Anne and I settled on nearby Mount Vernon Seminary, a girls' high school and junior college on Foxhall Road, still highly regarded but now known as Mount Vernon College, having since eliminated the high school and added the other two college years.

We enrolled Mary Lou there immediately, and Diane also enrolled as soon as she was eligible. Both did well there.

Mary Lou later went to Sweet Briar College in Lynchburg, Virginia, making the honor roll and Phi Beta Kappa. She was particularly adept at mathematics and was accepted for further education at Brown University in Providence, Rhode Island. I still remember our anxiety over trying to find Mary Lou the right place to live.

After driving to Providence, salesman Jack Morton took his daughter to all the private homes around the campus, knocking on doors. "My name is Jack Morton," I said. "This is my daughter, Mary Lou. We are from Washington, D.C. She is looking for a place to live while attending Brown."

We knocked on many doors before finding a charming lady who was pleased to have Mary Lou.

Mary Lou, like her sister, blessed with the good looks and charm of the maternal Mortons, never did put her mathematics to practical use. She attended Brown for about a year, then came back home and went to George Washington. She had a close friend whose family was close to President and Mrs. Johnson. Their influence led Mary Lou to be chosen as social secretary to the ambassador of Finland, a job she enjoyed for the couple of years she held it. She left to marry an executive of Southeby International Realty Corporation, Charles Seilheimer, Jr. They make their home in historical, beautiful (and more importantly, not too distant) Warrenton, Virginia, and have two children, Anne and Charles.

Mary Lou, successful not only in marriage and family, has been a visible and active member of the Warrenton community. She is a great gardener—hopefuly, after me—with prize-winning flower arrangements and displays that have attracted wide attention. She is also chairman of the board of the Highlands School, where she has been the inspiration for increased financial support and parent participation. She is an active member of the Virginia Historical Society, in which she has won many statewide friends.

Diane also did well at Mount Vernon and decided for her further education on Salem College in Winston-Salem, North Carolina. Here, Diane developed a special interest in art, and in her last year won the coveted President's Award in art. A few years ago, Diane resumed her interest in painting and today is quite accomplished, having shown her works many times and found a demand for her paintings.

Diane also has a good, successful husband and family. She is married to Lee Fentress of the Washington law firm of Craighill and Fentress, which specializes in the management of star professional athletes. They have four children, Andrew, Caroline, Dana, and Lee, III, and live in Potomac Falls, Maryland.

I have saved Billy for last, not because of the chivalrous notion of ladies first, but because he has played and continues to play a prominent role in Jack Morton Productions.

Billy's childhood followed the natural story line of practically every other boy in the neighborhood: cub scouts, athletics (a broken nose while playing football), patrol boy, summer camp, etc. He was active in the boys program at Chevy Chase Presbyterian Church, was successful as a youngster at gardening and was, I believe, an all-round typical boy.

When he was about twelve, Billy began to take an interest in the business and I would take him on sales calls with me, where he would meet business friends and associates and clients. I always made it a point to introduce Billy to all of these people, and every one of them, regardless of how important or successful, took considerable time to tell Billy something about himself and how he became successful. This, in itself, was an education you can't get in any business school.

Billy was not a scholar. Like most boys, he found automobiles, girls, his male friends, athletics, and other pursuits far more attractive than school books. And so while he passed and was graduated from Woodrow Wilson High School, he knew he would not have an automatic entry into the college of his choice. Anne liked to tell the children they could go to any *good* school anywhere in the country—so long as it was south of the Mason-Dixon line. And Billy picked the University of North Carolina. (I had dreams of going there at one time.) But frankly, his grades loomed as a giant stumbling block. Keep in mind that a state school limits the number of out-of-state students.

So, this eighteen-year-old traveled to Chapel Hill, made an appointment with the dean of admissions, and pled his own case for admission face-to-face. He was accepted. This was his idea—he did it on his own. I remember remarking to Anne after he returned home with the good news, "We are not going to have to worry much about him."

His talents as a salesman started showing when he began selling various items in the neighborhood. One time, for instance, I found him digging rich-looking dirt and peddling it as "top soil." The neighbors encouraged him by buying, too. I had one rule—I wouldn't buy anything and his mother wasn't supposed to—but I suspect she often violated the rule. My reasoning—which some people considered cruel—was, it doesn't test one's selling skills when selling to people who love you. The test of a true salesman is selling things to people who don't love you—or perhaps hardly know you. I still preach the same way to the new sales people in our company.

Billy's choice of major study was communications—motion pictures, televison, radio production, and allied subjects—and it proved highly beneficial, not only to him, but to our company.

His education was occasionally punctuated by mishaps and distractions—especially normal ones. He did very well as a freshman. I was so pleased and proud, I bought a sporty yellow convertible to provide "necessary transportation" in and around Chapel Hill. Anne and I were shocked when his grades tumbled in the first semester of his sophomore year. When his report card arrived, showing failing in two subjects, I couldn't get on the phone fast enough to tell him to park the car and leave it parked till he could bring it home. He recognized the problem and never questioned my judgment. More importantly, he responded, correcting his scholastic standing, even going to summer school to make up for the temporary failure. He has been on the right track ever since.

After graduation, Billy spent time in the Coast Guard fulfilling his military obligation, and when he returned home, I asked him what he wanted to do.

"I'd like to work for you," he said. Again, this was his idea, with no pressure from his mother or me, although I had quietly prepared him for this.

And so I sent him to work in our New York office at the lowest possible salary.

"Because of who you are, you will have to earn your own way so nobody can say you were favored for being the boss's son," I said. "We'll start you at $400 a month, $4,800 a year."

"Could you make it an even $5,000?" he asked. "Otherwise, I might have to do my own laundry."

Frankly, I didn't see anything wrong with his doing his own laundry; I did mine lots of times. But he got the $5,000.

It was while working in our New York office that Billy met a pretty airline hostess, Mary Kathleen Addis, of Fairbury, Illinois. They were married in 1973 and have given Anne and me two more grandchildren to dote on (for a grand total of eight—Anne Catherine, born in May 1973, and William Irvin Morton, Jr., born in December 1974.)

In the late '40s, the modern convention was emerging from its old image of smoke-filled rooms, free-flowing liquor, late-night bashes, and all-male audiences watching scantily-clad show girls popping out of frosty cakes. Industry people began to see conventions as a good place to do business. I had just successfully completed two major conventions. We had great shows, made some money, and the clients were happy. It dawned on me that this was a promising, exciting, profitable, and growing business, and I liked what I saw. Of course, the convention business didn't mature overnight, and many were still dubbed in the old-order image, where loose fun with sex, stag affairs, gambling, and a few other vices were commonplace. Nevertheless, the trend to clean up this image was apparent and growing and conventions were becoming proper, legitimate affairs. My upbringing during my early days in the theater and an inherent awareness of propriety and good taste were put to good use when I brought my services to the attention of meeting planners (many have said that Jack Morton was the pioneer in changing what people saw and did at conventions). It was more accident than deliberate that I entered the scene at the time customs were changing. Fact is, I merely saw an opportunity to expand our business, and I embraced it by deciding to open additional offices.

I opened them in Denver, Miami Beach, Dallas, Hollywood, and Detroit, and soon closed every one of them. There just was not enough business in Denver, Miami Beach, Dallas, and Hollywood. I had made a wrong assumption, i.e., I thought the convention town was the place to have the office, but I soon discovered it was more important to be located in close proximity to where the clients are located, no matter where they held their conventions.

Detroit was a one industry city, if the unions will pardon the expression, that was a closed shop. By that I mean they had their way of doing things there and needed no help from outsiders, thank you. It is my opinion that that kind of mindset led to a lot of their troubles when the Japanese and Europeans were demonstrating a "better way." Perhaps I am being too harsh, but at any rate Detroit sure did not cotton to this import from Washington.

Finally, through trial and error, we settled on offices in New York, Chicago, Houston, San Francisco, and Atlanta, in addition to our main office in Washington. These offices in the beginning were no more than desks and telephones and a secretary or answering help.

My first Chicago office was desk space I rented from a cartoonist for the *Chicago Tribune*, who would answer my phone for me. In New York, our first office was desk space in a building at 500 Fifth Avenue. All I got was a desk, a telephone, and a New York address.

Eventually, of course, we expanded our facilities and later, the cartoonist in Chicago rented space from us.

At the time Billy joined the firm, we were having problems with the New York office. The person in charge there was the

155

best existing example I ever knew on how *not* to run a business. I figured I could send Billy to New York, and he would be able to learn the right and wrong of it at the same time. I said, "Son, if you can make it in New York working for this person, you can make it anywhere."

That isn't the easiest way to learn how to do something right, working for someone who does it wrong, but it can be effective. In time, the employee was released and Billy was able to assume charge of that office. As I had hoped, all of his pent-up abilities came to the fore, and the New York office began to grow and succeed in spectacular fashion.

Up to that time, our business had been all entertainment and music, plus a little industrial theater. Billy took us into new directions, into the newly emerging audio-visual business, which today constitutes a major part of our total production.

Billy actually started our audio-visual enterprises by cutting a hole in a wall. Our offices on Madison Avenue were quite small, a few cubby-hole rooms, certainly not enough room to project a decent-sized picture on a wall. So, Billy cut a hole in the wall so he could project on the wall of the adjacent office and started us on the way to becoming one of the country's foremost communications-producing companies, utilizing the most sophisticated equipment and techniques, all under his guidance.

What we did was to take our vast experience in entertainment and marry it to industrial needs, producing slide shows and films for training, sales improvement, business education and the like, in a highly entertaining and imaginative fashion. This field is made up of hundreds of technical geniuses, who so often lack the practical know-how in business and entertainment. It is a field that requires not only technical skill, but good business sense and a lot of creativity. Billy has been able to bring it all together.

I think I am making our expansion into other cities seem easy. It was not. While it was my longtime ambition to have a real nationwide company, I did not have the experience, the capital, or even the complete support of my own employees. On several occasions, I borrowed money on our home. There was also the problem of finding, training, and installing reliable people in these various offices. As the business grew, those who stuck with me prospered. And so I was stunned and deeply hurt when two of

156

my key people in the Chicago office paid me back by almost ruining the company!

I trained these men in the business. I gave them liberal incentives, even turning over to them many lucrative accounts I had developed over the years and from which they immediately began reaping substantial commissions.

I had not been totally satisfied with the operations in that office. In fact, I had sent Chip Brown to Chicago from the Washington office, and it soon became apparent that he was resented and was being treated as an outsider. I made several trips to Chicago, as did Stan Brown, Chip's father and vice-president. We thought we might be able to create harmony where none existed.

But while the office situation was not perfect, the Chicago office was progressing.

Speaking of loyal employees, I must mention Bob Wolfe, who joined the company fifteen years ago as bookkeeper when managing our finances was a simple job. He has contributed to our growth, is now treasurer, and oversees more complicated fiscal affairs with computers and a large staff.

My relationships with people generally have always been so rewarding. I have mentioned over and over in this narrative the tremendous debt I owe to so many people who went out of their way to give me a helping hand. And though at the age of sixty-five I wasn't exactly naive, I was totally unprepared for the shock of that telephone call from Chicago on a cold February night in 1976.

I had just returned from a very successful week on the West Coast, producing shows for the Bank of America, when the phone in my home rang. It was one of the men in the Chicago office.

"Just wanted you to know, boss, Bill and I are resigning."

"You're what?"

"We're leaving."

I tried to get my thoughts together. "When?"

"Today. We're going out on our own."

By "going out on our own," they really meant going out with my business. Moreover, this man had been working for me for seventeen years. He was almost like a son to me.

These were our salesmen, our representatives with the clients. The loyalties of the clients are naturally more directly tied

157

to the salesman he has been dealing with. Moreover, the salesman is in a position to make the change seem completely above-board while at the same time taking over all the records and establishing his own organization.

I cannot begin to describe the total trauma of that time. Chicago had just become profitable after years of considerable cost of my time and money. And the defectors carried off with them all of the Chicago business. They carried off what it took us years to build. And they never had to invest a dollar for any of it.

I still shake inside a little thinking of it. Had I been a few years younger, I would have been better able to deal with it. But I actually thought I might have to dismantle the entire company. Had it not been for Bill Morton, Stan Brown, and Chip Brown, that is exactly what would have happened.

This may have been Bill Morton's finest hour. Filled with determination and optimism, he rolled up his sleeves and began to rebuild. A lot of people thought it couldn't be done. Billy said it could and would be done. And it was done.

I do not wish to imply that Billy did it all alone. The loyal people in the company all rose to the occasion. I already mentioned Chip Brown. Had Chip not been "in place," even Billy might have had an impossible task. Chip dug right in, rebuilt the Chicago client list and expanded it. Today our Chicago office is thriving in new quarters and studio. He has re-established our company in the Midwest on a very positive scale. He was able to attract and indoctrinate several very skilled and talented associates, particularly Jim Finger, creative director and production chief—a remarkably talented man. Our service and product in Chicago are top notch. The volume of business has grown beyond that of the best of the earlier years.

The Chicago incident had a sequel. About seven months later, we had two more defections—one in New York and one in Washington, who left to join the others.

This was not just coincidence. They had kept in close contact with the Chicago defectors from the beginning. I have never blamed anyone else for the problems in my life, so I have always felt that this incident was due to some shortcoming of my own. Nearly everyone has tried to spare me my feelings of guilt, saying that all of this was merely human nature, ambition, and greed. I was naive in believing that loyalty was stronger than opportunism.

Today, Jack Morton Productions is a highly successful, efficient organization with all offices, including the late-blooming Atlanta office, doing well. It is true the communications group has long since overtaken the entertainment side of the business, which is still a major part of our total company.

After the company was resurrected, I decided it was time to name Bill Morton president and turn over the operation to him. I asked Stan Brown, who had been with me almost from the start, to assume the title of chairman and work closely with Bill. I relinquished all titles, and although I am very active and still serve clients, I primarily help the young members of JMP.

The shows . . .

To me, that is where the excitement is. The shows—the music, the people, the great stars, the fantastic applause. And though I may be "getting along" in years, for Jack Morton, the show still goes on.

And while the show still goes on, I can look back on four decades of show producing. I can recall so many experiences, zany and sad, dramatic and upsetting, nostalgic and heartwarming. In the following chapters, I share these experiences with you.

The Morton Family out Nash Road, Wilson, North Carolina, 1915. Left to right: Nannie, Mama's mother; Ted; Mama and Mary; Charlie (on bike); Papa (seated with Fido); Otis (behind Papa); and I.L., Jr. (Jack).

Anne on her wedding day

The Morton/Morton wedding, an Anne Morton production, September 1, 1936

Anne and Billy, Diane and Mary Lou, 1950

Anne and Jack with Eleanor Roosevelt at Jaycee luncheon

Arranging the program with Victor Borge

With Ray Bolger in rehearsal

The Clown—my friend Red Skelton

With Art Linkletter in Miami for my first *big* industrial show

Bob Williams and that funny dog, "Red Dust"

Nelson Eddy and Gale Sherwood

Jane Morgan performing by candlelight, night of blackout in New York

Alan King with Food Brokers in New York

Author with Bobby Vinton

"Mr. Piano," Roger Williams

Lawrence Welk—America's most enduring musical personality

Rehearsing the show with Martha Wright in Miami

Shirley Jones after the wild ride at the Orange Bowl

Sandler and Young—cutting up, as usual

In Washington with George Burns, who told me to never retire!

Company President Bill Morton (left) and Founder Jack Morton flank
Col. (ret.) Walter J. Boyne, director of the National Air and Space Mu-
seum at the opening for "A Celebration of Flight."

The great and wonderful Jack Benny

Jack Benny

9808 WILSHIRE BOULEVARD, SUITE 204 · BEVERLY HILLS, CALIFORNIA 90212

November 6, 1974

Dear Jack,

I appreciated your beautiful letter
and sentiments.

I'm feeling fine once more and
"back on the road" as you said.
Thanks again for your thoughtfulness.

Best wishes,

Jack

Jack

Mr. Jack Morton
1225 Connecticut Avenue
Washington, D. C. 20036

/o

Andy Williams and Jack Morton

Friends and Charlie McCarthy, to whom I said, "Pardon me."

18

WALK INTO PRACTICALLY ANY GATHERING of two or more, and you will find at least one who could run the country better than the man elected to do it. Walk into any bar, and you will find any number of men who could do a far better job of managing the local baseball team or coaching the local football team.

The other guy's job always seems a snap to the uninitiated. And when it comes to entertainment, everybody has his likes and dislikes.

I learned a long time ago that if I am going to take the heat, I want to light the stove. I remember once, when my convention entertainment business was still young, I was invited to appear before a committee in Chicago to convince them why I should put on the show for their organization's annual banquet. There were about twenty men sitting around a long table, but I was prepared, for I had worked up a list of specific acts I wanted to recommend. But instead of doing that, I made the fatal mistake. I asked *them* what *they* liked. And they told me. More specifically, they told me what they did *not* like.

"You can take those stand-up comics," one said. "Bob Hope's the only one worth listening to."

"Please don't offend my ears with a soprano," said another.

"Nothing's deadlier than dancers at a banquet," chipped in still another.

"Gentlemen," I said when they were finished, "you have just eliminated every form of entertainment except circuses and burlesque."

They laughed good-naturedly and finally agreed to let me do the show. Naturally, it included some of their pet peeves, but it proved to be a good show and I was invited back.

These days we seldom have to deal with committees, because responsibility for entertainment is normally left to the judgment of the paid executive. I find it a lot easier to work with one intelligent and reasonable executive than a committee. Entertainment committees are a bit archaic.

What can happen when a committee makes decisions was brought home a few years ago at a convention of food distributers in Washington. The top executive, Henry King, and I had become rather close, and he always allowed me full rein in the selection of the talent. On this occasion, a committee got involved and insisted on putting on one man's favorite comedian.

Most comedians believe they have to be dirty, suggestive, risque—whatever you want to call it—because, I suppose, that's what is expected of them in the clubs in Miami Beach, Las Vegas, and other modern centers of frivolity. But not for our clients.

"He is what they want," Henry told me.

"I don't like it," I said.

"Well, they insist he'll know what is right and what is not right for our audience."

"I'm afraid it doesn't work that way," I said. "Some of these people need full-time keepers. But we can try to convince him."

And we did try.

I had three other top-notch acts. We gave the comic the number three spot. Just before he went on, Henry and I took him aside and cautioned him one last time. "This is not your typical Miami Beach audience," I told him for about the third time. "This is mom, apple pie, and church on Sunday."

He started out fine, but he wasn't getting any laughs (that's what comedians live on) from his clean jokes, so he slipped into his regular routine, a series of smutty one-liners. A pall fell over the audience. People began to squirm. Finally, the president of the association and his wife, seated at the table right in front of the stage, got up and left.

You could hear a faint buzz in the hall. The comedian continued with his routine, and the next thing I knew, Henry King was on the stage. Henry ordered the comic off the stage, turned to the audience and said:

"Jack Morton and I both want to apoligize for the bad taste displayed here." As he walked off the stage, Henry received the most thunderous applause of the night.

187

I personally absorbed the cost of the comedian, even though I had fought the decision to use him. But that is always the case. If you are the producer, you take the heat, regardless.

Still, I wasn't going to take this lying down. I withheld payment to the guy, knowing full well he would appeal to the American Guild of Variety Artists, which at that time controlled most of the variety acts in the country. We were signatories to the prevailing agreements between the acts and the producers. Predictably, AGVA conducted a "hearing" in Baltimore. The "jury" was three of their own members—two comedians and a strip artist from the infamous Oasis, in Baltimore, We were asked to state our complaint and testify to the material we objected to.

The "jury's" verdict: "We see nothing offensive in the material. Case dismissed."

I had to pay the comedian his fee. But I can tell you this: He never again worked in a show of mine. And I learned from that experience to say no to any suggestion I did not like and stick to it.

I have made my living for forty years by choosing talent and producing shows that please people and make the meeting planner look good to his members. It is a profession that is widely unknown and misunderstood. Most people relate it to the work of a booking agent. That is totally inaccurate. A booking agent sells acts and collects commissions, and he has no fundamental or continuing interest in the show or the client. All booking agents believe, rightly or wrongly, that their acts are "good." Perhaps they are good, but the question is, good for whom?

Unlike booking agents, we have no financial interest in any performer. Our commitment is to our clients, who pay us for choosing the kind of artists they can relate to. And because my clients and I are fashioned from the same mold, so to speak, I know that if I like an act, they probably will also.

Believe it or not, it is not just the act I judge; it is the person behind the act. I rarely hire any entertainer I do not personally like.

My personal values and tastes have stood me well.

I also believe that convention shows are the last bastion of good taste in public entertainment. At one time, it was the other way around, when conventions were mostly stag affairs with

188

entertainment that supposedly would appeal to all-male audiences. But when the wives began to accompany their husbands to the annual meetings, it upgraded the type of entertainment provided.

I remember, very early in the convention business, I picked up a stag dinner in Washington, and while I have never subscribed to lewd entertainment and did not have what you would call a "dirty show" that night, it wasn't exactly the kind of show you would put on for a mixed audience, either.

A friend of mine from a large trade association, whose convention business I had landed, was in the audience. After the show was over he took me aside.

"Jack," he said, "I don't want to presume to tell you what to do, but I want you to know that the show you put on tonight is not one you can be proud of. I know you need all the business you can get. But there are some people I work with who would be shocked over this. Let me put it this way, Jack. You already have a grand reputation for being a man of good taste. Do yourself a favor and don't do anything to mar that image. It's the kind of reputation that will take you far in your business."

I have followed that advice religiously over the years, and today Jack Morton Productions has an enviable reputation as a company with high standards and excellent taste. That is why Jack Morton Productions has been able to build and maintain the largest convention show production company in existence. It is also the reason we were able to attract Optimists away from the Miami Beach hotel promoters twenty-three years ago.

The Optimists International is a worldwide civic organization dedicated to public service, particularly in lending a hand to deserving and needy young people. Their membership represents a cross section of the professional and business communities. They are decent, work-oriented, and family-oriented people, and I was confident that I could put on the kind of show for their annual conventions that they would really like.

The first time I tried to sell the Optimists on my services, they were planning to meet in Miami Beach. I knew that was going to be a tough sell, because in those days, and to a lesser extent now, the hotel crowd in Miami Beach and Las Vegas thought they knew more about America's entertainment than anyone else in the world. They don't. But they think they do and that is one of the reasons entertainment in general has reached a new low in taste in recent times.

The Miami Beach hotel people sold the Optimists on the idea they could put on a fantastic show for them and do it a lot cheaper than any outside organization—like Jack Morton, for example.

They were half right. Their show was a lot cheaper than anything we would put on. But it was still priced too high. The entertainment they offered was their own lounge shows—all cheap and in bad taste. There are millions of people in this country who are not amused by this kind of entertainment, and they include members of the Optimist Club, who were understandably upset over the Miami Beach program.

The following year the Optimists held their annual meeting in Grand Rapids, Michigan, and Ralph Gentles and John Parker asked us to produce their show. This was a typical Jack Morton production—good, wholesome entertainment with the emphasis on talent, taste, and fun.

The following year the Optimists had their convention in Las Vegas—another place that was missing when God passed out standards of good taste. The hotel management there wanted to put on the show, and when they were told Jack Morton Productions of Washington was handling it, they almost broke out laughing. In fact, one of the newspapers there thought it so astounding they carried a story on it under the headline "Carrying Coals to Newcastle." "Imagine," the article said, "an organization from St. Louis hiring an unknown show producer from, of all places, Washington, D.C., to put on a show in, of all places, Las Vegas."

I imagine they stopped laughing when they learned the show we put on was a rousing success. The audience loved it. That show was not only a credit to our judgment, but a fitting commentary on our critics' lack of same. We are still working for Optimists after twenty-three years.

While I have always tried to avoid being influenced by "amateurs," it isn't always possible to do so. I recall the time the Teamsters Union was putting on a gala show to commemorate its new marble headquarters in Washington, and I was selected to do the entertainment in Constitution Hall and supply the music for the dedication ceremonies for the next day.

I suggested four artists, headlined by the then popular Earl Wrightson and Lois Hunt. I had a ninety-minute show planned. That is the right amount of time for a theater-type show. And then Dave Beck, the longtime union president, called me in and said, "Jack, I have good news for you. We have lined up a few movie stars for the program. Put them in the show."

Good news! I thought. Good grief!

The Teamsters are big in Hollywood. They furnish the drivers and helpers for transporting all the film, and so it was only natural that they ask the studios to send a few of their more illustrious stars as a favor to Mr. Beck.

Five came: Gregory Peck, Pat O'Brien, Dan Daley, Jack Haley, and Margaret Whiting.

Those were five of the biggest stars in the business, and you might think I would be very happy to have them. I was anything but happy. I already had an excellent show, and there was really no room for five stars, no matter who they were.

But I had no choice in the matter. Each of the five big names planned only to talk, to pay tribute to Dave Beck and the union and to congratulate them on their new headquarters building. So, I just alternated them with the acts. I knew it wouldn't work very well, but it was the only way I could use the movie stars.

These were "actors," not "acts." They were really out of their element. They were not there by choice, and they didn't seem too thrilled by it all. As each took his turn, the one "on deck" became edgy and highly critical of the one on stage. And none of them was able to say "a few words" in a few words.

I can recall only what one of them actually said back in the wings, waiting to go on—Dan Daley, who was the last to "say a few words." I repeat his analysis of a fellow star with a measure of reluctance.

"That son of a bitch," Daley said, "has done everything out there except take out his———and———on the stage."

If Dan Daley thought he was upset, he should have tried it from my end. My ninety-minute show grew into three hours and forty-five minutes of long periods of boredom interspersed with short periods of entertainment.

The audience stuck it out. There are some people who are actually enthralled by the very presence of a big star; some of them, I suspect, would remain glued to their seats forever for the chance to watch in person a Gregory Peck or a Pat O'Brien.

But I also suspect that the chief reason nobody walked out was that President Beck remained.

For the building dedication ceremonies the next day, I had Earl Wrightson again, this time to sing the national anthem, and a band to back him up. I was relieved that Dave Beck didn't want to squeeze in a few more of his Hollywood friends, but that relief was quickly dispelled by another development. The Teamsters Union, of all things, was having a serious labor problem. The office workers employed by the union belonged to another union and were having a problem over their new contract. In fact, they threatened to strike and picket the dedication ceremonies.

This concerned me particularly because entertainers and musicians are very labor conscious, for the most part, and I feared my musicians and even Earl Wrightson might well refuse to cross the picket line.

However, one of Beck's lieutenants assured me everything would be fine. "You got nothing to worry about," he said. "We got a few people we're bringing from New York to take care of any troublemakers."

Later I received a telegram from James C. Petrillo, president of the American Federation of Musicians, and another from the president of the American Guild of Variety Artists, telling me to ignore any picket lines.

But at that point, I would have made book there would be no picket lines and there wasn't. The Teamsters Union, one of labor's great organizations, would never permit it.

That overly long show for the Teamsters was in direct contrast to another show I put on in Washington. I had some good entertainment lined up, but the show wasn't supposed to start until after a U.S. Senator had given a speech. I was told he would talk about thirty minutes, and so I informed the entertainers and the orchestra what time they should be on hand.

The dinner was concluded and the chairman introduced the guest speaker, who walked quickly to the lectern.

"Ladies and gentlemen," he began, "it is a real pleasure to be here with you tonight. Thank you very much for inviting me."

With that, he walked off the stage and took his seat in the audience.

It is the first time I can recall any speaker—particularly a politician—not having anything to say. It's hard to say who was the most shocked—the audience or me—but rounding up the musicians who were on their break and getting the show started was like a Mack Sennett comedy of bygone days. It was another hard-earned lesson in coping with surprises.

One of the most embarrassing moments in my years of producing shows took place at a large banquet in the Americana Hotel, in New York. As soon as they had finished dinner, the 2,000 or so people pushed back their chairs, sipped on their coffee, and awaited the entertainment. Quite a few of them lit up cigarettes or cigars. It was a time to relax and enjoy.

The star of our show was Vicki Carr, the charming and talented young lady whose records have sold millions. Her performance was superb, as I knew it would be. What I did not know was her aversion to smoking.

After acknowledging the thunderous applause she received after a few numbers she then proceeded to take all the smokers in the room to task for destroying their lungs and polluting the air. The smokers in the audience just stared back at her. A few of them put out their cigarettes and lit new ones.

I wanted to disappear. Such an antismoking lecture would be bad enough under any circumstances. But what made this embarrassing was that one of the sponsors of the show, the one paying the entertainer to sing and not to wage war against cigarettes, was the Philip Morris Tobacco Company!

Fred Waring, whose music has thrilled millions over the years, was another antismoking crusader, but he had a different approach; not necessarily better, just different. I learned this in the main ballroom of the Waldorf-Astoria, scene of a dinner put on by General Motors for the American Trucking Associations' convention.

Sitting down front near the stage and not too far from where I was sitting, was a trucking company executive smoking a cigar. The orchestra had just finished a number, and when the applause had stopped, Waring pointed to the man and said, "I sure would like to have that cigar you're smoking." Waring then pulled out some money and said, "I'll give you a dollar for it."

The man accepted the offer, pocketed the dollar and gave Waring the cigar. Waring made a big production out of putting out the offending weed. The trucking executive then pulled out another cigar and lit it. Exasperated, Waring pleaded, "Will you please and will everyone in this room please stop smoking?"

It was a bad scene, and it happened many years back, before the surgeon general's report and at a time when smoking was considered by most people, even the majority of nonsmokers, as an innocent, albeit stupid, preoccupation. Finally, Waring went back to leading his orchestra, an activity far more suited to his talents than crusading. All he had accomplished was to alienate his audience.

Alienating the audience is not very smart. Neither is alienating the sponsor.

At a show in Washington, one of the entertainers put his foot in the mouth, and once again I found myself in trouble with Phillip Morris.

Phillip Morris at that time was part of an organization that called itself the "Big Six," a group of six big companies that combined to sponsor entertainment at certain conventions.

It was a good show, an excellent show as I recall, and when it was over, all the M.C. had to do was say "thank you and good night." Instead, he had to thank each and every one of the six companies—but he left out Phillip Morris and substituted Liggett & Myers!

I was standing offstage and looked at the head table. As I expected, a Phillip Morris official was looking at me—not tenderly, I might add. I immediately rushed on stage, took over the microphone and as tactfully as I could, corrected the blunder. But if I thought that was bad, all I had to do was wait a year.

Once again, I was hired to produce the show for the Big Six, this time in Chicago. The chairman of the program, who was with the McCormick Tea Company, reminded me of the boo-boo the previous year. "Jack," he cautioned, "make sure your entertainers stick to entertaining. They don't need to do any commericials."

I agreed wholeheartedly. In fact, I made a point of stressing that taboo during the afternoon rehearsal, with the tea company man standing by and nodding.

"Don't say anything about the companies or their products," I said.

The rehearsal for the show, which starred singer Gordon

MacRae, went off extremely well. But rehearsals do not include everything—for example, what singers say or talk about when they are not singing.

Gordon MacRae is a first-rate performer. But sometimes he did more than just sing. He told funny stories and he did imitations. "And now," he said, "here's that man, Arthur Godfrey." And then, with the McCormick Tea man staring in disbelief, MacRae launched into the famous Lipton Tea song. He sang it not once, but twice!

There was no way I could go up on stage and try to repair the damage. It was irreparable. I am still hearing about that one.

For another show, at the Edgewater Beach Hotel in Chicago, for the B.F. Goodrich Company, I booked a man who was superb with sound effects. He imitated everything from an airplane taking off to pouring a drink over ice and then drinking it.

"Don't mention B.F. Goodrich," I said. "They do not want any credits."

But he did have a routine that related to tires. He had tires screeching going around corners, he imitated perfectly the sound of someone repairing a flat, and capped it off with a few blowouts.

"Now here is a blowout to end all blowouts," he said.

It was. It was realistic, loud, and dramatic, even to the thumpety-thump sound of the car coming to a stop.

"You know whose tire that was," he said. "That had to be a Goodrich."

He meant *Goodyear*, of course, the name of the sponsor's competitor, but the damage was done. This only proved that when entertainers start talking, no one knows what will come out.

The first time I ever worked for the Reserve City Bankers—the elite of the banking society—was in Atlantic City at the Haddon Hall Hotel, which is now Resorts International, the first to bring legal gambling to that city. The entertainment chairman was William (Bill) Day, president of the First Pennsylvanian Bank and Trust Company of Philadelphia. He was a gentleman and admitted his inexperience in arranging entertainment. With a good recommendation on Jack Morton from an important customer, his confidence was established, and working together was a happy experience. Bill briefed me on the kind of entertainment they had

195

had, none of which was impressive. He agreed to leave the choice of talent entirely to me, told me the date and place and approved the budget. The negotiations were the simplest I had ever known. I understood his good taste and guessed his would represent that of the other members. I chose two accomplished singers—a man and a lovely girl—both of whom had opera and Broadway musical experience.

Come the night of the show, the bankers had had a lively cocktail reception, an elegant dinner and were in a great mood. Bill was there, of course, and was a bit nervous about how things would go. In his efforts to prepare me for something less than a smash hit, he told me not to worry if the people talked and paid no attention to the entertainers. That was upsetting enough, but his last words before I was introduced, were that last year the bankers had thrown rolls at the performers—including the emcee, which I was playing that night. With that advice, I was literally in shock when I walked on stage. My worry was dispelled as soon as the pretty soprano started to sing. She captured the audience, and for a moment I thought that after she finished would be a good time to stop since nobody had thrown any rolls! The operatic tenor who followed her was a handsome man with a tremendous voice. He could do no wrong—every number was a hit. To climax the show, the pair sang two duets and received a standing ovation.

One of my treasured letters is from Bill when he learned that I was relinquishing the presidency of JMP. He reminded me of our success and happy times and the night the bankers *did not* throw rolls!

You might not think so, but there are few things that make an audience feel more uncomfortable than an obviously pregnant performer onstage. It happened to me twice. Once should have been enough. There will never be a third time if I can help it. If I discover after I engage a woman to perform that she is pregnant, I will cancel her rather than let her go on. I think it should be obvious that I am not against motherhood—my own mother and my wife both have engaged in it—but there is something about a pregnant woman onstage singing or dancing that just seems ludicrous if it's not designed to be funny.

The first time it occurred was at the Convention Center in Denver. I engaged a talented but not too well-known girl-boy singing team. I knew the woman was pregnant when I signed them on, but I had no idea how pregnant she was. She appeared in one of those expensive maternity dresses that go straight down from the chin and are supposed to hide the evidence. But everybody was painfully aware of what was behind it.

They sang beautifully, and you might be wondering why the lady's condition was so disconcerting. I don't know if I can answer that. All I know is everybody in the audience was conscious of her condition. And with the two of them chanting romantic lyrics, the embarrassment was compounded.

There they were, then, waltzing together and singing "I Could Have Danced All Night" when the music faded a little and he began to talk to the audience:

"You know, Lillian and I have been singing together for a long time, and people often wonder if we are married or if we are just sweethearts."

He paused and then said, "We are both."

You could almost hear the collective sigh of relief rising up from the audience. From somewhere in the back I could have sworn I heard someone gasp, "Thank God!"

On the other occasion, I had booked Anita Bryant months in advance for a show scheduled for the Armstrong Cork Company in December in Lancaster, Pennsylvania. Sometime in October, Anita called to tell me she was pregnant. "It's pretty obvious," she said, "and if you want to cancel, I will surely understand."

That is the proper thing to do. I thanked her for her candor and told her I would get back to her.

Well, Don Goldstrom, the spokesman for the company said they had already made the announcement and would prefer a pregnant Anita Bryant to a substitute. After all, she was one of the biggest entertainment names at the time.

They wanted a pregnant Anita Bryant and they got a pregnant Anita Bryant. Watching her get on and off the stage was awkward for everyone. I remember noting that she looked like three people. And though she did her usual fine job of singing, the pregnancy overshadowed everything.

Don, a great guy, and I both agreed afterward that we should have accepted Anita's offer to withdraw. Hindsight is always twenty-twenty.

But the story has a most happy ending. Two months after the show, Anita Bryant gave birth to twins.

No wonder she looked like three people. She *was* three people.

19

I HAVE ANOTHER RULE OF SHOW PRODUCING: Always expect the unexpected. It won't do much good in preventing it. The unexpected
will still happen, bringing near-disaster with it, but learning not
to be so shocked by it is the best way to live long enough to write
a book about it.

There was the evening in the Commodore Hotel in New York
when a grand feeling of confidence came over me. That should
have been the tipoff right there. Up until then, I had been nervous.
After all, I was in charge of the entertainment at one of the most
prestigious events of the year—the National Business Publications
Association's Silver Quill Award dinner. This year's recipient of
the award, given to one of the nation's outstanding business leaders, was Ben Fairless, chairman and chief executive officer of the
United States Steel Corporation.

As I looked around that vast room, with a slight feeling of
satisfaction, I saw about a thousand men and women elegantly
dressed in black tie and dazzling evening gowns. They repre-
sented the top drawer in business, professional, and government
circles.

I had been given a generous entertainment budget, about
$20,000, if I recall correctly. I engaged topgrade entertainment,
led by opera stars Felix Knight and Mimi Benzell and including
a couple of dancers and a large orchestra.

The rehearsal that afternoon had gone superbly. The stage
was decorated exquisitely. The lighting and sound had been
checked and re-checked. Nothing, I reassured myself, could possibly go wrong.

Finally, the dinner was over and it was time to sit back and enjoy the festivities, which would include introductions of the head table and other guests, two or three speeches lauding Mr. Fairless and finally, the presentation of the award. Following the presentation, the toastmaster would announce the start of the entertainment and would introduce me. I had agreed to act as the M.C.

The program proceeded without a hitch. Some of the speeches were overly long, but that is almost always the case. The actual presentation of the award was extended to accommodate the photographers, also expected. We were pretty much on schedule.

As Mr. Fairless began his acceptance remarks, I made my way unobtrusively to the wing of the stage to await the toastmaster's introduction.

As Mr. Fairless took his seat, the Silver Quill Award in hand, the toastmaster waited patiently for the applause to subside. I was ready to move quickly to the stage and start the show. The performers were tense and anxious to get started.

"Ladies and gentlemen," the toastmaster said, "that concludes our festivities; thank you and good night!" Whereupon hundreds of guests began pouring toward the exits.

Somebody shouted. It might have been me. At any rate, the toastmaster, recognizing what he had done, began to shout into the microphone for the people to return to their seats. Most of them did not hear him. I took the microphone. "We have a show," I said. "Please return to your seats." Most of them didn't hear me, either.

Of the thousand people who had sat in that ballroom only moments before, about 100 remained to see the show. But those 100 were in for a real treat.

I asked everybody to move down front near the stage. "We have a fine show, so come down here where you can really enjoy it."

And they did.

Felix and Mimi and the rest of the cast threw away the original script, or at least a portion of it, and made it a lot less formal, a lot more intimate. They conversed and joked with the audience, and it was like having a great production of classical music and dancing right in your own living room.

200

When they were through performing, Felix said: "We have really enjoyed this. You have been a wonderful audience. How about joining us up here on the stage for a few minutes so we can get to meet you."

That was the icing on the cake for those who had remained.

For me, it was a nerve-racking experience, and my client was ready to commit suicide!

On the other hand, I have been the unfortunate producer of other shows where the audience stayed and wished they had not.

One had to do with a "show in the round," a production I avoid at all costs if conditions are not perfect. You may recall we put one on in Cleveland, with Jack Benny as the star, and it had been a rousing success. But there is too much that can go wrong with such a show, and when the following year the convention manager of the Super Market Institute asked for a repeat in the round for the annual banquet in Houston, I demurred. He insisted. I pointed out that conditions in Houston weren't like Cleveland. He insisted. I pointed out such shows are costly. He insisted. I finally agreed to do it, although going against my better judgment. (I don't go against my judgment anymore.)

The show was to be held in a large hall adjacent to the Superdome. As you know, a show in the round means the stage is in the center of the hall and the audience is seated all around. It may sound simple, but the arrangement presents special challenges for lighting and sound and staging. The sound must radiate from the center stage 360 degrees and must be uniformly amplified. Spotlights have to be placed at a very high angle so as to hit the performers while not blinding part of the audience. There is the added complication of a canopy over the stage for the housing of other lights for the special onstage effects. And finally, there is the problem of getting the acts to and from the stage. They must go through the audience, which takes an eternity in show time.

The program included a girl singer, a comedy act, and Rouvan, who at the time was the "Englebert Humperdinck of Las Vegas."

The afternoon's rehearsal went off well. I finally put aside most of my misgivings and made the twenty-minute walk to my hotel.

On my return for the real thing, I had just left my hotel when

201

a sleek, black limousine pulled up alongside me and the man in the back offered me a ride. It was Lee Bickmore, president of the National Biscuit Company, sponsor of the entertainment.

"Everything all set for tonight?" he asked.

"It's going to be a great show," I said. And I was sure it would be. Nothing, I told myself, could possibly go wrong.

The first thing that went wrong was the lighting. All the people sitting in the first half dozen rows all around the stage were blinded. The big arcs hit them square in the face. They weren't able to see their hands in front of them, let alone what was happening on the stage.

I called the operator. "We're working on it," he said.

The spotlights were reduced in intensity and the overhead lights raised. Now the people in the front rows were no longer blinded. However, nobody else could see what was going on on the stage.

They couldn't hear very well, either. When they adjusted the sound so the people up front could hear, the people in the back could not. When they turned up the sound so the people in the back could hear, the people in the front were almost blasted out of their seats.

It was a disaster. We were never able to get the lighting and sound systems to work properly. The more we tried, the worse things seemed to get. I tried to shorten the program, but that is almost impossible to do once the show gets underway. I did eliminate the traditional encores.

When it was all over and the disappointed audience moved out of the hall, I had to remain behind and take the abuse. Some of the officials were very kind and understanding. One was not. When he got through giving his opinion of the show and my abilities as a producer, the air was purple, and my complexion was red. But in conforming to my rule, I accepted the criticism.

Finally, after everyone else had gone, a young man who was working as my assistant and I started walking back to the hotel. However, the gate through which we had come was locked. We then walked across the parking lot in search of another way outside and along came a truck.

"How do we get out of here?" I asked the driver.

"Where are you going?" he said.

I told him. He offered us a ride and we accepted, standing up in the back of the truck.

As we neared the hotel, I said to the driver, "You don't have to take us to the front door. Just drop us off here."

"No problem," he said.

"But I insist," I said.

"No problem," he said, driving that unsightly truck up through the circular driveway and stopping in front of the main entrance. We got out of the truck in front of a full audience, including people I knew. It was downright embarrassing, but still it got more laughs than the show!

I remember later thinking how appropriate it all was. I travelled to the show in a Cadillac limousine and came back in a trash truck.

There is another night I will never forget and neither, I would wager, will Shirley Jones. I suppose we both wanted to hide, but it is very difficult to hide inside the Orange Bowl in Miami with glaring spotlights shining down and thousands of people booing.

I had a bad feeling about this from the beginning, when I learned I was going to have the second night of two nights of entertainment. The host was Lions International, and those in charge thought it would be nice to split the entertainment between myself and a competitor.

The problem was, the competitor was putting on a similar show the night before mine, built around music and some stand-out entertainers. He had other advantages, too, including the use of several high-school and college bands that came to Florida to pay tribute to the incoming Lions president, a native North Carolinian. There was also on the first night a tremendous fireworks display. You could say we were starting from a losing position—except for one thing—we had Shirley Jones, the star of the Rodgers and Hammerstein musical *Oklahoma!* At that time, the movie version was at the height of its popularity.

We had several other acts, plus a chorus to sing and dance, and, of course, a large orchestra.

Having people sing to orchestra music is great when both are amplified. But when the voices are amplified and the orchestra is not, you wind up with a tremendous time lag and the effect is a terrible assault on the ears and nerves. So, while the singers and the players were in synchronization onstage, they were completely out of synch when the sound reached the audience in the grandstand about 100 feet away, and that 100 feet made the disastrous difference! On top of that was the noise of the airplanes, roaring on takeoff from nearby Miami International Airport. These were propeller planes, not jets, so by the time they reached the Orange Bowl, they were still only 500 feet or so in the air. The noise they made drowned out everything.

On top of all that, the show seemed to go on forever. Every official of the Lions International wanted to get into the act, and most of them did. They introduced everybody they knew and people they didn't know, gave speeches, told boring stories, and then insisted on providing one of their entertainers, a blind girl who sang. At least she picked an appropriate number, "The Lord's Prayer," which by that time I should have been reciting.

By the time we reached what I had hoped would be a winning climax to a spectacular show, the audience had just about had it. With the sound out of synch, the airplanes roaring overhead, the oppressive heat and humidity, and a show that already was longer than *Gone With the Wind*, it is no wonder the audience was on edge.

Still, I had hopes that the final act, featuring Earl Wrightson and Shirley Jones in a scene from *Oklahoma!*, would salvage something out of the night. The big number was going to be "The Surrey With the Fringe on Top," one of the hits from the play. Shirley was to ride in the surrey from the far end of the field. Onstage would be Wrightson and the chorus. As the horse and surrey moved from the far-off goalposts, the orchestra would strike up the familiar medley and Earl and the chorus would sing, and then, as the surrey pulled up in front of the stage, they would go down, lift Shirley out of the surrey, and she and Earl would go up to the stage and sing together.

It was one of my more brilliant ideas.

Everything was ready. The horse and surrey were in place, the driver nodding in the front seat, and Shirley in the back dressed in calico and a wide white bonnet, waiting for the start of the act.

Suddenly, the operator threw the klieg lights onto the horse and surrey, which scared the daylights out of the horse, who had (naturally) gone to sleep. That horse took off down the foul line, and not even navy's Joe Bellino in the 1961 Orange Bowl game against Missouri ran down that field any faster. The horse didn't stop anywhere near the stage. He kept going all the way to the other goal post for a sure six points. The driver couldn't seem to get him under control and Shirley Jones was a wreck, her bonnet having blown off somewhere in the vicinity of the forty-yard line.

The horse finally stopped and Earl Wrightson and the chorus hurried all the way down to the end zone to take Shirley out. That walk back to the stage was one of the longest in show business history. This was all great comedy. Unfortunately, it wasn't planned to be.

By this time the audience was in an uproar. They were screaming and throwing everything they could get their hands on, but fortunately the targets were out of range.

I made the newspapers. There was the complete description of my debacle . . . the poor, frustrated producer, lost in his own production, plagued by every possible curse and mistake. It was a sad night indeed.

The next day I "disappeared" to Cuba, where three days of R and R, reinforced by certain potions, helped me forget—at least for a while.

Two unexpected developments resulted in my virtual banishment from a certain hotel in Boca Raton, Florida. I was producing the entertainment for a drug manufacturers' convention there and scheduled for the final-night dinner, an outdoor Western party, with a Western show featuring a rope artist, some singers, and the headliner, "Tex and his Trained Bull."

I had never seen Tex and his bull, but they came highly recommended from an agent who told me the bull was a miniature. It was trained to count, pray, and nod his head and stomp his feet in response to questions from Tex.

Late that afternoon the first unexpected development occurred—black clouds moved in, and it became obvious that it was going to rain on our party. So, it was decided to move it indoors.

"Can you do the same show inside?" my client asked me.

"We'll sure try," I said.

Some of the scenery we had outside would not fit inside, but we figured we could get along without that. Everything seemed to be in order, and when I returned to my room the phone rang. It was Tex, who had just arrived.

"I would like to come down and see your bull," I said.

When I arrived out front, I noticed a moving van about twenty feet long.

"What's that?" I asked.

"That's my van," Tex said.

"What's in it?" I said, almost afraid to ask.

"My bull," he said.

"Your miniature bull?" I asked.

"Yep, that's right," he said opening the side panel and revealing an animal that reminded me of Babe, Paul Bunyon's pet bull. He must have been at least twelve feet long. And he had horns. Big horns. Real big horns.

"If that's your miniature bull," I told Tex, "I sure don't want to see any of your big ones."

He assured me the bull was always a big hit. "Our finale is when I ask for a volunteer to ride the bull out. I have my wife planted in the audience, and she volunteers and rides 'em out. The audience always gets a big kick out of it."

Having that animal perform outside was one thing. But inside? I wasn't sure. I checked with the social director of the hotel, a very pleasant woman who had been in her job for a number of years.

"Fine," she said. "We need a little excitement around here."

Tex and his bull waited at the van outside the hotel until it was time for them to perform. Theirs was the final act. And when it was time—after the singers and rope artist and the other performers had finished, I had someone go out to tell Tex it was time, while I went through the banquet room making sure there was a path between the tables from the doors to the dance floor where they would put on their act. I also thought I should let the audience know what was coming through.

"The bull is safe," I assured them. "We just want to get him on the dance floor."

"A dancing bull?" someone asked.

Well, Tex brought his bull through the front doors of the hotel, through the lobby while desk clerks, bellhops, and guests gaped in amazement, down the hall and through the banquet

206

room. As he came through the room, everyone was laughing in obvious enjoyment at the strange spectacle of the gargantuan bull walking docilely, almost tiptoeing, through the large dining hall.

And Tex and his bull were superb.

"Now," Tex announced at the conclusion of the act, "I want a volunteer to ride this wonderful and peaceful bull out through the hall and outside."

A woman immediately volunteered, a smiling attractive blonde. She came forward, and with Tex's help, awkwardly straddled the bull and rode him outside to the accompanying cheers and applause of the onlookers.

It was a beautiful moving climax to a highly successful show and everyone, including Jack Morton, left the room with a grand feeling.

But I wasn't feeling too grand the next morning. That is when the second unexpected event occurred. As I was checking out of the hotel, an assistant manager approached me. He had the look and demeanor of, well, a mad bull.

"Are you the one who brought that bull into the hotel last night?" he demanded.

"Yes, I'm Jack Morton," I said. "I was the producer of the show."

"Well, you won't be producing any more shows in this hotel if I have anything to say about it. The very idea. Bringing a big, dangerous bull into this hotel."

"He behaved better than some of the people," I replied.

I learned later that the social director, who said they "needed a little excitement" around there, was fired. While no hotel would want a 2,000 pound bull running around its facilities, this particular animal was highly trained, was never out of control of his trainer or the trainer's wife, and on any given night was far less likely to create a disturbance than some of the guests one encounters in a typical bar. That was the last of my "bull" shows.

Sometimes the unexpected can produce bizarre results.

I will never forget the dinner in the Statler Hotel in Washington. Once the dessert was finished, the M.C. introduced a speaker, a man, he said, who, though not extremely well known to the general public, had served three presidents in high level positions and was considered an expert on Asian affairs.

207

The speaker began first of all to recount some of his experiences of years ago as a roving correspondent in China. The audience found it most interesting. And then suddenly someone in the back of the room shouted: "Who cares?"

The audience turned around almost as one.

The heckler then got out of his seat and began to harrass the speaker. He was obviously not too sober.

"And another thing," he said, "I spent some time in China myself during the war . . . the big war . . . World War Two . . . "

"Please, sir," the speaker said, "I'm the guest speaker here. Would you please sit down and listen?"

"No, I ain't gonna sit down and listen. . . . "

Some of the men in the audience shouted:

"You heard him, sit down!"

The stooge persisted. "I'm gonna tell you somethin'. . . . "

The audience began screaming at the heckler to sit down and shut up. Finally, four or five men, their patience exhausted, lifted the man right off his feet and swiftly carried him out of the room.

I rushed outside in pursuit. They had the man in the lobby pushed up against a wall.

I was horrified.

Not only were they physically assaulting one of my performers, they were also ruining the act.

"Let him go!" I said. "He's part of the act."

"He's what?" asked one.

Then, someone recognized me. "Hey, that's Jack Morton," he shouted. "He's the show producer."

Embarrassed, they released the "heckler," who went back into the hall, staggered up the center aisle, shouting at the man on stage, who by this time didn't know how he was going to end his act.

But they were able to pull it off well and both got tremendous applause.

Incidentally, that is the kind of act you can pull off only on occasion. As Lincoln said, "You can fool some of the people some of the time. . . . " But while I have seen that act and similar ones quite a few times, never had I seen anyone in the audience taken in as much as those men who thought they were coming to the rescue of the "lecturer."

There was another occasion when audience participation was *invited* and almost turned into disaster.

This was at the fiftieth anniversary banquet of the National Tire Dealers Association in Atlantic City. While I had arranged the entertainment, it was my good friend, Bill Marsh, the chief executive of NTDRA, who supplied the extra touches. And he was good at it.

For this golden anniversary, Bill had the room colorfully decorated, had the head-table guests all in formal attire, and featured a gourmet menu. He told me he wanted top entertainment, and I brought in the highly popular "Young Americans," the great singing group from Hollywood, as the featured act.

Bill and I waited patiently as head-table introductions and the few brief speeches were made, for Bill had planned a dazzling climax for the dinner—the cutting of a huge anniversary cake, while the thousand or so guests stood and swirled lighted sparklers, creating a fairyland of swirling lights.

"Ladies and gentlemen," Bill announced, "here is our cake!"

There was the huge, beautifully decorated pink and white cake, with two lovely ladies standing beside it, knives in hand, ready for the cutting.

"And now," Bill said, as the house lights dimmed, "please take the sparklers there on your table, light them with the matches that are there, and stand and wave them." The audience responded.

But the fairyland effect didn't come off. Instead, a thousand and one sparklers in the overly-warm banquet room set off enough smoke to send Fred Waring into permanent orbit. The air was thick and black with smoke. Nobody could see. Marsh was choking and coughing. I was choking and coughing. The audience was choking and coughing. More importantly, the Young Americans were choking and coughing.

Hotel security rushed in, thinking the place was on fire. One of the security people ordered everyone to douse their sparklers in water.

"The sprinkler system could go off any second," he said.

Doors and windows were opened and in about half an hour we were able to proceed with the show.

Bill and I have joked about that night a number of times. And

209

we speculated over what would have happened had the sprinklers gone off. We were told it wouldn't have taken much more heat and smoke to trigger it.

It was an excellent show, but I am sure those who saw it remembered the incident of the sparklers longer than the show.

I never think about the night of the sparklers without also remembering one of most fantastic performances I have ever had the pleasure of witnessing by a fantastic performer under any circumstances—Jane Morgan. I had the pleasure of engaging her for the closing banquet of the annual convention of the National Milk Producers Federation in the fifty-story Americana Hotel in New York. The date was November 9, 1965.

Jane was supported by a specially assembled orchestra and a couple of other acts, a specialty team that did imitations using recorded music and sound effects, and a standup comedian.

Jane's personal conductor and the orchestra gathered in the huge ballroom at 4:30 P.M. for a rehearsal. Suddenly, right in the middle of "Fascination," Jane's block-busting record-seller, the lights went out. We were in total darkness.

When power was not restored after about twenty minutes or so, I went outside onto Fiftieth Street. It was an amazing scene. The city of New York was in total darkness except for the endless headlights. Confusion reigned. Traffic was hopelessly snarled because the traffic lights had gone out. I discovered later that the subway also was out of action. Flashlights and candles were beginning to appear.

I remember one wag in the hotel lobby suggesting, "The candle-makers did it; their business has been off ever since Edison got his light to work."

I phoned Mike Norton, head of the Milk Producers Federation, in his suite on the fiftieth floor.

"Jack," Mike asked, "what can you do about the entertainment?"

"Well," I said, "let's not cancel just yet. The power should be restored soon."

"I'll instruct the hotel people to remain on standby," Mike said. "You do the same so everyone will know we have not cancelled. I'll have the staff contact our members."

As banquet time approached, it was still dark. I called Jane Morgan.

"Jane, how are you doing?"

"Oh, Jack," she said, "what a mess! What are you going to do? Are we going to have a show?"

"Jane," I said, "I need your help tonight. Do you think you could please come over here and we'll play it by ear?"

"I'll be there," she said. She was too much of a trouper to cancel!

Of the 1,500 expected guests, we got about 500, who were actually having a marvelous time eating by candlelight, while the orchestra entertained with such old "blackout" favorites as "Black Magic," "Dancing in the Dark," "When the Lights Come on Again All Over the World," "A Kiss in the Dark," and "Moonlight Becomes You So."

Jane arrived (she had to walk down eight floors and several blocks). With her tremendous sense of theater, Jane chose not to wear the usual glittering bejeweled evening gown, but an attractive everyday kind of dress. It was the right touch.

Because there was no amplification, we had to cancel the supporting acts. Jane was the show. Also, there were no speeches.

"Ladies and gentlemen," I said, "let's everybody move down front and bring your candelabras with you. We need them for footlights."

The audience, caught up in the drama of the occasion, responded. Candelabras were placed on the stage, and it was reminiscent of old theater when there was no electrical amplification and all the lighting was done by oil lamps and lanterns.

"Ladies and gentlemen," I announced, "you've heard of singing in the rain. . . . Well, here is Jane Morgan singing in the rough."

Jane came out to a relatively small but highly enthusiastic audience. It was a magnificent performance. She sang a lot of the old favorites, inserting several numbers on the spot with mutual agreement with the musical director. She sang "Fascination" twice and a couple of other songs she had made into hit recordings, including "The Day the Rains Came," and "With Open Arms." I am sure everyone in that audience agreed with me that the show itself was "fascination."

It all began when someone made a faulty setting of a relay at an electrical distribution plant in Ontario, near Niagara Falls. The resulting massive electric power failure blacked out 80,000

211

square miles in the northeastern United States and southeastern Canada, an area containing twenty-five to thirty-five million people. New York City was the hardest hit, and parts of it were without electricity for as long as thirteen and one half hours.

After the show, Jane and her agent-manager, Jerry Weintraub, and I sat down at a table in the banquet room and were served dessert and coffee. Jerry's management company was on the rise and later handled such stars as John Denver, Dorothy Hamil, and John Davidson. He also embarked on a movie producing career, producing *Nashville* and *Oh, God*, starring George Burns and John Denver.

But the smartest thing he ever did, in my opinion, was to promote himself to Jane. They married, and when I last talked to them, they were still happily married, with children, living in Beverly Hills.

As we finished our dessert, Jane turned to me and said, "Jack, how in the world did you get into this business? You are not like any of the others I know. You seem more like a lawyer to me."

I said it was a long story. Jane replied, "Some day you should write about it." That was the second time a star had made this suggestion.

I returned to my room that night, tired but contented. I had to walk, carrying a candle, thirty-nine floors! I entered my darkened room and was struck by the bright lights coming in from the window. I looked out. The moon was shining brightly down from a clear, crisp November sky. Across the river the bright lights of New Jersey twinkled like a fairyland. It was a strange and hauntingly beautiful view from a Manhattan hotel. It was fascinating.

As I went to sleep I could still hear the strong, clear voice of Jane Morgan, singing "Fascination."

20

I HAVE ALWAYS HAD a particular fascination for magicians, the greatest ones, that is. Everyone stares at the performer in unblinking concentration—like Jack Nicklaus over a putt—not wanting to miss a thing and in hopes of "catching" a glimpse of the secret. The good ones are so skillful, no one ever does.

Dick Cardini was a good one. I met Cardini in Washington when he was playing at the Statler, and I started to book him soon after. He was always a smash hit.

Magicians are actors, too. They just don't "do tricks." They perform. And Cardini was a superb performer.

Dressed in tophat and tails and very properly British in his manner, he would come on stage accompanied by his wife, Swan, in pageboy attire, and spellbind the audience with his card and cigarette tricks.

Other magicians have done the cigarette thing since—pulling lit cigarettes out of the air, out of their hats, out of their hair, etc., but Cardini originated and perfected the act. I don't know how he did it, except I do know he had to light the cigarettes in advance, just before going on, so timing was essential. On one occasion I remember the preceding act took one encore too many and Cardini almost set himself on fire in the wings.

For his card tricks, Cardini had another assistant, an amazing parakeet named "Cecil."

Cardini would shuffle the cards and let someone from the audience pick a card, look at it and give it back in the usual manner as Cecil watched while perched on the magician's shoulder. Cardini would again shuffle the cards and put them in a plastic container and hold the container high over his head, whereupon

213

Cecil would take off from Cardini's shoulder, fly around a second and then light on the plastic container. The bird would then reach into the card-holder with his beak and pull out a card. Invariably it was the card chosen by the participant from the audience.

So, you can imagine my consternation the day I thought I had—unintentionally, of course—murdered Cecil.

Cardini, Swan, Anne, and I were driving from Washington to the famous Greenbrier resort in White Sulphur Springs, West Virginia, where I was producing a show featuring the great magician. We put all the baggage in the trunk and put Cecil, who was in his cage, on the floor in the back of the car.

We stopped in Lexington to have lunch. It was one of those typical summer days for the region, hotter than a griddle, with a humidity reading right up there with the temperature.

Out of habit more than anything else, I made sure the car was all closed up and locked securely.

We had a nice lunch and lingered a while over dessert and ice tea. As we walked out of the cool comfort of the restaurant into the blazing noontime heat, I was struck with a bolt of fear. "Oh, my gosh," I muttered.

"What's wrong?" Anne asked.

"I forgot about Cecil."

We ran to the car. I quickly opened the doors and found Cecil in his cage, flat on his back, his feet stretched upward, looking as dead as a doornail.

Cardini pulled the bird out of the cage and began massaging him gently while muttering, "Cecil, Cecil, speak to me, Cecil," as I stood there feeling like Lucretia Borgia.

Fortunately, the fresh air revived Cecil and that night he performed as well as he ever did.

But while that old trooper, Cecil, went on as scheduled, I had one star performer who did not, causing me all kinds of problems. He was in jail.

George Kirby, a black comedian, was at the zenith of a fantastic career. Through television, he was known and loved by millions and was in great demand by clubs and conventions. I managed to book him for the final night banquet of the American Mining Congress convention in Pittsburgh. With a comedian of Kirby's stature and talent, you really don't need any other acts, and so he was going to be the whole show.

And then, early on a Sunday morning, three days before Kirby's scheduled performance, the telephone awakened me at home. It was Glenn Jackson, the AMC vice-president.

"I hate to bother you, Jack," he said, "but have you seen the papers this morning?"

"No," I said.

"George Kirby's in jail. He has been arrested on a narcotics charge in Las Vegas."

My first thought was one of gratitude that George didn't wait until Wednesday morning to get arrested.

"Are you there, Jack?" Glenn asked.

"Yes, Glenn, I'm here. I'm just dumbfounded. Fortunately, we've got time. This is Sunday. The show is Wednesday night. There isn't a heck of a lot I can do about it today, but I'll get on it first thing tomorrow and get back to you."

I got hold of Kirby's agent Monday morning. His response was all too typical for agents. "He'll get released," he said. "Besides, this is America. He's innocent until proven guilty."

"I'm not trying him," I said, "but my client may not like someone fresh out of jail performing at his convention—guilty or not."

"Look at your contract," he said. "There's no escape clause covering that."

When there is money involved, some agents have a noted lack of sympathy. He said he would call me when he knew more about the situation.

I then began calling other agents. What I wanted was one standout act on a level with Kirby or, failing that, I would settle for two or three lesser acts and just build an entirely different kind of show.

Like I said, when it comes to money, some agents have a noted lack of sympathy. I got the expected baloney about short notice and so-and-so has other important plans. So-and-so had no important plans at all—he was unbooked—but anything to jack up the price.

However, let me emphasize not all agents are in this category, and by Monday night (I was in Pittsburgh by then), I had a number of fine acts who would be available if I needed them.

Late Monday night, Kirby's agent called me.

"I think he'll be out in time," he said.

"Not good enough," I said. "We have to put on a show and I can't wait any longer to see if your man is going to be able to perform.

"We have a contract," he said.

His client is in jail, he doesn't know if he is going to be out in time to make the date, and he's talking about contracts.

"We want out," I said.

"A contract's a contract," he said, and then mentioned the possibility of a lawsuit if we used someone else and Kirby was not paid in full.

Al Overton, the president of the American Mining Congress—like most of my clients—has a high sense of morality and propriety, and he didn't want Kirby now even if he were available.

"How much is it going to cost if we have to pay him?" he asked me.

I told him. I said I might be able to get the cost down some.

"Let's do it," he said. "We'll absorb the cost."

Tuesday morning I told Kirby's agent we were cancelling.

"We want to be paid," he said.

I didn't want to pay him. I wanted to fight it all the way to the Supreme Court if necessary. But Al Overton understandably did not want to get involved in that kind of a public dispute. I did manage to get the settlement figure lowered.

On Wednesday night in downtown Pittsburgh, we put on a revue-type of show with three excellent variety acts, and it was one of the most rewarding shows I have ever produced. The audience loved the show and the client was happy, and that is really what matters.

It turned out Kirby could not have made it anyway. He didn't get out in time.

Then there was the time I had to cancel another show—because *I* didn't want to go to jail. But if you think that upset me, you should have seen the look on an Abercrombie and Fitch salesman when he got the news.

Off and on I had been in contact with Walter LaBorie, the vice-president of sales for the U.S. division of Lever Brothers, one of the big sponsors of entertainment at the big food conventions.

216

One day I got a call from Walter to come see him in the Lever Brothers offices in their brand new building on Park Avenue in New York. I grabbed the train from Washington with hopes high that I was going to land the Lever Brothers contract for one of their big shows.

And sure enough, I did. But this one was a little different than anything else I had ever done.

"We're putting on this party in Miami Beach," Walter told me. "What we have in mind is a gambling party. We would like you to put it on. You'll need music, decorations, gambling equipment, the personnel to run it, and prizes."

They were willing to spend upwards of $50,000, with about $25,000 or more going for prizes—a princely sum in those days. Walter said they wanted prizes of good quality, nothing cheap.

And so I went over to that exquisite merchandiser of fine quality, Abercrombie and Fitch. A salesman, walking softly over deep carpet, asked if he could help me.

"Yes," I said, "I want to pick out a few things, about $25,000 or $30,000 worth."

That would have sounded most impressive in Woolworth's. The Abercrombie and Fitch salesman didn't even blink, though I am sure his brain was doing a quick calculation on the commission.

I explained my mission. The salesman and I went around the store picking out all kinds of gifts—silver urns, watches, exquisite hand-painted lamps, clocks, electric appliances, etc. We made a list of all the things I wanted, and I told the salesman to hold onto the list and I would be back in a few days to make it official. First, I wanted to make all the arrangements in Miami Beach.

I flew to Miami Beach the next day, looked over the facilities at the hotel where the convention was being held and then found a company that specialized in gambling parties. They would set it all up—roulette, dice tables, blackjack, poker, the works.

Everything seemed to be set. But then someone—I don't remember who, probably someone from the hotel—said that the authorities had been cracking down lately on illegal gambling activities and perhaps I should check with the sheriff's office, just to be on the safe side.

So, I went to the sheriff's office and explained the entire

217

operation. It would not really be gambling, because the patrons would not be playing with real money.

The sheriff said he understood. "But you still can't do it," he said. "Oh, you can do it, I guess, but if you do, we will have to come and break it up and put you and your sponsor and the operators in jail."

Well, there went my first big show for Lever Brothers. They still asked me to put on some entertainment, a little music and dancing. You might say in the big gamble that is show business, I lost that one. But I had company in the salesman from Abercrombie and Fitch. That was the worst part, having to go in there and cancel the order.

The salesman was in the back of the room, and when he saw me enter, he made a quick start and, realizing who and where he was, began to walk slowly, deliberately, toward me. Only the gleam of his eyes suggested any anticipation.

And then I had to ruin his day.

His commission would have been considerable, and I remember walking out wondering if he had already spent any of it. Probably not, I concluded, but perhaps he had spent every dime of it mentally.

I did a number of shows after that for Lever Brothers, and Walter LaBorie and I became friends. In fact, he and his wife later moved to Europe, and Anne and I visited them there on two occasions.

And then there was the time in Buffalo when for a few mintues I really thought I might again be going to jail.

I produced the entertainment for the banquet of the National Retail Hardware Association, and Russ Mueller, the director of the association, as was his custom, invited members of the cast and me to the dinner. Cast members rarely accept such invitations before performing, but a couple of them joined me at one of the tables, where we sat with a group of association members and their wives.

It was a good banquet and the show went over well.

After the show, one of the cast and I went out on the town. In Buffalo that doesn't take long. As we walked across the lobby of the Statler Hotel on the way to our rooms, a portly, dour-looking man and a smaller, distraught man approached us. The smaller man pointed a finger at me and said, "That's him. He's the one." The stout man happened to be the hotel security officer, and he invited us to come with him to his office in the rear.

"This gentleman," he said to me, "says you stole his wallet."

"That gentleman," I said, "is crazy." I told him who I was and that I was in no need of the gentleman's wallet, and I wasn't in the habit of stealing other people's things.

My accuser began to weaken. He said I was sitting at a table with him at the banquet. On second thought, he wasn't absolutely sure. He was obviously under the weather and had been "out on the town" himself. He ended up apologizing and after he left, we concluded that he had lost his wallet while "out on the town" and was trying to create a fiction that he could half-believe himself and pass off on his wife back home with a measure of conviction.

It was at about that same time, back in the 1950s, that I was faced with a strange puzzle. The same shows that thrilled audiences in Chicago, Los Angeles, and other places, invariably died in Dallas.

I could not understand it. The clients could not understand it. Where genuine laughter and rousing applause greeted acts in other places, in Dallas the very same acts found themselves competing with an audience that seemed indifferent to what was going on onstage.

During one such occasion in Dallas, I stood off to one side of the big ballroom surveying the scene. The show had started out fine, but now I noticed the volume of audience noise had increased considerably. I could hear the rattling of ice cubes, the clinking of bottles and glasses, and a definite rise in crescendo of conversation. My eyes focused on a scene at a nearby table. A man was pouring a drink out of a bottle in a paper bag. That was it. I knew they did that in Dallas, but I had never made the connection between Texas' strange drinking laws and the audience response to my shows. But there it was, and it was unmistakable. The audience—or a significant portion of it—was focusing its collective attention on the thing at hand—drinking. The show had become secondary.

In those days you could not buy a drink in a public place in Texas. But drinking out of a bottle was legal. "You can't buy a drink," they used to say in Dallas, "but you sure can buy a drunk."

Ordinarily— and now even in Texas—people are sold liquor

219

by the drink, which places a measure of control of drinking during convention shows in the hands of the client. That control is important. I always advise the client to have all food and drink service stopped during the show. No talent in the world can compete with liquor, food, and bustling waiters.

So long as that peculiar drinking ordinance remained in effect in Dallas, I could not control that situation, so I did the next best thing. On subsequent shows there, I just cut down on the length of the show so that it would end before the audience attention was significantly transferred from the stage to the table tops.

It was not the best solution, but it worked until such time that the Texas lawmakers were able to see the folly of drinking laws that encouraged people to get soused.

But if I thought Texas was bad, all I had to do to dispel that notion was to take a show a little farther south, into Mexico.

I was asked to produce a show in Acapulco for a leading American carpet manufacturer. We had to transport from the New York area stage sets, lighting and sound equipment, operating personnel, and a live cast, along with two truckloads of carpet for a sales display we also agreed to set up.

I am convinced it is easier for a rich man to get to heaven riding a camel that has passed through the eye of a needle than for two trucks to get through Mexican customs.

It took an entire day, while every item was cataloged and we argued with the customs officials over import taxes they wanted to levee on everything brought into the country. The crowning offense was when our technician was ordered to open the chest carrying his tools and instruments essential to his work. This was at the airport in Acapulco, and the custom people asked for $400. After a long delay they settled for $100, but asked that our man pay in twenty dollar bills so the loot could be evenly divided. And it happened right then and there with no apology, explanations, or embarrassment. After the money was paid, it was all "Gracias, gracias, gracias, Señor."

The show went well enough, but as we were loading the trucks for the return, someone noticed that about half of the carpets were missing. The police came and were very official and meticulous in their note-taking, but nothing was recovered.

When the trucks reached the border, the drivers were asked to account for the missing carpets. They reported they had been stolen. The customs official grinned and detained the trucks for a day. The rental costs on the trucks plus the $100,000 worth of equipment was considerable, so the client ended up paying an "import" tax on the carpets that had been stolen.

The Bahamas wasn't any better. When our equipment landed at the Freeport Airport, officials impounded it—musical instruments, projectors, films, sound and lighting equipment—everything we needed to put on our show. We were able to get the equipment only after making a large cash deposit, which was returned to us on our way out. We also had to pay a "work tax" on all personnel. That was to encourage the use of local labor, musicians, and technicians—which you couldn't use anyway, because none were qualified.

On the other hand, European countries are far more cooperative and helpful, for they have a better understanding of the benefits of having such a show imported.

I found Canada to be the most pleasant of all. There are certain restrictions, but no unreasonable ones, and competent help is readily available.

It was in Canada where we produced one of our more memorable and more satisfying shows.

The International Minerals and Chemical Company of Skokie, Illinois, the world's largest producer of potash, hired me to put on a Christmas show for its workers at its chief potash mine in Esterhazy, Saskatchewan. Esterhazy is about 100 miles from Moose Jaw and a considerably farther distance from Broadway.

What made this show both memorable and satisfying was the remote, frontier-like setting and the fantastic reception we received. The audience could not have been more enthusiastic had we brought an all-star lineup of top flight acts. We had Bob Lewis, a banjo playing, singing comic and his wife Ginny, heading a cast of five. Don't misunderstand me—it was a good show, but it wasn't Bob Hope or Perry Como.

Six of us—the cast and I—made the trip, flying from Chicago to Toronto on a regular passenger plane and hopping from Toronto to Moose Jaw on one of those small commuter craft. From Moose Jaw, we had a three-hour bus trip over bumpy dirt roads over hill and dale and through some of the densest woods I have ever seen.

Esterhazy was what you would expect—a small clearing in

the woods, so to speak, an assortment of frame dwellings and shops, a couple of white churches, a small schoolhouse, and a meeting hall, where we performed. Our hotel was not in the Hilton chain. It was clapboard building similar in appearance to the "tourist cabins" of the '30s and '40s, two stories high and considerably larger than a cabin. There was one bathroom down the end of the hall, but it was clean and surprisingly snug, considering the near-zero temperature outside!

We ate our meals in the town's only cafe, where the fare was also what you would expect, not gourmet, but good, wholesome, and plentiful.

We spent three days there, putting on four shows, two at night and two matinees to accommodate the school children and the different work shifts at the mine. Some people attended all four shows.

While we had no orchestra—only Bob Lewis on banjo and a piano player—the emphasis was on music with a Christmas theme, and a lot of sing-along numbers. The townspeople loved it. I have never seen such a radiance of goodwill and good cheer. There was nothing but welcoming, smiling faces everywhere we went, and the applause and cheers were so tumultuous I thought that the meeting hall was going to fall down.

We left there a few days before Christmas. As we boarded the puddle-jumper airplane to take us from Moose Jaw to Toronto, Ginny Lewis said, "That was great; I have never felt more Christmassy in my life." And I had to agree. I believe that is what Christmas is about. We went up to the wilds of Canada to give the folks in a frontier town a little Christmas spirit, and they gave it right back to us.

21

WHEN I LOOK BACK ON MY YEARS in show business, I don't think only of incidents; I think of people—the performers, people like Bob Hope, Jack Benny, George Burns, Red Skelton, Arthur Fiedler, Ray Bolger, Vic Damone. I suppose if a national poll were taken on who was the greatest of all, Bob Hope would win by a wide margin.

You would probably have to go to the wilds of Borneo or deep up the Amazon to find anyone who didn't know Bob Hope. I don't believe anybody in the history of show business ever remained so high in the affections of the people for so long a time.

For those who do not know Bob personally, it may be comforting to know that the personal "nice guy" image he portrays is the real thing.

He is also one of the most conscientious performers I have ever known. I remember a number of years ago I booked Bob to perform for the second year in a row before the same group. He did not realize he was performing before virtually the same audience twice in one year until the rehearsal the day of the performance. Bob reads newspapers and listens to radio and television news accounts and stays right up to the minute so he can insert topical material into his act. But much of his material is durable, and while after a year his repeat material may have seemed fresh to the audience, Bob would not risk that. He ended up throwing out most of his script and building a completely new act just hours before going on. It was a totally new and fresh act.

"Wasn't he terrific?" I said to the top executive of the client corporation.

"I don't think he was nearly as good as last year," he said.

223

In my judgment he was every bit as good, if not better. But I learned a valuable lesson—never bring a performer back before the same group until after an interval of a few or more years. It doesn't matter how good he is; in show business, familiarity breeds discontent.

Bob Hope is a real trouper. There was the time I had him booked for the annual meeting of the U.S. Chamber of Commerce in the Washington Hilton when he suffered a recurrence of an eye problem. He called me from New York to tell me his appearance at the Chamber affair was in doubt.

I had to line up a contingency show and arranged for two acts to come to Washington and stand by. The client, of course, agreed to the additional expense.

Meanwhile, Bob made the trip to Washington, taking a suite at the Mayflower Hotel. His appearance at the Chamber banquet was still doubtful. His condition had left him feeling concerned. But he was still going to try.

On the day of the show Bob called me. "Look, Jack," he said, "I'm sorry, but the way my eye feels, I just can't possibly make that rehearsal today."

Well, I figured, that was that.

"How about having the conductor come over here," Bob asked, "and we'll run through my act—just in case I can make it tonight?"

We had two rehearsals, one at the Hilton featuring the substitute acts and one at the Mayflower for Bob, meanwhile still figuring there was little chance of Bob's making the show that night.

And that presented another problem. The Chamber had planned to present Bob with a special award of commendation for his longtime contribution to the entertainment world. So, we made provisions to do that by telephone. The Chesapeake and Potomac Telephone Company installed special equipment with a direct line from the Hilton ballroom to Bob's suite in the Mayflower. Appropriate speakers were installed in the ballroom so the audience would be able to hear the phone presentation.

The show was to begin at 9:00 P.M. Everything was set. The substitute acts were in the wings waiting to go on. The phones had been checked out. And then, about 8:30, the direct-line phone onstage unexpectedly rang. It was Bob Hope asking for me. "Jack," he said, "I'm on my way."

When Bob arrived, he was accompanied by a prominent Washington eye surgeon recommended to him by his New York doctor. Having the doctor agree to accompany him to the show, Bob told me, gave him the reassurance he needed to go on.

And, incidentally, Bob Hope had never performed better. He was his usual very funny, sparkling self, with no hint that he was under any kind of pain or apprehension.

Bob is like that. He is also very punctual. He will usually arrive just two or three minutes before he is due to go on and will be on stage for the exact time requested. When you want a sixty-minute show, you get a sixty-minute show. If you wanted forty-eight and a half minutes, you'd get forty-eight and one half minutes. Bob is never surrounded by an "entourage" and handles all his own business. I have always negotiated directly with him, not through an agent, and I like it that way. He is scrupulously honest, fair, and cooperative.

There are a lot of lesser lights who could take lessons in courtesy and just plain getting along with people from Leslie Townes Hope.

Dolores, Bob's wife, is a gracious, lovely lady, and I've had the good fortune to get to know her. Dolores was a performer in Broadway shows before she and Bob were married. I believe her theatrical experience has been helpful to them both because Bob is truly one of the world's great travellers—always on the go and under pressure.

It was an accident—or a situation—that I got to know her. Bob was scheduled to do a show for me in New York when his eye problem recurred—this time in Ohio where Bob had gone to receive more honors. While there, he was stricken again and Dolores flew to Ohio to be with him. They then went together to New York, where Bob has long availed himself of the expert skills of a certain famous ophthalmologist.

Bob called me several days ahead to tell me the problem and the possibility of having to cancel. But Bob has the knack for coping with whatever gets in his way. He recovered sufficiently to do my date, but the extra treat was his suggestion to put Dolores on the program. It didn't take me long to pay off and and cancel the girl singer I had booked to appear with Bob. (Usually we have a singer to open and then Bob kids around with her and they end by doing "Buttons and Bow.")

Bob very personally and proudly presented Dolores during his act, and she gave her rendition of a song she always dedicates to him. The audience showed their enthusiasm and warm appreciation with standing ovations.

I selfishly believe that Bob did this then and on two other occasions for me. Of course, Dolores has appeared with Bob on several of his special television productions, but I doubt if he has done this on other shows for private audiences. Together they are an unbeatable pair!

Bob has a world of friends, but one in particular comes to mind because he was the speaker at one of the earlier conventions for which I provided the entertainment. He was a spokesman for the General Electric Company, but his message related to big government, the deficit, and other things of current interest. I recall two of his examples in making his points: One was that getting the government to reduce the budget was like trying to go over Niagara Falls—up; the other described how high a stack of $100 dollar bills would be to equal the amount of the public debt. The speaker got a standing ovation, and afterwards we all lined up to shake his hand and congratulate him, and many commented on what a great opportunity he would have in national politics. Many said he was presidential material. His name was Ronald Reagan.

The late Arthur Fiedler was another joy to work with, a man of great talent and personal charm. Considering his unquestioned position in his field, he also had a remarkable tolerance and understanding for those less gifted.

The Chamber of Commerce wanted Dr. Fiedler for its annual banquet in Washington once in the mid-1950s. Those in charge of the entertainment knew they could not get the entire Boston Pops Orchestra, but they were determined to get the maestro, and I found myself one winter morning on the phone to Arthur Fiedler to see if he was available. He was not.

"That date," he said, "it is impossible. That is the second night of our new season. See if they can change their date."

And so I dutifully reported the declination to my client, who

226

still would not give up. Of course, it was impossible for the Chamber to change its date, which had been locked in for some time.

"Call him back," I was instructed. "Tell him we will up the ante. Tell him we need him. Tell him anything."

"Dr. Fiedler," I said—he preferred being called Arthur, but somehow I could not bring myself to call him anything but "Doctor"—"I know the date is inconvenient for you, but the Chamber is most anxious to have you and would be willing to increase your fee if there is a chance you can make it."

Dr. Fiedler chuckled. "Well, call me back. Let me see what arrangements I can make here."

I called him back the next day. "Dr. Fiedler, how about if we double your fee?"

"Well, that is good and fast work," he said. "Were you ever a salesman?"

I laughed. "As a matter of fact, yes, a long time ago."

"I thought so. Okay, for you I will do it."

The Chamber's program chairman wanted a couple of opera stars on the show, a baritone and a soprano. I also had to line up an appropriate orchestra—fifty-five musicians who could somehow play like the Boston Pops. I would have had a quick solution to that problem had the National Symphony been available. It was not. Furthermore, the ballet was also performing, causing an additional drain on the top musical talent in the area. I will not go into detail, but obtaining fifty-five musicians approaching the caliber needed taxed all our resources. I do not know how many man-hours we spent on telephones alone just to put together an acceptable orchestra. And then we were still left with the nagging fear that it really would not be acceptable after all. I am not a musician, but I know something about music, and I knew in my heart that we were asking the great Arthur Fiedler to step down in class. I only hoped he would understand.

The singers also posed a problem, for we were asking two established opera singers to step out of their milieu as well. Generally speaking, opera singers go two ways—they perform to the accompaniment of a substantial orchestra, utilizing established music and routines, or in the case of special performances, they reduce it all down to piano accompaniment. We were asking them to sing with a complete orchestra, a new and unfamiliar orchestra.

To bring the two together—orchestra and singers—suitable orchestrations were essential. Dr. Fiedler had none that would have been suitable. It actually took us an entire month to locate six orchestrations that could be used—two for the baritone, two for the soprano, and two duets.

A word about an all-musical show—it's tricky. No matter how beautiful the music may be, it will not hold the interest of a general audience over an extended period of time, save for the few zealots who may be there. Such a show normally does not have the variety, the excitement, the laughter, the highs and lows of a general kind of show. But there is a time and place for such good all-musical programs, if not done too often, if it is part of an entertainment mix offered at a convention, and if the blend of leader, artists, and selections are good.

No one was better at selecting music that would sustain audience interest than Arthur Fiedler. He was a master at it.

The morning I picked him up at National Airport was one of those absolutely gorgeous spring mornings. The cherry blossoms—that great pink panorama that symbolizes spring in Washington—were in full bloom along the Tidal Basin; other trees and flowers were in bloom; birds were singing; and I felt confident that despite the way it was "thrown together," the show would be a great success.

We drove to the hotel and I accompanied the maestro to his suite. I was happy to see that the flowers, cigars, and bottle of bourbon I ordered for Dr. Fiedler had been delivered. He was not a pretentious or demanding man. I found out he liked an occasional cigar and a drink of bourbon—two drinks, in fact—one just befor the concert and one at intermission. I never knew him to drink liquor at any other time. (I had some misgivings that once he heard the orchestra we put together for him, he would drink down the whole bottle and order more, but I need not have worried.)

Dr. Fiedler allowed me to assist him in making the musical selections. I can't remember all of them, but there was a nice variety of easily recognizable pieces—including, appropriately enough, "April in Paris," and "It Isn't Even Spring," along with some of a more classical nature.

Arthur Fiedler was a medium-sized man with snow white

hair, twinkling Santa Claus eyes and a whimsical smile. He seemed to view all of life with an engaging sense of humor.

When he got to the rehearsal that afternoon, he needed all the humor he could muster. The rehearsal lasted all afternoon. It took that long to put together a show that would last about fifty minutes. For one thing, the orchestra, as I feared, was not up to standard, and Dr. Fiedler made a number of changes in the musical selections.

It all came off all right. For one thing, a general audience is not that discerning and will not even notice the graduations in quality that would be obvious to the professional or serious student. I do not consider myself in either class, but standing in the wings during the performance, even I was pained by the noise emanating from the harp. I couldn't help but wonder how that woman ever got the job of playing a harp.

The next morning, I picked up Dr. Fiedler to take him to the airport and apologized for the poor quality of the music. "Yes," he said matter-of-factly, "it wasn't what we would have liked, but . . . "

"The harpist," I volunteered, "it sounded to me like she was playing the wrong notes."

"No," Dr. Fiedler replied, "she wasn't playing the wrong notes. She just didn't know how to tune the damned thing."

Some time later, I ran into a friend who knew Dr. Fiedler. "I saw Arthur Fiedler a short while back," he told me. "I asked him about the Washington show he did for you and he said it was great."

I was amazed. "He actually said it was great?"

"No, come to think of it. He didn't really say it was great. He said he's never heard anything like it before."

Later on, I had occasion to use Dr. Fiedler again, at a Sunday night banquet in May in Chicago, but this time things were different. We were able to engage the 100-piece Chicago Symphony, and we also had as the accompanying singing star the exquisite artist, Kathryn Grayson. I remember watching Kathryn perform that night, and I wondered whom she had finally gotten to do her hair.

Early that day I had called Miss Grayson and found her to be rather uneasy about the performance, which was understandable; she had never done conventions, she would be performing with unfamiliar artists, and there would be just the one rehearsal that afternoon.

"Tell me more about the program," she said.

I explained to her, besides Dr. Fiedler, herself, and the Chicago Symphony, there would be a male singer, a baritone, who would do two or three solos early in the show and would join her in a couple of duets later in the show.

"I don't know this man," she said. "I'm not comfortable singing duets without a lot of preparation."

I had had a lot of experience listening to on-edge artists. "Well," I said, "George [I believe that was the baritone's name, though I can't recall his last name] has sung at the Met. He really is an accomplished artist, and with Dr. Fiedler conducting, everything will be fine. We have three hours of rehearsal and if you are not satisfied with the duets, we can drop them."

"I need a hairdresser," she said. "I just couldn't go on looking like this."

"I don't have a hairdresser on staff," I said, "but I will try to find one."

Have you ever tried to find a hairdresser in Chicago on Mother's Day? I never did find one. Not even the hotel could locate one on such short notice. But Kathryn Grayson must have found one, or else she did it herself.

It was an excellent show. The young man proved to be an excellent soloist and singing partner for Miss Grayson. The Chicago Symphony was superb. Everything was harmonious. Even the harp was in tune.

But there was another show in Chicago that ended on a sour note, due to a star's ego. While even commoners have been known to regress to such unattractive piques in times of wounded pride, such infantilism seems more common among performers. Perhaps it is the nature of the work. After all, in no other work does one place himself squarely on the line for judgment by a mass of strangers. And favorable judgment from the masses is heady stuff. The ego just naturally expands. With longtime success, the adored one can either mature and settle into a kind of wise, easygoing, good-grace acceptance of one's good fortune, or remain demanding. In other words, a star can be a nice person, a spoiled brat or, what is more likely, a mixture of the two.

230

Fully aware of star temperament, I nonetheless was totally unprepared for the performance of one of my favorite people—Ray Bolger.

At that time, Ray, the singing, dancing scarecrow of *The Wizard of Oz*, was an institution. Louie Armstrong, the inestimable "Satchmo," was fresh off his great success with Bing Crosby, Frank Sinatra, and Grace Kelly in *High Society*. While Ray was a star of great magnitude, Louie was newer to the heights and was enjoying newfound popularity. His picture was gracing the cover of *Life* magazine at the time of the convention. Also, Louie's act consisted of six or seven other musicians and performers. So, taking everything into consideration, I thought Satchmo was the natural closing feature, and I planned the show accordingly. A singing team would open the show, Ray would do about thirty minutes, and then Louie and his act would wind it up.

Bolger didn't like it.

"I always close the show," he said.

"Louie's got seven people in his show," I said. "It really works better this way."

Ray finally agreed to do it, but it was obvious he did not like it. I reasoned that he was a real trouper and would cooperate. I reasoned wrong. What was scheduled as a thirty-minute performance, lasted over an hour. I soon learned that my decision on the programming was wrong, and never again have I put other acts on Ray's shows. This great artist does it all—alone.

And while it was a great performance, it was far too long. Audience attention spans are notoriously brief; even the greatest of entertainers can hold an audience for just so long. Some people had left during Ray's performance, and when he finished there was a general exodus. It was getting late; time for bed. Louie Armstrong agreed. He was asleep backstage.

Louie was awakened, and he and his supporting cast put on their show before a handful of people. It was anticlimatic.

I swore I would never book Ray Bolger again, but time tempered my pique, as it did his, and I later found myself in his Beverly Hills home negotiating contracts with this very talented man.

We were in his studio, where he spent a few hours every day to keep his routines sharp and himself in the best of shape. Many people have the idea that a performer, once he or she makes it

231

to the top, merely performs, with perhaps a little time for rehearsing thrown in now and again. Performers—singers and dancers, musicians and acrobats, comedians and actors—are like athletes. They need to put in long hours on a daily practice routine to retain the sharpness that seems so natural onstage.

While we talked, Ray danced. We talked about a lot of things while Ray danced, a superbly conditioned, graceful figure who belied his years. We broke for coffee, finished up our business, and talked some more.

Neither of us mentioned the Chicago incident.

Most artists will balk at any departure from the routine, as witness Jack Benny's reluctance to perform on a rotating stage Similarly, Ray Bolger was not in the least receptive to the idea of a scrim curtain. A scrim curtain is like a two-way mirror; it screens out from the audience view anything behind it and is an excellent way to show off in solo splendor the performing artist while rendering invisible other performers, like the orchestra, that are in the background.

"It works real well," I explained to Ray, but he wasn't having any. Ray works very closely with his pianist-conductor and said he wanted to be sure his pianist-conductor could see him at all times. We assured him he could, but Ray still balked. This was at a show in Washington, and we finally abandoned the scrim curtain idea. Later, for another show, Ray agreed to use the scrim curtain.

After the show, he was enthusiastic. "That thing is fantastic," he said. "All those musicians back there and the audience can't even see them. We should have been using this thing all along."

For Vic Damone, it was the orchestra pit. Or rather, as was the case with Jack Benny and the turntable, it was the manager, more than the star, who objected. For Vic Damone's show in Chicago, we had the band in the pit instead of onstage. Vic's manager and road show director dropped in early the day of the show. Vic wasn't even there, but his manager made up for that.

"We don't perform with the band down there," he said. "Change it."

"I can't change it," I said. "It's too late to make major changes like that. Besides, it will work out fine."

"We're not going on then," the manager said.

I went to my client and he backed me up. "If Damone won't perform, don't pay him."

Vic's conductor decided to go ahead with the rehearsal, and when Vic arrived, I explained to him the advantages of having the orchestra in the pit. The manager still didn't like it, but Vic agreed to to it, and the show turned out to be a real winner.

After the show, Vic's manager was again in the process of telling me he didn't like it when Vic came up and said, "Jack, this is the best date I have ever done. If you ever want me again, just let my manager or agent know it's for you and I'll do it."

I met Alan King during the war, when, as just a youngster, he was appearing at the Trade Winds nightclub in Washington, where I provided the orchestra. I thought Alan was the funniest fellow I had ever heard, and I booked him to appear at a private dinner for a group of doctors. They paid us sixty-five dollars, which amounted to forty dollars for Alan, fifteen dollars for the accordionist, and ten dollars for me. We have worked together many times, and Alan has enjoyed a phenomenal career, but his price has certainly gone up!

I remember watching painfully as another star was not going over very well, but the genius of Benny Goodman prevailed, and he turned potential disaster into overwhelming success.

Benny was the headliner and closing act at a convention in New York, but the talents of his orchestra and the particular artistry of Benny on the clarinet were not receiving the response they truly deserved. The audience had had dinner, a few drinks before and during dinner, and had responded quite well to the preceding acts. Perhaps the crowd was just "responded out." Whatever the reason, Benny Goodman and his orchestra were competing with the conversational buzz of an audience that had been lost.

Halfway through the scheduled thirty-minute performance, Benny asked the audience for quiet and then announced:

"I bet you people would like to dance. Shove the tables aside and let's dance!"

The response was immediate and fantastic. Within a few minutes, the whole room was hopping as just about everybody was dancing to the famous Goodman swing music, around tables and chairs, and out into the aisles.

Instead of a thirty-minute concert, Benny Goodman put on a dance show that lasted for well over an hour, and when it was finally over, the applause and cheers went on for a full five minutes.

It was my only show with Benny Goodman, and I have regretted that, for he is truly a tremendous musician and performer.

There is another star who *never* performed for me—and for that I can blame only myself. For the banquet finale to a large convention in New York, we had a good show lined up, including a girl singer of some renown. Because of an illness in her family, she had to cancel, leaving us only a couple of days to get a substitute.

Paul Kielar, our production chief in New York, called me to tell me he thought he had found someone. I flew up to New York, and Paul and I decided to view this virtually unknown singer at work. At the time, she was performing at the Blue Angel.

"I think she's terrific," Paul said after we listened to her.

"I don't really care for her style," I said, and we ended up getting some other singer. I don't even recall the name of the singer we finally settled on. I certainly remember the name of the singer whose style I didn't care for—Barbra Streisand.

That incident reminds me of the time I got to know another star too well—so well, in fact, that I conferred on him qualities he did not possess. When we ennoble others far beyond their due, it can cause great embarrassment, pain, and disillusionment.

There is no doubt that Edgar Bergen raised ventriloquism to new heights. He was a true artist, an astute showman, and a very funny guy. He was also—and let me emphasize this—a first-class gentleman in every respect, always courteous and considerate and very easy to work with.

But still, none of us likes to feel foolish, and while you might say that it really wasn't Edgar's fault, I still rankle every time I think of the time in Las Vegas, in full view of a half-dozen people, when I was walking backstage, making my way in and around packing cases and trunks and people who were standing and sitting and talking, and there to my everlasting embarrassment, I actually said, "Pardon me"—to Charley McCarthy.

22

LIKE BOB HOPE, Red Skelton and George Burns seem to go on forever. Red has been the classic clown, earning his living by making the masses laugh while his own life has been marred by tragedy, including the death from leukemia of his young son, his divorce from Georgia, and later Georgia's own death.

When Georgia died, Red was scheduled to do a show for me in San Francisco, but called me and told me what happened and that he could not go on. I had no trouble lining up a suitable replacement, a man who was more than willing, even on short notice, to be a substitute under those circumstances. Who else but Bob Hope?

I remember the first time I had booked Red Skelton for one of my shows. I will never forget it, for right before he was due to go on, he almost induced in me a heart attack. He told me a very dirty joke.

"Don't you think, Jack," he said, "the audience here will like that one? I think I'll tell it."

At first, I thought he meant it. He didn't, of course. He had heard about my aversion to any kind of smut in my shows, and Red was a great practical joker. Red is still one of the greatest artists of our times.

What can I say about George Burns? I have worked with him often, and he has always been the same, a warm, considerate gentleman, who, in his eighties, still has that same memorable sense of timing that has marked his performances for sixty years. As of this writing, he is near eighty-eight years of age (he was born on January 20, 1896) and is still going strong. He once told me: "Jack, don't retire. Never quit, just keep going."

Jack Benny was another whose star shone brightly for a half a century, or until the day he died. He was a kind and gentle man and seemed so ordinary offstage you would never know he was a great star. When he arrived for a rehearsal, he made it a point to go around and introduce himself to all of the musicians and kid with them and was warm and personable with everyone he came in contact with.

I remember the time, long ago, we were making a promotional audio-visual presentation for our company, and I asked Jack if he would be willing to record a message for it. He gave us about five minutes of tape, an excellent commentary sparked by the famous Benny wit, and clients and prospective clients were most impressed that we had the famous Jack Benny doing a commercial for Jack Morton. But he would not take a dime for it.

When he was stricken, I wrote him a letter wishing him good luck and predicting he would be "back on the road" shortly. A few weeks later, I received a letter from him thanking me. "You are right," he said, "I will be back on the road very soon." That may have been the last letter he wrote. He died shortly after that on December 26, 1974.

Not all stars shine so brightly for most of their lives. Some burn brightly for a short time and then for one reason or another quickly fade, and it is difficult to recall how popular they once were.

Eddie Fisher is a case in point.

Back in the 1950s, he was one of the biggest names in show business, and when he and Debbie Reynolds became what Hollywood columnists used to call "an item," all the young people in the country went bananas.

I was caught up in that madness when Coca-Cola decided to put on a show featuring Eddie and asked me to produce it. The word also "leaked out" that Debbie would appear with him. The show was to be held in Miami as part of the National Soft Drink Association convention.

We knew there would be a lot of young people on hand for that one, not only the under thirty-five members of the association, but the offspring, relatives, and friends of the older members. There was no point in trying to put on an Eddie and Debbie show in a hotel. What we needed was something big—like an aircraft hangar. And that is what I got—an aircraft hangar at the Miami marina. We had to build a stage and bring in all the lighting and sound equipment and provide a large orchestra. No expense was spared. We did not provide seats, purposely. The audience would stand and be able to move about while watching the show. We roped off an area in front of the stage to discourage anyone from getting too close to the performers.

The biggest mistake I made with this show was booking two acts to precede Eddie. Ordinarily, there is nothing wrong with that; it is routine. But here we had a case of national hysteria. There is no explaining young America's insane obsession with the Eddie-Debbie duet, but unknowingly I did a great disservice to the performers who opened that show. The audience would not applaud; they didn't even know the stage was occupied by real live performers. All they knew was the stage was *not* occupied by Eddie and/or Debbie, who were not due to arrive until forty minutes into the show.

Well, the king and queen of romance arrived on schedule, and when Eddie came out on stage, all bedlam broke loose. The crowd tore down the ropes that were supposed to hold them back and poured onto the stage. They screamed. They grabbed; at one point I thought they were going to tear Eddie Fisher apart, but somehow he managed to restore a semblance of order. He kept pleading with them. "I can't sing unless I have a little breathing room, folks!" It took a while, but the crowd finally receded and settled down, and Eddie belted out a few of his hit recordings. Incidentally, Eddie Fisher was a great performer. He had that certain charisma or dynamism that made his in-person perform-ances something special. I don't know whether his one-time adorers ever forgave him for leaving Debbie for Liz or what, but in my opinion, his star faded long before its time.

After singing a few songs, Eddie told the audience he had a "special friend" with him and would like them to meet her—and you would have thought he had just announced he and Debbie were going to spend a week in each and every one of their homes. I will not attempt to describe the noisy demonstration that fol-lowed. Debbie came onstage, she and Eddie talked and sang to-gether, and the crowd went into an absolute frenzy.

When the show ended, a police escort helped the stars out

of the place, but not before both of them had been subjected to a pawing, clawing, squeezing attack that left them looking like they had been wrestling grizzly bears.

Still, nobody was really hurt, and all in all it was a tremendous success, and I continued to produce the Eddie and Debbie Show for the Coke people in various parts of the country. They were always a great hit, and I began to accept the accompanying bedlam as "normal" for this act. There was one thing I never did after that first night in Miami: I never booked any supporting acts. Eddie and Debbie really didn't need any help.

There has been a parade of people in my life—it still goes on—stars and ex-stars and stars-to-be, and plain, ordinary people with extraordinary qualities, practically all of them making a mark on the life of Jack Morton.

I remember with a glowing feeling the "family" type entertainers—the Lennon Sisters, who were so young when they worked with me that I would escort them to the stage and adjust their microphones to help them feel a little more self-assured after their usual prayer prior to the performance. There was the Alberghetti family, with the father conducting, the mother playing piano, and Carla and Anna Maria singing, and a six year old brother, who also conducted. Anna Maria is still a delightful, talented singing star today. I first worked with the famous-to-be Osmonds when there were only three of them singing, dancing, and clowning. The fourth one was too young to be in the act, but he would dart on stage after his brothers' performance, take a bow, do a cute little dance step and disappear—always to big applause. The big turning point in their career was when Andy Williams put them on his weekly television show and gave them national recognition—and stardom. I have followed their career all these years and still work with them. Instead of the Osmond Family of the past, they now comprise three acts; Marie, Donnie, and the Four Osmond Brothers—each a star and all are doing very well. Just importantly, their business success equals their other talents. The family built fine recording and film studios in their home town—Provo, Utah. They are a remarkable family.

I can still see a vivacious and talented young woman singing and dancing and doing a commercial-type dialogue with a male partner for the first industrial show I had ever produced. It was for the National Automobile Dealers Association in Washington, sometime in the early or mid-50s. I don't remember the young man, but I surely will never forget the outstanding Carol Burnett. She received $275 for her work. A great reason for Carol's phenomenal success is her pure, unadorned naturalness. Nothing phony about this talented woman. To illustrate what I mean, I go back to a time when Anne and I were at the Elbow Beach Hotel in Bermuda. I spotted Carol with her husband having dinner, and on the way out stopped to introduce myself and remind her of the show she did for me. I had hardly started before she assured me that she remembered not only the show, but me, too—name and all. Such a lady!

I remember a long time ago another vivacious youngster, younger than Carol was, still in his teens, a singing, dancing, joke-cracking Sammy Davis, Jr., who performed as part of his uncle's group, the Will Mastin Trio.

I recall the time in New York when we were rehearsing a show for that evening and we got to the point where we could do nothing but wait and wonder what happened to the headline performer, a newcomer to this country from Denmark named Victor Borge. He was two hours late, and we could only conclude that he had gotten lost in the big city and was probably somewhere in Brooklyn confused and bewildered—and we were right. He finally showed up all apologetic and excited, too, for he had forgotten the time while he watched, enthralled, confused, and bewildered, the Brooklyn Dodgers play the New York Giants in baseball.

Such a parade also includes Lawrence Welk, marching to his own wonderful tune of proper conduct. No bums, no dirty comics ever worked for Welk. There was Perry Como, as easygoing offstage as on; Eddie Arnold, the country singer with the cosmopolitan voice, about whom Frank Sinatra said, "I'm glad he stuck with country music." Martha Wright—there are a lot of people today wondering whatever happened to Martha Wright, the pretty, talented Broadway musical star. I worked with Martha on more than one occasion, and I know what happened to her. She walked away from it all, from the glitter, the glamour, the ex-

239

citement, and the fame, to take on the role of wife and mother, a woman who knew where her priorities were and had the self-assurance to stick to them.

There is so much that could have gone into a book like this, so much about so many people, people like the opera stars Robert Merrill, Beverly Sills and Roberta Peters; Tennessee Ernie Ford; Tony Bennett (another of Sinatra's favorites); Al Hirt, the great jazz trumpeter who led orchestras for me in New Orleans for twenty-five dollars a show; Bob Newhart, who once worked for me for $200, a tiny fraction of what he commands today; Roger Williams; Florence Henderson; Bill Cosby; Glen Gampbell; Sandler and Young; the Ames Brothers, the McGuire Sisters . . . all of them fantastic people and each carrying that special burden in his or her own special way, for talent is a burden, an awesome responsibility that brings rich rewards, but also extracts a severe price, including too often lives that are overwhelmingly complicated.

My parade also includes the not-so-famous people, acts, unknown entertainers, agents, businessmen, and hotel officials all too numerous to mention and, of course, all those other tremendous people, bosses and co-workers, schoolteachers and relatives, going all the way back to a ramshackle farm in eastern North Carolina, where a hardworking, corn-likker-drinking and sometimes profane man managed to instill into a small boy a sense of moral obligation, of duty, of responsibility.

And, of course, at the head of this parade is Anne, who has been with me all these years, through the uncertain, hard times when I really didn't know where I was going or what I was doing, and still with me today, always thoughtful, always encouraging.

Putting these memoirs together has convinced me more than ever of the truth of John Donne's observation that no man is an island. For this really is not Jack Morton's story, nor even the story of the success of one company. It is really everybody's story, for in the final analysis, we all travel the same road together; we are all in the same big parade. We do the best we can with what we have, whether it's digging a well, or laying out a ballfield, or producing a show, or singing, or playing the piano, or selling appliances. We do the best we can. And we will be judged, finally,

240

not on how much money we have made nor on how many people knew our name, but on how we have treated those who walked with us.

If their treatment of Jack Morton is an example of how they treated others, then most of the people mentioned in this book will be judged kindly.

To all of them, I am grateful.